The Making of the Black Country

A Unique Industrial Landscape

GEOFF MARSHALL

Copyright © 2024 Geoff Marshall

The moral right of the author has been asserted.

Apart from any fair dealing for the purposes of research or private study, or criticism or review, as permitted under the Copyright, Designs and Patents Act 1988, this publication may only be reproduced, stored or transmitted, in any form or by any means, with the prior permission in writing of the publishers, or in the case of reprographic reproduction in accordance with the terms of licences issued by the Copyright Licensing Agency. Enquiries concerning reproduction outside those terms should be sent to the publishers.

The manufacturer's authorised representative in the EU for product safety is Authorised Rep Compliance Ltd, 71 Lower Baggot Street, Dublin D02 P593 Ireland (www.arccompliance.com).

Troubador Publishing Ltd
Unit E2 Airfield Business Park
Harrison Road, Market Harborough
Leicestershire LE16 7UL
Tel: 0116 279 2299
Email: books@troubador.co.uk
Web: www.troubador.co.uk

ISBN 978 1 83628 051 4

British Library Cataloguing in Publication Data.
A catalogue record for this book is available from the British Library.

Printed and bound in Great Britain by 4edge Limited
Typeset in 11pt Garamond Pro by Troubador Publishing Ltd, Leicester, UK

Contents

Introduction		v
One	Coal	1
Two	Iron	22
Three	Glass	58
Four	Chains	72
Five	Nails	84
Six	Locks and Keys	91
Seven	The Chemical Industry	102
Eight	A Multitude of Industries	112
Nine	Canals	145
Ten	Railways	171
Index		183

Introduction

Elihu Burritt was born in Connecticut in 1810 and began life as a blacksmith. In 1864, Abraham Lincoln appointed him United States consul in Birmingham and it was at this time that he wrote *Walks in the Black Country and Its Green Border-Land*. In his book, Burritt captured the very nature of the Black Country's unique industrial landscape with his now-famous phrase, 'black by day and red by night', referring to the smoking chimney stacks turning the sky black with smoke by day to be followed by the red glow from iron furnaces at night. Burritt continued by observing that 'the Black Country cannot be matched, for vast and varied production, by any other space of equal radius on the surface of the globe'.

So, where is the Black Country? It has no defined borders as such but is enclosed within an area which runs south from Wolverhampton to Stourbridge, then east from Stourbridge to Halesowen, then north to West Bromwich and Walsall. West of Walsall is Willenhall and so back to Wolverhampton once more.

Birmingham is not in the Black Country, nor is Stoke-on-Trent.

The land on which the Black Country stands was blessed with abundant deposits of iron ore, coal and limestone, and it was upon these raw materials that the area's wrought-iron industry was founded. The Black Country has seen many innovators. Abraham Darby, who smelted iron ore with coke rather than charcoal, was a Black Country man, born at Wren's Nest near Dudley in 1678. It was in the shadow of Dudley Castle at Tipton where Thomas Newcomen came in 1712 to first install and publicise his groundbreaking atmospheric steam engine. James Watt installed his first steam engine fifty-four years later at the Bilston iron works of John 'Iron Mad' Wilkinson, justifiably called the father of the iron industry. Although Henry Cort can be credited with inventing the puddling furnace, it was a Black Country man who was to make real advances in puddling. Joseph Hall was born in Tipton in 1789 and was successful in developing the technique known as 'wet puddling'. The list goes on. In the early nineteenth century, John Gibbons from Sedgley improved blast-furnace design; John Urpeth Rastrick of the Stourbridge firm of Bradley, Foster and Rastrick built the *Stourbridge Lion*, the first railway locomotive in America; Aaron Manby of the Horseley Iron Works built the first iron ship to go to sea in 1822; and in 1851, Chance Brothers supplied all the glass for Joseph Paxton's Crystal Palace, centrepiece of the Great Exhibition.

There have been many authors of books and articles about the vast number of individual Black Country industries – iron making, coal mining, glass manufacture, nail making, chain making and lock making to name just a few. *The Making of the Black Country: A Unique Industrial Landscape* attempts to bring all these industries together, concentrating on the nineteenth century when the Black Country really was black by day and red by night. Particular thanks are due to these authors: W.H.B Court, Rex Christiansen, John Chubb, Graham Fisher, W.K.V. Gale, Charles Hadfield, J. Ian Langford, Ron Moss, Bev Parker, Harold Parsons and Ray Shill. There are many more, particularly those who have contributed to *The Blackcountryman*, the indispensable magazine of the Black Country Society.

The book is fully referenced. Where websites are quoted the relevant industry can be found with the websites search facility.

Thanks are also due to the staff of the British Library for retrieving heavy volumes so efficiently, and to Jane Humphrey at Dudley Archives for providing images. I would also like to express my appreciation to the following for their encouragement: Keith Hodgkins (also for providing photographs), Malcolm Dick, Simon Briercliffe, David Eveleigh and Keith Robinson, but emphasising that any errors and omissions are my responsibility.

ONE
Coal

Throughout the Middle Ages, wood was used for domestic heating and also to produce charcoal to smelt metallic ores. There is no mention of coal in the *Domesday Book*, but in the thirteenth century it began to be gathered where it outcrops to the surface, particularly on the Northumberland coast – hence the term 'sea coal'. Coal also outcropped in South Staffordshire and in the thirteenth century was gathered in Wednesbury and Dudley. Bell pits are recorded in Pensnett Chase as early as 1292, valued at 12s 4d[1]. In 1540, the antiquary, John Leland, recorded coal being mined in Walsall and Wednesbury.

Dr Robert Plot, in his *Natural History of Staffordshire* published in 1686, records:

'I was told by Mr. Persehouse of Nether Gournall, that in his grounds at Etingsall in the parish of Sedgley, in a place called Moorefields, the bed of coal lies at 14 yards thick; in so much that in some acres of ground have been sold hereabout for a 100 pound per acre; I was informed of one acre, sold for 150 pound, and well indeed it might be so, since out of one single shaft there have sometimes been drawn 500 pounds worth of coal.'[2]

Plot was referring to the South Staffordshire coalfield, the so-called ten-yard coal or the 'thick coal' that, for much of the area, lies very close to the surface. The seam extends from Walsall and Wolverhampton in the north to Stourbridge and Halesowen in the south and is divided by the Russell Hall Faults between Rowley Regis, Dudley and Upper Gornall. To the north the Bentley Faults separate it from the coalfield centred on Cannock. The eastern boundary fault runs from east of Walsall to West Bromwich and to about one mile east of Rowley Regis. The western boundary fault extends from Wolverhampton to Sedgley, Pensnett and Stourbridge.

Thomas Smith has described how the order of stratification is similar throughout the area but that the distance from the surface varies. He notes that the first coal beneath the surface is called brooch coal, this is followed by the thick coal, the upper measures when detached are known as flying reed. Then comes the heathen coal, the rubble coal, the stinking or sulphur coal, the new mine top and fire-clay coal and the new mine bottom coal. Of these strata, the brooch and the thick coal are preferred to the lower beds owing to the large proportion of sulphur in the lower coals.[3]

Coal was first worked in South Staffordshire in 'bell pits'. These were shallow shafts, no more than twenty yards deep, and hollowed out at the bottom in the shape of a bell. Miners dug out in all directions until the pit was abandoned when the roof began to collapse. Other bell pits were then dug nearby. Coal was also extracted in drift mines – horizontal tunnels dug into the side of a hill – to give access to the seam. King has published a detailed account of Black Country mining before the Industrial Revolution.[4]

Dud Dudley, in his book *Metallum Martis* written in 1665, informs us that within a ten-mile radius of Dudley Castle there were twelve or fourteen collieries and twice that number were idle; that each colliery produced about two thousand tons every year and that the pits were no more than 24–120ft deep. He continues to say, 'Where the coles is deep and but little earth upon the measures of coles, there the colliers rid of the earth, and dig the coles under their feet; these works are called foot-rids.'[5]

From the beginning there were accidents; the Sedgley Parish Registers record that Robert Aston was 'kild in ye colepits' in 1658, as was Blind John Elwell four years later.[6]

In time, deeper shafts were dug, and coal was gathered by the so called 'pillar and stall' method. Passages were cut out horizontally from the bottom of the shaft, forming a series of galleries or stalls from which the coal could be extracted. Pillars of coal were left in place to hold up the roof, to form a network of pillars and passages radiating out from the shaft. This process was known as 'working in the whole'. When the boundary of the coal was reached, the process was reversed and, 'working in the broken', the miners would remove the pillars and gradually move back to the shaft.⁷ An alternative technique, first developed in Shropshire, was the longwall method. As the name implies, a long wall of coal, perhaps a 100-yard section, was removed and supporting walls of stone or timber installed at right angles to the face with access passages from the shaft. When all the extracted coal has been removed another wall was mined and the supporting shafts moved forward.⁸

Extraction of Water – The Stationary Steam Engine

Plot, in his *Natural History of Staffordshire*, noted that if pits are dug 'the workmen are prevented by waters', or in other words, deep mines tended to flood. Plot had highlighted a problem that was to bedevil the mining industry. It got worse as deeper shafts were sunk and measures had to be taken to rid the mine of water. If the topography was suitable, a sough or adit was tunnelled from the base of the shaft at a gradient, allowing water to drain away to a valley outside. Alternatively, water was removed by a series of buckets hauled up the shaft either manually or with the help of a horse gin. When a horse gin was used, the buckets were attached to an endless leather belt which passed over a pulley at the top of the shaft. The pulley was connected via a cog mechanism to a rotating drum turned by a horse (or horses) walking round endlessly in a circle. Such a device was constructed by John Fidoe, a wheelwright, who was engaged by John Gibbons in 1720 to 'build erect and set up a good engine or gin that shall draw, keep down and drain the water in the coleworks at Ettingshall'.⁹ Fidoe was paid £80 for his gin and given a retainer of £150 per annum to maintain it. If it broke down, Fidoe was fined, and to avoid competition, he was barred from installing his gin at any mine within two miles of Gibbon's Ettingshall mine. Flooding continued as a perennial problem, only alleviated by the invention of the steam engine, which enabled water to be pumped from the mine. In 1698, Thomas Savary patented an invention 'for raising of water and occasioning motion of all sorts of mill work by the impellent force of fire which will be of great advantage for drayning mines'. Savary's engine, which he termed 'the miners' friend' was a forerunner of Thomas Newcomen's atmospheric steam engine. Originally intended to drain the tin mines of Cornwall, Savary brought his engine to Wednesbury to drain one of the town's coal mines. Regrettably, it failed:

Black Country Gin Pit (Dudley Archives)

'The engine could not be brought to answer the end proposed; for the body of water being so great, such a quantity was to be raised, and so large a fire was required, as rent the whole machine to pieces, so that after much loss of time, labour and money, Mr. Savary was forced to give up the work and the machine was laid aside as useless and the scheme for raising water was dropt as impracticable.'[10]

These difficulties didn't discourage Thomas Newcomen from erecting his atmospheric engine in South Staffordshire in 1712. There has been much debate over the years as to the location of Newcomen's engine, the first application of this revolutionary machine not only in Staffordshire but in the world. Some argued it was employed by a Mr. Back of Wolverhampton to draw water from his coal mines between Wolverhampton and Walsall at the Parke. The Parke may be 'on the left-hand side of the road leading from Walsall to the town over and against the half milestone'[11] The weight of evidence, however, suggests a site near Dudley Castle. Rolt, in his biography of Newcomen, refers to an entry in the Bilston parish records of 1725 referring to 'Thomas, ye son of John Hilditch, mangr of ye Fire Engine at Tipton'. In addition, there is an entry in the diary of one John Kelsall, who in the same year recorded 'there is near Dudley Castle an extraordinary fire engine'. There is also a print, engraved by Thomas Barney in 1719, of Newcomen's engine with Dudley Castle in the background.[12]

Martin Triewald, a Swedish engineer, came to England in 1716 and described Newcomen's engine:

'Mr. Newcomen built the first fire engine in England in the year 1712, which erection took place at Dudley Castle in Staffordshire. The cylinder of this engine measured 21 inches in diameter and was 7 feet 10 inches high. The boiler was 5 feet 6 inches in diameter and 6 feet 1 inch high. The water in the boiler stood 4 feet 4 inches high and the volume of the water was 673 gallons. The machine makes 12 strokes a minute and delivered 10 English gallons a stroke. The mine was 51 yards deep.'

Based on this information, Rolt has concluded that Newcomen's engine was erected on a nine-acre site at Coneygree Coalworks, part of Coneygree Park in Tipton and well within sight of Dudley Castle, later confirmed by recent research. The engine was a sensation and was visited from far and wide. But Newcomen was anxious to protect his interests. The Spanish ambassador, who made a special journey from London, was denied sight of the wonder, despite offering a reward![13,14]

There were other engines erected across the coalfield, but regrettably the Newcomen engine had shortcomings. The cylinder was heated and then cooled with successive stokes, making it very wasteful of coal. James Watt addressed this problem by incorporating a separate condenser, enabling the main cylinder to be kept permanently hot, thereby reducing the quantity of coal required. Richard Nernham tells how, in 1765, Watt went out for a Sunday afternoon stroll and 'the idea occurred to [him] that as steam was an elastic vapour it would expand and rush into a previously exhausted space and if [he] were to produce a vacuum in a separate vessel and open a communication between the steam in the cylinder and the exhausted vessel that such would be the consequence'[15]

In 1766 Watt met Matthew Boulton and three years later took out a patent for 'A New Method of Lessening the Consumption of Steam and Fuel in Fire Engines'. Boulton and Watt, in 1776, installed their first commercial steam engine at Bloomfield Colliery in Tipton. Aris's *Birmingham Gazette* takes up the story:

'On Friday last a steam engine constructed upon Mr. Watt's new principles was set to work at Bloomfield Colliery, near Dudley in the presence of its proprietors… and a number of scientific gentlemen, whose curiosity was excited to see the first movements of so singular and powerful a machine and whose expectations were fully gratified by the excellence of its performance… according to custom a name was given to the machine, viz., Parliament Engine... This engine is applied to the working of a pump 14 inches and a half diameter which it is capable of going to the depth of 300 feet or even 360 if wanted with one fourth of the fuel that a common engine would require... The cylinder is 50 inches in diameter and the length of the stroke is 7 feet.'

The Black Country can thus lay claim to have pioneered both the first Newcomen and the first Watt engine in the world. However, Watt was not entirely satisfied with the Bloomfield engine. Because of leaks at its valves and joints, he was in the habit of referring to 'ye Bloomfield disease' whenever he faced problems with other engines. Ironically, Watt's engine was not taken up in the Black Country as much as elsewhere (the Cornish tin mines for instance), and the Newcomen engines survived for many years. Boulton and Watt charged a fee for their engine based on the saving of coal. But in the Black Country, in contrast to Cornwall, there was coal a plenty.[16]

The Dudley Family

The Dudley family owned vast estates in South Staffordshire and were important coal proprietors. Development began in earnest with John, 2nd Viscount Dudley and Ward in the late eighteenth century. He was lord of the manors of Dudley, Himley and Sedgley. Much of his estates were taken up by common land, where, according to ancient custom, commoners (local people) had certain legal rights, such as freedom to graze their cattle, remove wood for fuel and to fish. Enclosure acts, authorised by Parliament, removed these rights and Lord Dudley benefitted from three enclosure acts passed between 1776 and 1784, particularly the Pensnett Act and the Dudley Wood Act, which allowed him to exploit his land for mining and to build canals and roads. By 1788, coal and ironstone mining were concentrated at Coneygree (Tipton), Parkhead (Dudley), The Level (Brierley Hill), and Brockmoor (Brierley Hill).[17]

Dudley's method of operation differed from that in other coal fields. In Newcastle, for example, it was more usual for the landowner to lease his land and receive a royalty on coal gathered. Lord Dudley was a coal proprietor in his own right. Because of the myriad of small mines in the Black Country, a system of subcontracting, known as the 'Butty System', was frequently practised. Its origins are obscure, but it was particularly prevalent in Staffordshire. It has been defined as such: 'the workmen are the servants not of the proprietor or lessee of the colliery, but of a contractor (the butty) who engages with the proprietor of the mine to deliver coal or ironstone at so much the ton, hiring the labourers requisite, using his own horses and supplying all the tools necessary for working the mines.' The management of the pit, underground, would then be put in the hands of a 'doggy', who would report directly to the butty. The system suited the coal owners because the butties would possess first-hand mining knowledge. It was possible with this mode of operation for miners to move through the ranks, progressing from loaders to pikemen to doggy and finally to the butty himself.

In 1797, Lord Dudley hired Charles Beaumont as his mineral agent. Beaumont was from Tyneside, was something of an expert and had authored a book, *A Treatise on the Coal Trade*. Beaumont defined the responsibilities of the butty. They were experienced miners, and it was their job, under the terms of a charter of 1797, to represent the interests of the proprietors on a day-to-day basis at the colliery. They were paid by the amount of coal they brought to the surface, employed the colliers directly and supplied winding equipment, horses, ponies and carts and provided the men with tools. Butties employed the 'doggies' and at the surface, the 'banksman' who would check the amount of coal gathered. Ponies were used underground at the larger pits to draw as many as six

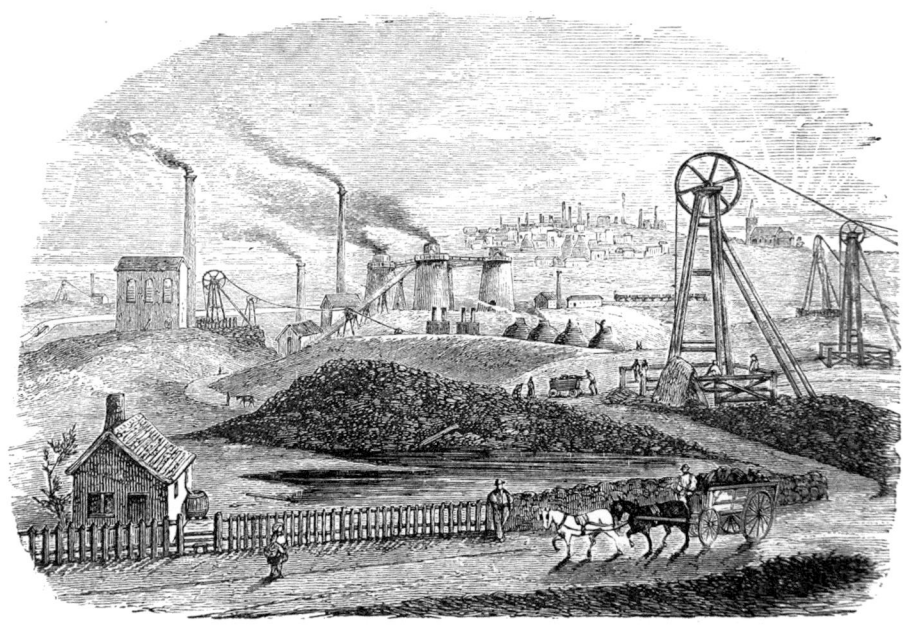

Earl Dudley's Coal Fields (Samuel Griffiths, 1873)

to twelve tubs of coal at a time to the shaft. They were also employed to operate horse gins for winding equipment at the shallower seams.[18,19] But the butties were often in it for themselves. There was much competition amongst them, profit margins were small and accordingly, corners were cut and safety ignored. The system was frequently open to abuse. Sometimes the men would be paid in tokens which could only be redeemed in so called 'tommy shops' owned by the butty himself. The butty system was eventually to come under attack from the trade unions and from a parliamentary select committee deliberating on accidents in coal mines. Later, the Coal Mines Act of 1872 specified that every colliery should have a qualified mine manager. Both of these factors contributed to the decline and eventual demise of the butty system.

It cannot be said that Beaumont was greatly impressed by Lord Dudley's mines, at least not in comparison with those he had left behind in Newcastle. He commented: 'I find the works almost wore out, none of them puts out half

Underground Work at Earl Dudley's Salt Wells Colliery (Samuel Griffiths, 1873)

of what they might.' He considered them as 'the most barbarous which could be invented to lose the most coal'. He deplored the fact that the four steam-pumping engines on the estate were not pumping water from the lowest levels of the seam, thereby allowing the mines to flood. But in a comparatively short period of time, Beaumont improved the efficiency of Lord Dudley's mines. Proposals were submitted to increase the efficiency of the pits. Better shafts were sunk, trap doors installed to improve ventilation, tubs provided and a horse-drawn tramway built from Brockmoor pit head to the Stourbridge canal at Pensnett. By price saving, he set about to find wider markets for Dudley's coal, both in Birmingham and via canal to the borders of London, even competing with coal from Newcastle[18]. Significantly, Beaumont wanted to do away with the butty system and for the miners to be employed directly. Seemingly, despite the potential influx of scores of miners from Newcastle, the miners themselves were in favour of direct employment and supported Beaumont's proposals. Plans were fiercely resisted, however, by the butties and there were even threats to burn down Dudley's house at Himley, forcing Beaumont to leave. In 1833, the Dudley estates were placed in the care of trustees who commissioned a report to investigate the state of his pits and to return them to the efficient way of operation that they had enjoyed under Beaumont. Richard Smith was appointed mineral agent, and his principal recommendation was that the

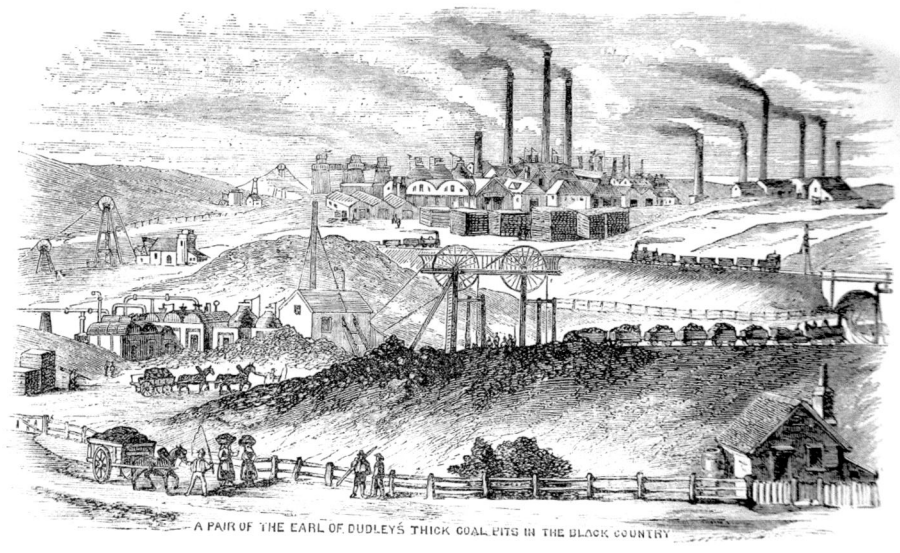

A Pair of Earl Dudley's Thick Coal Pits in the Black Country (Samuel Griffiths, 1873)

trustees should let pits out on royalty. Given that ironstone and coal are found together, many lessees were iron companies such as the British Iron Company, Messrs, Blackwells, Izons and Co., and Bramah and Cochrane.[20]

Ventilation

Ventilation was always a problem in Black County coal mines. In the very early pits, it was clearly very inefficient. Eventually, twin shafts were sunk and, exploiting the fact that hot air rises, a fire was sometimes lit beneath the upcast shaft to provide a draught and so remove foul air. Later, in larger pits, steam-powered fans were installed at the surface to circulate fresh air. But too great a circulation of air could cause its own problems. There were always large quantities of coal dust and slack at the foot of the mine. Johnson, writing in 1866, noted that large amounts of air enhance the decomposition of slack and coal dust and cause spontaneous combustion, the so-called 'gob fire'. However, he also mentioned the positive advantage that the heat from the smouldering gob fire produces, causing a difference in temperature between the upcast and downcast shafts and so improving ventilation.[21]

Gas was an ever-present hazard. Carbon dioxide was known as 'choke damp', which as the name implies, while not flammable, restricted the miners' air supply. Methane was appropriately called 'fire damp' and was flammable. Black Country mines were relatively free of fire damp, and this probably persuaded many miners to dispense with Humphry Davy's safety lamp. It was inconvenient to handle, and, because of this, many miners used a candle instead – a blue halo indicating the presence of methane. Perhaps more significantly, candles allowed more coal to be gathered and therefore more pay. Safety lamps were used, however, in the so-called explosive district (in the West Bromwich area) in the ominously named 'slaughter pits'.[22]

The majority of Black Country mines were less than 250 yards deep, and pairs of shafts were seldom more than 300 yards apart. Coal was retrieved from the bottom of the shaft by skips hanging freely by ropes or chains and the same method was used to transport the colliers.[23] Shaft guides were introduced in the mid-nineteenth century, soon leading to cages suspended by wire ropes.[24]

Working Conditions

The Black Country coal industry reached its peak in about 1860. That coal mining was a tough and unhealthy job goes without saying today. It was realised as such. A colliery manager noted at the time:

> 'I have known many men constitutionally old and finished at 34 years of age in consequence of working on pillar and stall. Besides the extra labour in this sort of work there is a certain amount of oppressiveness owing to the small and confined space in which the work is performed – men not only breathe the same air but inhale a great amount of coal dust, so much so that their discharges are as black as coal'.[25]

It comes as no surprise, therefore, that life expectancy for a miner was ten years less than the national average.

Women worked in the pits until the Mines Act of 1842 restricted them to working at the surface. They were known as 'pit bank wenches'. Small boys as young as seven worked underground until 1843, when the minimum age was

Black Country Miners at Work (Dudley Archives)

increased to ten. The treatment they received depended on the attitude of the butty; some were treated well but others were put in harm's way when 'men sent them where they would not dare to go themselves'[26]. They often worked at the surface in various occupations, such as driving the gin horses. By 1887, the age limit was raised to twelve, to thirteen in 1900 and fourteen by the Coal Mines Act of 1911.[27]

Yet, because of the tough and dangerous working conditions, miners were paid more than most workers. In the early nineteenth century, pikemen (men at the coal face who extracted the coal manually with handheld pikes) typically earned between three and four shillings per day. Boys got between 6d and 8d for opening and shutting air doors and between five shillings and fourteen shillings per week for driving the pit ponies. Skip loaders got twelve to fifteen shillings per week. [28]

William Troughton described his life as a collier in 1842 thus:

'I was 18 last March. I carried dirt or slack from the men holing the coal back into the gob (waste area). I crawled under the coals and with a rake filled a basket and then crawled out and carried the basket back about 20 yards and emptied it out. I came by half past 5 and got down by six and went to work. Men crawled under to take out the big coal and rolled and pushed it out and loaded the skips and then the boys crawled in and filled the basket with the slack, being small coal and dust. If the coal be as big as an orange, it is taken up by the men for the forges and furnaces, but if the coal is only as big as an egg it is not worth taking and the men leave it… the doggy is always a good workman, but he is very strict over the others. He has 5 shillings a day and all he does is walk about in the pit and make other people work. Some of them would not work if it were not for the doggy.'[29]

As well as being unhealthy and tough, the life of a Black Country miner was dangerous. There were far more accidents than in other mining districts. Eleven men died in an explosion at Five Ways Colliery, Rowley Regis in 1844, five at Fire Clay Pit, Deepfields Colliery, Bilston in 1866 and even though it was thought to be a low-risk mine, nineteen perished at Round's Green, Oldbury in the same year. One year later, five died at Yew Tree Colliery, Rowley Regis and in the following year, twelve were killed at Heathfield Colliery in Darlaston. The list does not end there![30] Fatal accidents were caused by falls of coal or rock from the roof of the mine, faulty winding gear causing men to fall down the shaft, gas explosions, fires and flooding. Many accidents went unreported, and it could be unwise for a collier to raise safety issues if they wanted work. One collier commented: 'If you know there is a danger and say you won't go, the butty will say then you must go up and there's no more work for you.'[31].

In time, central government was prompted to concern itself with mine safety. Because of a series of fire damp explosions in the north of England, a select committee of the House of Commons was set up in 1835 to consider mine safety. Its recommendations were minimal, and fatalities continued. In a five-year period in the mid-nineteenth century, 610 colliers were killed in accidents of one sort or another. In 1849, a select committee of the House of Lords recommended that mines should be inspected and in 1850 the Coal Mines Inspection Act became law. By the terms of the act, mine inspectors were authorised to inspect collieries and mine owners were required to keep plans of their underground workings. Fatal accidents were to be reported to the Secretary of State within twelve hours. A further Act of Parliament was passed in 1855 specifying that sufficient ventilation must be provided, that shafts should be properly lined and protected, and that signalling should be provided when winding. In 1860, another Act stipulated that places where there was no working should be fenced off; safety lamps were to be examined and overhead

Haden Hill Colliery (Keith Hodgkins Collection)

covers put on the skips which carried the men up and down the shaft. More safety features were implemented, and in 1872 every mine was required to be under the supervision of a qualified manager and copies of underground plans had to made available in a central location.[32]

By present-day standards, the attitude to safety seems positively casual. Johnson, writing in 1866, comments in a manner which would be unacceptable today:

> 'Where an explosion has unfortunately occurred its effect has rarely extended beyond the particular chamber in which it took place, the workmen in other chambers having escaped injury… Out of 540 collieries in 1864, only twelve people were killed from explosions of gas, and at most only two per explosion while 50 or 60 in the same pit went unharmed. Out of 10,200,000 tons of coal mined this equates to one death per 850,000 tons – a small risk.'[33]

Much information on individual mines can be found on the Black Country Muse website (www.blackcountrymuse.co.uk), including details of accidents. It is a matter of regret that the pillar-and-stall method for extracting coal was used so extensively in the Black Country. It was widely accepted that the longwall method was safer, as highlighted in 1857 by the Mines Inspector for South Staffordshire and East Worcestershire, who in his annual report lamented that eighty-eight lives had been lost and yet 'not one single death in getting the coal by the longwall'. As well as safety issues, he also observed that 'thousands of tons per acre of coal would be liberated over and above the proportion obtained by working in the accustomed manner of pillar and stall'.

Yet despite all these measures, accidents persisted unabated, including one of quite dreadful proportion in Northern France, where over one thousand men perished. In response, a Royal Commission was set up in 1907, culminating in the Coal Mines Act of 1911. By the terms of the act, rescue stations, staffed by trained rescuers and equipped with appropriate apparatus, were made compulsory. They were required to be sited within 10 miles of any mine with more than one hundred employees; the one covering the Black Country mines was at Trindle Road in Dudley. The Act also specified a working day of no longer than eight hours, ruled out the employment of children under the age of fourteen and made provisions for the welfare of pit ponies.

Decline

By 1860, the Black Country was producing over five million tons of coal every year from 440 pits employing 28,000 men. But there was a problem. Black Country mines were small, badly equipped and older seams were exhausted and prone to flooding. By the late nineteenth century, many parts of the Black Country were peppered with disused shafts and subsidence was a major problem, even to the extent of 'pit-pulled' cottages sinking into old workings. Black Country mining was described as 'extensive mining of the most elementary character, vigorously prosecuted for centuries, with no regard to the damage done to surface or contiguous seams… a water-logged rabbit warren'[34] Ironically, the definite advantage of coal being so close to the surface had encouraged a race to exploit it, with only short-term profit in mind. Vast numbers of shafts were sunk with un-recorded workings, with the consequence that large quantities of flood water became trapped in abandoned pits. To compound the problem, the position and workings of disused pits was often unknown. Inundation by flood water therefore became a serious issue. In 1859, water burst in from old workings into the Pump House Colliery, West Bromwich, and two lives were lost. Three years later, seven men were killed in a similar incident at Old Bradley Colliery in Bilston[35]. The extent of the problem was illustrated in a paper written in 1866. The author laments about the immense amount of water pumped from mines finding its way back there, only for it having to be pumped out again. He estimated that 50 million gallons of water were raised every day in the whole coalfield of approximately 125 square miles. The cost of the steam-powered pumping equipment to achieve this translates to an increase of 3¾d per ton of coal raised. He identified the need for combined action but regretted that the principal difficulties were the absence of a combined effort on the part of various proprietors and the want of a method of apportioning costs in proportion to the benefit gained.[36]

In 1854 colliery owners made their first attempts to club together to drain and rid mines of floodwater. The scheme didn't get off the ground; those who contributed resented paying to drain the mines of those who declined to join the scheme. Then in 1873, the South Staffordshire Mines Drainage Act was passed. A levy of 1d was imposed for every ton of coal raised. But bickering continued. Oldbury and Bilston lobbied to be excluded, claiming their area – in contrast to Tipton – was relatively free of flooding. In 1886, the levy was increased to 9d per ton of coal mined. The Tipton firm of **Lee,**

Howl & Co. was founded in 1880 and operated as hydraulic engineers. They designed and made water pumps which were used to drain flooded mines. The factory stood by the Birmingham Canal, next to Tipton Railway Station. Edmund Howl was a director of the company; he was also manager of the South Staffordshire Mines Drainage Commission[37]. It all led to inevitable decline; by 1920, forty tons of water had to be removed for every ton of coal won. The outcome was 150,000,000 tons of submerged coal left abandoned beneath the ground.[38]

The mining industry was prone to periods of recession and when the demand for coal fell it was the custom to reduce the colliers' wages. Stoppages were the consequence and there were many strikes. In 1878, a Bilston miner summed up his fate in a poem,[39]

They tell us very plainly too,
They mean to use their powers
To bringing us poor miners back
To slavery and long hours
But should reductions come again
I feel it duty bound
To ask that those should be reduced
Who get their thousand pounds
The masters and the public say
The trade has left the land
Both coal and wages must come down
If not, the work must stand.

There was a serious strike in 1921, and rioting miners overturned loaded coal trucks at New Hawne Colliery. Deserted pits were flooded and many never reopened, including New Hawne, after the General Strike of 1926.[40]

Later Collieries

So intensive had mining been, that many Black Country collieries were exhausted by the mid-nineteenth century. But there was always hope that coal could be recovered beyond the eastern and western boundary faults. The prominent mining engineer Henry Johnson was optimistic that thick coal could be found, and proposed sinking a trial shaft, beyond the eastern boundary fault beneath Sandwell Park, on land belonging to the Earl of Dartmouth. As part of the deal, the earl would get a royalty on the amount of coal produced.

A meeting was held at the Queen's Hotel in Birmingham with the intention of raising £20,000 in two hundred shares of £100 each. Johnson, now appointed engineer at £200 per year, began work on the 2nd of May 1870, with the hope of reaching the thick coal at a depth of 350 yards. There was a scramble for shares when a thin seam was reached, only to be followed by a 'South Sea Bubble' panic when hard rock restricted sinking to only 4ft per week. Shares tumbled from £205 to £50, but Johnson was undeterred. His sinkers were induced to persist, with the offer of a quart of ale and a leg of mutton every week if they dug more than eight yards. Brooch coal was found first at 380 yards and then on the 28th of August 1874, at a depth of 418 yards, the thick coal was reached.

The mine was close to the Great Western Railway line from Birmingham to West Bromwich, as was the Birmingham Canal Navigation. A wharf was built by the canal to connect with the colliery via a five hundred-yard tramway. A second shaft was soon sunk which reached the thick coal at 425 yards and by 1883 a third shaft was in place. Plans were made for a second colliery to ensure continuity of supply when the first colliery became exhausted. Between 1897 and 1909, at Warstock Fields, about a mile north of the original colliery, two shafts were sunk, the Jubilee Shaft and the Primrose Shaft. Coal was transported along a tramway to the old colliery and thence to the railway.[41,42]

In 1875, encouraged by the Sandwell Company's discovery of coal beyond the eastern boundary fault, the Hamstead Colliery Company purchased land from the Hon. G.C. Calthorpe of Perry Hall and on the 29th of June of that year began their search for coal. It was found at a depth of about 630 yards and for a while Hamstead was the deepest colliery in the world. Isaac Meachem became the colliery manager. He was a brave man and risked his and his son's life while supervising rescue operations after a serious fire in 1898. Meachem and his son were trapped but he kept his spirits high by singing his favourite hymn, 'Lead Kindly Light', until rescued. After the fire, the colliery was forced to close for a while, putting many men out of work. Some relied on the charity of soup kitchens while others sought work elsewhere, in some cases as far afield as the Yorkshire mines. A very serious fire struck on the 4th of March 1908 and twenty-six men lost their lives. To mark the centenary of the tragedy, a monument was unveiled in 2008. Poems were written as well.[43]

The Hamstead Mine Disaster by Ron Treharne
On Spouthouse Bridge, I stood at dusk and scanned
The Village, round, and I drove my gaze t'where
The Pit-head stood, as, hard, the fisted-hand
Of disaster struck with grief and despair
On the few, who ventured down the shaft
Of death, with, pick and shovel for the coal-
Packed earth, where a broken cry, from the craft
Of toil, told of a flame, And the whole
Of the land of Hamstead stirred, as the blade
Of the driving knife of smoke stabbed and tore
Through the breathless lungs of the men who prayed
And slipped into death and a darker core
As the eye of pain, upon Hamstead, bled
Down six and twenty tears for the dead.

Following the success beyond the eastern boundary fault, attention was focused on the search for coal beyond the western boundary fault. The Earl of Dudley owned the land and there seemed every prospect of finding it, particularly as the journal, *The Engineer*, had written in 1869 that 'it is the opinion of most geologists that there is every evidence of coal existing beyond the fault, and it will no doubt be found by the never tiring energy of the Earl of Dudley's agents'. A site at Baggeridge Wood, about a mile west of Sedgley, was selected and boring began in 1896.

Unfortunately, the first attempts failed; the bore rods broke, leaving behind expensive industrial diamonds underground. Success was achieved with another boring and thick coal was discovered at a depth of six hundred yards. The first shaft was begun in 1899, finding coal in 1902. Problems arose when the second shaft was sunk. It took until 1910 to complete because of the ingress of 'a perfect sea of water', only alleviated by a special method of brick lining to keep the water at bay. Baggeridge could win over three thousand tons of coal in every eight-hour shift. Coal was transported by extensions of the Pensnett railway and GWR to Round Oak steel works and the canal at Ashwood Basin.[44]

Yet despite new modern collieries at Sandwell Park, Hamstead and Baggeridge, the Black Country coal industry entered a period of terminal decline in the mid-nineteenth century. In 1860, there were about 440 collieries

Baggeridge Colliery (Dudley Archives)

extracting about five million tons of coal every year but, as we have seen, in the main they were small-scale enterprises, the majority of which were less than two hundred yards deep and each employed only a handful of men. By 1913, output had slumped to about three million tons per year. The number employed fell in line with the fall in output: 28,000 were employed in 1872, falling to 10,000 in 1913.[45]

Baggeridge was the last Black Country colliery to close. A commemorative medal was struck to mark the occasion, and so it was that at 5.30 am on the 2nd of March 1968 the winding gear at Baggeridge hauled the last shift of miners to the surface. Black Country Society members were there to witness this poignant event.[46] They drank a toast to the memory of Baggeridge Colliery and to all those who worked there over the years and after taking a group photograph and presenting a commemorative medal to the longest serving miner, Mr. B Fellows, that was that.

References

1. John Hemingway, Illustrated Chronicle of Dudley Town and Manor, MFH Publishing, 2009, p. 56
2. Robert Plot, The Natural History of Staffordshire, Oxford, The Theatre, 1686.
3. Thomas Smith, The Miners Guide, Privately Printed, Sandy Fields, nr Sedgley, 1836
4. P.W. King, Black Country Mining Before the Industrial Revolution, Mining History: The Bulletin of the Peak District Historical Society, 2007, 16, 34
5. Dud Dudley, Metallum Martis, 1665.
6. W.J. Jenkins, The Early History of Coal Mining in the Black Country and Especially Around Dudley, Trans. Newcomen Society, 1928, 8, 107.
7. William Jones (ed.), Dictionary of Industrial Archaeology, Sutton, 1996, p275.
8. ibid., p233
9. B. Poole, Mines Drainage, Blackcountryman, 1969, vol.2, p23.
10. R.A. Lewis, Coal Mines in Staffordshire, Staffordshire Education Committee Local History Source Book, 93, 1982.
11. Stebbing Shaw, History and Antiquities of Staffordshire, part 1, 1798-1801, p120.
12. L.T.C. Rolt, Thomas Newcomen, David & Charles, 1963, p 48.
13. ibid., p46-48
14. J.H.Andrew & J.S.Allen, A confirmation of the Location of the 1712 'Dudley Castle' Newcomen Engine at Coneygree, Tipton, International Journal for the History of Engineering &Technology, Vol 79 (No 2), 2009, p.174-82.
15. Richard Newnham, The Bloomfield Colliery Engine 1776, The Blackcountryman, 1976, IX, (4), p45.
16. ibid., p49.
17. T.J. Raybould, Lord Dudley and the Making of the Black Country, The Blackcountryman, 3 (2), 1970, p. 53-9
18. Richard Stone, The Collieries and Coal Mines of Staffordshire, Phillimore, 2007, 17-19.
19. Howard Gauden Hill, The Pit Ponies, The Blackcountryman, 1979, XII, 61
20. T.J.Raybould, The Development and Organization of Lord Dudley's Mineral Estates, 1774 – 1845, Economic History Review, 1968, Vol. XXI, 529
21. Henry Johnson, South Staffordshire Coal Field. Method of Working – Ventilation, Extent and Duration, in The Resources, Products and Industrial History of Birmingham and the Midland Hardware District, ed., Samuel Timmins, Robert Hardwicke, 1866. p21

22. T.E. Lones, The South Staffordshire and North Worcestershire Mining District, Transactions of the Newcomen Society, 1930/1, XI, p. 42-54.
23. T.E. Lones, History of Mining in the Black Country, Printed at the Herald Press, Dudley, 1898, p 21.
24. T.E. Lones, 1930/1.
25. D. Anderson, A Pictorial History of the British Coal Industry, David & Charles, 1982, p 29.
26. T.E. Lones, 1898, p. 43
27. Richard Stone, p. 33
28. T.E. Lones, 1898, p. 36
29. R.A. Lewis, p. 20
30. Richard Stone, p. 37
31. Lewis, p. 23
32. T.E. Lones, 1898, p.49-60.
33. Henry Johnson, 1866. p. 23
34. G.C. Allan, The Industrial Development of Birmingham and the Black Country, 1860-1927, London, Cass, 1966, p142.
35. T.E. Lones, 1898, op.cit.
36. Samuel Timmins (Ed.), The Resources. Products, and Industrial History of Birmingham and the Midland Hardware District, 1866, p38
37. Bev Parker, Tipton Industries, in www.historywebsite.co.uk
38. Richard Stone, 2007, op.cit. p. 31
39. ibid., p.84
40. Peter Barnsley, New Hawne Colliery, Blackcountryman, 1971. IV, 48
41. Nigel Chapman, A History of the Sandwell Park Colliery, Heartland Press, 1997.
42. D. Dilworth, Sandwell Park Colliery Company, Blackcountryman, 1973, VI (4), 41-44
43. www.miners.b43.co.uk
44. R. Newnham, The Sinking of Baggeridge Colliery, Blackcountryman, 1968, I, 21
45. G.C. Allan, 1966, p142 and 281
46. John Brimble, Blackcountryman, 1968, I, (3) 5.

TWO
Iron

The Black Country's industrial history is largely a reflection of the area's underlying geology of coal, iron ore and limestone. These naturally occurring minerals are relatively easy to extract and were the raw materials for the burgeoning iron industry of the eighteenth and nineteenth centuries, for which the Black Country is justly famous.

Iron occurs naturally in combination with oxygen as iron oxide and has been excavated as iron ore from very early times. The early iron workers heated the ore with charcoal to form a spongy lump or bloom of iron. (Charcoal, obtained by heating wood in the absence of air, releases the metallic iron from its oxide by reacting with the oxygen.) The bloom was then forged (hammered) into shape and wrought iron was the result, a form of iron that, when heated, can easily be shaped. For many years, wrought iron was the only form of iron.

The area that is now called the Black Country was not a major centre of the iron industry in the medieval era. The centres then were the Weald of Sussex and the Forest of Dean. Nevertheless, iron was worked in the area. Robert Plot, in his *Natural History of Staffordshire*, published in 1686, mentions that ironstone outcrops in Dudley and Walsall[1]. As early as the fourteenth century in Walsall, Adam the Bloomer was granted one acre of wasteland by the Lord of the Manor, Roger de Morteyn. It is likely that there was smelting north of the town in Birchills. A bloomery was also discovered at the end of the nineteenth century in Bescot when the former sewage disposal plant was built. The site is now occupied by Bescot Stadium, home of Walsall Football Club[2].

In time, water-powered bellows were introduced to blow air into the iron ore and charcoal mixture, increase its temperature and cause the iron to melt. So was born the early blast furnace and cast iron was formed in the process. The iron was run in liquid form into long depressions in sand, known as sows. There were side arms in the sows, known appropriately as pigs, hence pig iron. Pig iron (cast iron) contains 3–4% of carbon and as a liquid can be poured into moulds to form the shape of the mould. But pig iron cannot be shaped in the forge and so it was fed, as a solid, to a finery – a furnace where the iron is melted again, and the carbon expelled as carbon dioxide by pumping air in with bellows. Any residual carbon was expelled in another furnace, known as a chafery.

The blast furnace was known in the Midlands by the end of the sixteenth century. A court case concerning a series of affrays in 1597 provides the evidence. A group of labourers and yeomen from Wednesbury, led by Thomas and Richard Parkes, broke into a blast furnace mill at Perry Barr and occupied it for many weeks. The men from Perry Barr retaliated and attacked Parkes' forges in Wednesbury and other places, taking away forge hammers, chafery and finery bellows and large quantities of iron bar. The trouble did not stop there, but the details of the case show that the new blast furnace technique had reached South Staffordshire. It would soon supplant the older bloomeries[3].

It is easy to see why the Sussex Weald and the Forest of Dean were early centres of iron making. Both are heavily wooded and therefore suitable for the manufacture of charcoal. There was in fact a shortage of iron in the Midlands in the late-medieval period, insufficient for the thriving manufacturing industry developing in the area. Knives and cutting tools were made in Birmingham; there were lock makers in Wolverhampton and Willenhall; stirrups, buckles and bits were made in Walsall and nails just about everywhere. Iron was, therefore, imported from the Forest of Dean. Andrew Yarranton, in 1697, describes how 'sow iron is sent up the Severn to the forges of Stourbridge, Dudley, Wolverhampton, Sedgley, Walsall, and Birmingham and wrought and manufactured into all small commodities and diffused all over England and sent into most parts of the world'.[4] And it was not only the Forest of Dean that supplied the Midlands; Swedish iron was imported as well, again via the River Severn.

The problem the early iron makers faced was the vast amount of wood needed for charcoal production. This had serious implications because forests were becoming denuded, and wood was needed by the navy to build ships. In 1615, King James I issued a proclamation forbidding the glass makers of the Sussex Weald from using wood for charcoal production. Lack of wood hampered the development of the iron industry in the Midlands as well. Although it seems a bit of an exaggeration, it was claimed that at the end of the seventeenth century, 'within 10 miles of Dudley Castle there be near 20,000 smiths of all sorts of iron works… decayed for want wood'.[5] The breakthrough came in 1709 when Abraham Darby first smelted iron ore with coke. But first we must introduce Dud Dudley.

Dud Dudley

Instead of charcoal, Dud Dudley claimed to have smelted iron ore with coal. He was the illegitimate son of the wealthy landowner, Edward Sutton, 5th Baron Dudley. Dud was born in 1600 and at nineteen years of age went up to Balliol College, Oxford. In 1665, he wrote a book, *Metallum Martis*. In it, Dud relates how he attempted to smelt iron ore with coal:

> 'Having seen many of their failings, I held it my duty to endeavour, if it were possible to effect and perfect so laudable, and beneficial, and also so much desired inventions, as to making iron into cast works and bars with pit-cole, sea-cole, peat and turf.'

He goes on to say:

> 'Having former knowledge and delight in iron works at my father's when I was but a youth; afterwards at 20 years old, was I fetched from Oxford, then of Bayliol College, Anno 1619, to look and manage 3 iron works of my father's, 1 furnace and 3 forges, in the Chase of Pensnett, in Worcester-shire, but wood and charcole, growing there scant, and pit coles, in great quantities abounding near the furnace, did induce me to alter my furnace, and attempt by my new invention, the making of iron with pit cole.'[6, 7, 8]

It is little surprise that local charcoal producers did all in their power to thwart Dud. Undeterred, after his experiments at Pensnett Chase, he substituted coal for charcoal at a furnace at Cradley. Unfortunately, this furnace became victim of a serious flood, prompting a move to furnaces at Himley and Sedgley.

It was here that Dud Dudley claimed to be able to make seven tons of iron per week with his 'new invention'. His apparent success did not go unnoticed. A mob, prompted by the charcoal masters, took it upon themselves to destroy Dudley's furnaces. The Civil War then intervened, and Dud Dudley took up the cause of Charles I and the royalists. After the Restoration, he was back in Staffordshire, living in Kingswinford and smelting iron ore with his 'perfect invention', at furnaces at Green's Forge, Swin Forge, Heath Forge and Cradley Forge.[9]

Dud took out two patents, but it is the conclusion of most experts that he failed to make wrought iron, the reason being that coal can contain as much as 4% sulphur, which would have rendered the iron useless (red short or hot short), thus preventing it being forged without breaking up or splitting.[10] (As a rider, the author points out that some Black Country coal has a low sulphur content thereby perhaps enabling Dudley to make iron of an inferior quality.)

Abraham Darby and Thomas Newcomen

Abraham Darby was a Black Country man. He was born in 1678 at Old Farm Lodge, Wren's Nest, near Dudley, the son of the Quaker, John Darby, who, in common with many at the time, combined farming with the life of a nailer. Abraham was apprenticed to a malt-mill maker in Birmingham before setting up in business in Bristol. In 1706, he moved to Coalbrookdale in Shropshire, involving himself in various enterprises.[11] In the same year, he is credited with smelting iron ore with coke rather than charcoal. Coke is produced by heating coal in the absence of air. In Darby's case, he heated heaps of coal covered with layers of ashes. Gases are driven off and the hot mass then cooled with water to produce coke, a pure form of carbon.

Darby did not publicise his innovation and in consequence it was slow to reach the Black Country, so preventing the area from fully exploiting its natural resources. But there was another difficulty that the Black Country faced and that was the lack of a ready supply of water to drive the water mills which powered the blast furnaces. At the time, there were only three ways of doing physical work (such as working the bellows of a blast furnace). These were muscle power (those of a horse or a man); wind power (windmills) and the power of a flow of water (water mills). Another innovation was needed, and it came from Thomas Newcomen.

Thomas Newcomen was a blacksmith from Dartmouth. He invented the atmospheric steam engine, whose original purpose was to pump water out of the local Cornish tin mines. But it was to the coal mines of the Black Country where Newcomen headed in 1712 to install and publicise his groundbreaking invention at a site near Dudley Castle (see chapter: Coal). James Watt was later to improve the efficiency of Newcomen's engine by providing a separate condenser. Watt went into partnership with Matthew Boulton and further improved the steam engine by pioneering the so-called sun and planet gear which enabled rotative motion to be achieved. (Newcomen's engine was only capable of reciprocating motion.)

Newcomen and Watt's inventions enabled energy from a steam engine to power the bellows, so releasing the area from its reliance on a flow of water! By so doing, Newcomen and Watt kick started the industrial revolution. The impact in the Midlands was immediate – what we understand as the Black Country became a reality.

John 'Iron Mad' Wilkinson

There is a large literature about John Wilkinson (1728–1808). In this section, the following sources were consulted. [12,13,14,15]

'If there is a manufactory of more importance to England than another – it is that of making iron with pitcoal.' These were the words of John Wilkinson, in instructions to his trustees in 1806. John Wilkinson can be styled, with all justification, the 'father of the Black Country iron industry.'

He came from an iron making family; his father, Isaac, was chief caster at Backborrow Iron Company in Furness, North Lancashire. John Wilkinson went to school at Dr Caleb Rotherham's Dissenting Academy in Kendal. In 1753, Isaac Wilkinson left Lancashire and headed to North Wales to work at the Bersham furnace, near Wrexham. He was joined shortly afterwards by his son.

When Isaac Wilkinson arrived at Bersham, the blast for all furnaces was provided by leathern bellows depressed by the power of a water wheel. In order to increase the volume and intensity of the blast, Isaac Wilkinson invented the iron bellows. He answered his detractors by informing them, 'I grew tired of my leathern bellows and determined to make iron ones. Everybody laughed at me. I did it and applied the steam engine to blow them'. Isaac's mention of the steam engine is significant. John Wilkinson was quick to realise the flexibility of the steam engine and how it could be used to exploit the potential of South Staffordshire as a centre of iron making, now released from its dependence on water mills. In 1757 (some claim it was 1767), he arrived at Bilston. There he built his first blast furnace at Bradley, more specifically 'near Fireholes'. He called it the 'Old Furnace'. Fortuitously, in 1768, Parliament passed an Act allowing a canal to be built between Birmingham and the Staffordshire and Worcestershire Canal, passing through Bilston. Wilkinson then erected another furnace adjacent to the canal (the Birmingham Canal Navigation) at Upper Bradley. Expansion continued apace and by 1770 the Bradley works extended to twenty-six acres.

Lack of a flow of water to power a water mill at Bradley meant that Wilkinson was obliged to use a steam engine to blow his furnace. First, air was pumped to accumulators, large vessels known as 'regulating bellies', to even out the flow of air to the furnace. It was then applied to the bellows. (His first engine was almost certainly an atmospheric engine similar to that pioneered by Newcomen; eight years were to pass before Boulton and Watt went into business at Soho in Birmingham, thereafter providing Wilkinson with a Watt engine.)

Wilkinson obtained his coal from the local Hallfields Colliery at Bradley and Barebones and Heathfield in Darlaston. Gubbin and New Mine iron ore were used, and by 1772 he succeeded in using raw coal in his furnaces, writing to his clerk at his furnace at Broseley (Shropshire) to say, 'I am happy to acquaint you that I have at last succeeded in using coal in my furnace. The coal is got on my estate and answers well. The produce of the furnace is now 20 tons instead of 10 tons formerly'. Wilkinson was no doubt helped by the fact that South Staffordshire thick coal is relatively low in sulphur; secondly, because there was an increase in blast furnace temperature caused by the stronger blast from the steam engine; and thirdly because limestone was added to remove any residual sulphur.

In 1775, the famous firm of Boulton and Watt was founded at Soho in Birmingham. A letter, sent at the time to James Watt, indicated that the firm were having difficulties in obtaining good quality iron: 'The people of Coalbrookdale sent us castings for the circular machine only a month ago. They were unsound and totally useless and done over with some stuff to conceal the defect.' The letter continues: 'An eminent caster has settled during the summer at Bilston. We were obliged to have recourse to him.' The eminent caster was John Wilkinson and so was born the working relationship between the two firms.

Wilkinson made iron of the highest quality. He also invented an accurate boring machine, taking out a patent in 1774 'for a new method of casting and boring iron guns or cannon'. Previously, the rotating boring head was held stationary and the item to be bored placed on slides and drawn towards it. Wilkinson reversed the process by rotating the object to be bored and then feeding the drill towards it. Much better cylinders were produced, ideally suited for Boulton and Watt steam engines.

The relationship between Boulton and Watt and Wilkinson was not always harmonious. To the irritation of the Soho firm – they held patents on their steam engine – Wilkinson began building engines of his own without permission or by paying the appropriate royalties. But Boulton and Watt were dependent on Wilkinson. Although he was expensive: 'I observe your charge for fitting is much higher than similar goods from Coalbrookdale,' complained the Soho firm; they were ready to admit, 'I must do Mr Wilkinson justice to say nobody excels him as an engine iron founder'. They also insisted that their customers bought from Wilkinson.

In 1777, Wilkinson decided to branch out and produce malleable iron, i.e. wrought iron. For this he declared 'he was going to work the forge way'. But to make wrought iron, he would need a charcoal-fired finery and charcoal was in short supply. (Henry Cort had yet to develop his puddling furnace which would eventually enable cast iron to be converted to wrought iron.) But we know from a letter James Watt wrote in 1784 that the puddling furnace, when it was developed, was late coming to the Black Country: 'As to Mr Cort's process I have never seen it as it is not practiced in this neighbourhood, the iron being made mostly by the Wright and Jesson's process, which answers very well.'

Richard Jesson and John Wright were ironmasters in West Bromwich. They improved upon a process originally developed by Charles Wood of Egremont in Cumberland and his brother John Wood in Wednesbury. In 1773, Jesson and Wright took out a patent for their process, whereby pig iron was melted in a refinery but using coke instead of charcoal. After the bulk of the carbon had been removed, the iron was hammered, first hot then cold, to break it into small pieces which were placed in a series of clay crucibles and heated in a reverbatory furnace for four or five hours. The crucibles broke up and ran out with the slag leaving pure iron to be hammered into a ball or transferred to a chafery.

(In 1777, Jesson and Wright acquired premises which they called Wren's Nest Forges on the Linley Brook at Broseley, near the River Severn in Shropshire.)[16] Wilkinson may have used a process like Wright and Jesson. If not, may be the technique developed by the Crannage brothers from Coalbrookdale, whose patent for making pig iron or cast iron malleable used a reverberatory furnace with pit coal.

Wilkinson approached Boulton and Watt in the early 1780s, requesting a steam engine to raise a stamp on his forge. The Soho firm made several attempts without success until on the 27th of April 1783, James Watt wrote:

'We have had a trial of our new forge engine at Bradley; cylinder 42 inches diameter and 6 feet stroke, makes from 15 to 50 (even 60) strokes per minute at pleasure, works a hammer of 7½ cwt raised 2 feet high which makes 6 strokes per stroke of the engine and has struck 300 blows per minute; we are, however, going to make it strike only 4½ blows per stroke'.

This was the first time a steam engine successfully forged iron and it continued as the method of choice until Nasmyth invented his direct-acting steam hammer.

We know from other correspondence of Boulton and Watt that John Wilkinson had slitting mills and rolling mills at Bradley: 'We have never erected any engine for slitting or rolling of iron, but our friend, Mr Wilkinson, has by licence from us annexed a slitting or rolling mill to one of our engines.' This enabled Wilkinson to make boiler plate and by 1786 he was making boilers for both Boulton and Watt and their customers. It took him a couple of weeks to complete a boiler and within ten years orders came in at a greater volume than Wilkinson could cope with.

'Iron Mad' is a very apt sobriquet for John Wilkinson. Everything had to be of iron; he made an iron pulpit for the Wesleyan church in Bilston and constructed an iron barge. Wilkinson died in 1808. It was his wish that he should be buried in an iron coffin near his stately home at Castle Head near Ulverston. Obviously, an iron coffin had to be provided, but when his corpse arrived at Castle Head the coffin turned out to be too small. The Bradley works were immediately instructed to make a larger one; meanwhile, Wilkinson was buried in the garden to await its arrival. Difficulties continued, for it was suddenly realised there was an insufficient depth of soil, so before the poor man could be finally laid to rest, explosives had to be found to blast a hole in the rock.

Legends abound about 'Iron Mad' Wilkinson. It was prophesised that seven years after his passing he would reappear at his beloved blast furnaces mounted on a white horse. Apparently, thousands gathered at Bradley on the due date, full of expectation.

The Bradley works fell into terminal decline after Wilkinson's death, caused in no small way by the general depression in the iron trade. But many have blamed the demise on the fact that Wilkinson never took up Henry Cort's new puddling method for producing wrought iron from pig iron.

Henry Cort, Joseph Hall and the Puddling Furnace

Henry Cort was born in Lancashire in about 1740 and began his working life in London as a naval agent. In 1775, he took over a forge at Fontley in Hampshire and began making naval ironware. His fame rests on his invention of the puddling furnace, used to remove carbon from pig iron and convert it to malleable wrought iron. He took out a patent in 1784, describing a reverberatory furnace where the fuel (coal) and metal were kept apart in separate compartments. The products of combustion (flames and smoke) passed over a fire bridge of refractory bricks between the two compartments, to the furnace containing the metal before being exhausted via the flue (chimney). Pig iron was placed in the bed of the furnace and when it became molten was stirred with an iron bar inserted through the furnace door. The current of air so produced oxidised the residual carbon to CO_2 and wrought iron was the product.[17,18] Although taken up rather slowly in the Black Country, the puddling furnace was a very significant advance in iron making. But there were disadvantages. Cort's process was only effective with so called 'white iron', i.e. cast iron with low carbon and silicon levels. A form of pre-treatment was therefore required in a finery to reduce the carbon level. It was also common practice for the bottom of the furnace, containing the molten iron, to be made of sand. Sand was cheap but proved to be an unsuitable choice. Under these conditions, magnetite formed in the melt and combined with the silica in the sand to form excessive amounts of slag. Cort's puddling furnace was, therefore, wasteful of iron. The problem was addressed by S.B. Rogers at Nantyglo, South Wales, who substituted iron oxide for sand as the furnace bottom.[19] The molten iron was now in contact with a material rich in oxygen which aided removal of carbon.

It was a Black Country man who was to make real advances in puddling. Joseph Hall was born in Tipton in 1789 and was successful in developing the technique known as 'wet puddling', as opposed to the 'dry puddling' of Henry Cort. In 1856, he described to the *Birmingham Journal* how his new process came about. It was all down to an old shoe heel!

> 'One day, in coming out of the forge, I met one of my employers on his way to the refinery with an old shoe heel in his hand, full of old hob nails, worn once probably by a poor collier. I felt surprised on seeing such a thing in his hands and watched to see what was to be done with it. To my surprise he threw it into the fire of the refinery which was close at hand. After a few seconds I saw the object of his carrying the old shoe heel. Naming the circumstances to the refinery man he said O yes, he often brings a similar bit; it is to save that much iron.'[20]

Witnessing this chain of events prompted Joseph Hall to reflect on the quantity of waste iron he had discarded in the past. He determined to mend his ways and to save as much iron as he could. But he went further and began collecting the waste slag found in the puddlers' boshes. (Boshes were the water tanks used to cool the iron workers' tools, not be confused with the boshes of the blast furnace.) The slag, known as bosh cinder, contained appreciable amounts of iron oxide. Joseph Hall decided to add the bosh cinder to the molten metal in his puddling furnace. A violent reaction immediately set in and as Hall explained:

> 'I became much alarmed for the consequences, and thought the furnace would have been burned down, for whilst the boiling went on the furnace appeared literally full, the contents ran over into the standing plate on which the puddler stands to work… and I promised myself not to attempt the like again.' But to Hall's surprise 'on trying the bloom of iron produced by the above experiment, I found it to be the best piece of iron I had ever seen.'[21]

What Hall had done was to speed the removal of carbon by reacting it with the oxygen of the iron oxide in the slag to give off carbon monoxide, which oxidised to carbon dioxide, emitting a blue flame, known to the iron workers as 'puddlers' candles'. Hall's process had a further beneficial effect; phosphorus was removed in the slag which would otherwise render the iron so called 'cold short', i.e. brittle when hammered cold. There was a slight difficulty which Hall quickly overcame. Hall found that unless he first roasted the bosh cinder, it was prone to attack the cast-iron furnace bottom. When roasted, however, it lined or 'fettled' it. The roasted cinder was known by the name 'bulldog'. In time, other materials were used for lining the furnace such as haematite and iron pyrites. There were two further benefits of Hall's 'wet puddling' process; there was now no need to first subject the cast iron to the finery and the vigorous boiling action in the furnace alleviated the manual labour of stirring the mixture.

Bloomfield Iron Works[21]

Joseph Hall worked for the same employer between 1806 and 1830 and it was in this period that he did his ground-breaking experiments with 'wet puddling'. He then joined with Thomas Lewis and purchased land at Bloomfield near Tipton, where he built an iron works and equipped it with three 'wet puddling' furnaces. Lewis soon left and Hall was then joined by Richard Bradley. Within the year, the firm was producing fifty tons of iron every week. But extra capital was needed, and this was provided by William Barrows who joined in 1834 and took control of the finances leaving Hall in charge of technical matters. Thus, was born Bradley Barrows and Hall (BBH). They were soon to diversify, and with a group of bankers took over a colliery near Tipton. But trouble lay ahead. Local miners had had their wages reduced and even though BBH did not cut their men's pay, the 'flying pickets' of the day with a group of bankers succeeded in preventing the BBH miners from working. Joseph Hall responded by ferrying his iron workers in a boat down the Birmingham Canal to the colliery to guard his miners. Eventually, peace was secured after Hall assured the striking miners that his colliery would only supply his works and not any other. The pickets were satisfied and dispersed, shouting, 'Hall forever'.

But BBH's troubles were to continue when the bankers failed. James Foster of Stourton Castle, himself an ironmaster at Stourbridge and a member of the committee looking after the bank's affairs, offered to save the day by offering Hall a considerable amount of money. He described Hall's misfortune as a 'cursed shame' and continued, 'Mr Hall, I repeat what I have said many times

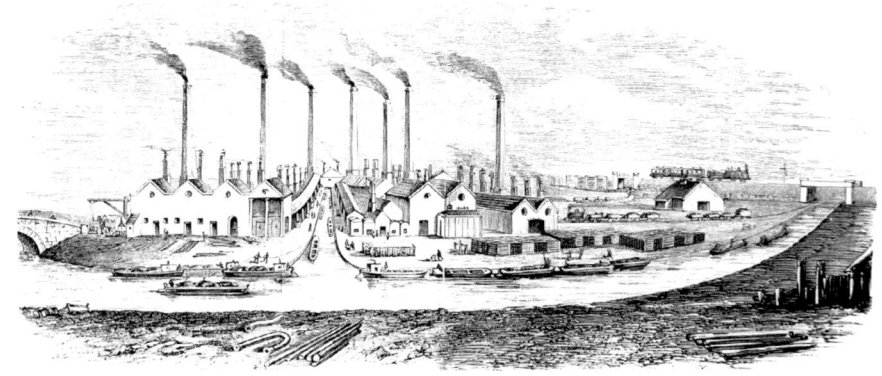

W. Barrows & Sons Bloomfield Iron Works, Tipton (Samuel Griffiths, 1873)

W. Barrow & Sons Factory Works (Samuel Griffiths, 1873)

behind your back, that you have done more for our trade than anyone before you, and I don't think anyone after you will do more'. Hall declined Foster's kind offer and in the event an arrangement was made whereby Joseph Bramah (son of the renowned Joseph Bramah of hydraulic power fame), joined the firm.

Before long, Bramah died and Bradley left, leaving Hall and Barrows at the Bloomfield works. Joseph Hall died in 1859 and within the year so did William Barrows. The firm then passed to Joseph Barrows and expanded to build other works at Tipton Green and the Factory Works, also at Tipton. Over one thousand men were employed, producing one thousand tons of iron every week.

John Gibbons

The Black Country was to produce yet another innovator. John Gibbons (1777–1851) came from a long-established Sedgley family. They were originally involved in the coal trade and acquired much land in the Black Country, where they expanded their interests. In the mid-eighteenth century, John's grandfather, also John, leased a series of forges in the Stour Valley and the Gibbons family entered the iron trade. John Gibbons Jnr. had a series of blast furnaces at Millfields (Bilston), the Levels (Brierley Hill), Ketley Hall (Kingswinford) and Corbyn's Hall (Pensnett).[22] Blast furnaces in use at the time had to be relined after about four or five years of continuous operation. When Gibbons came to reline his furnaces, he noticed that the original square furnace had been rounded off to a circle by the action of continuous heat. He mused, 'a fiery finger has written knowledge on these walls; I will try to decipher it.' John Gibbons recorded his experiments in a book he wrote in 1839, *Practical Remarks on the Construction of the Staffordshire Blast Furnace*,[23] where he noted, 'If I at once make room which the furnace makes for itself by a rougher operation, I might probably preserve thereby a considerable portion of my hearth and boshes.' He tried his idea out at Corbyn's Hall and succeeded in making 236 tons of iron per week as compared with the previous seventy-five tons. Gibbons' new blast furnace with its circular hearth quickly spread throughout the region. John Gibbons made a further innovation in 1844, when he wrote, *Practical Remarks on the use of cinder pig in the puddling furnace and on the management of the forge and mill*.[24] Here, Gibbons charged his blast furnace with the ironrich waste from the puddling furnace, as well as with iron ore. [25]

John Urpeth Rastrick

Vast quantities of heat are lost in the manufacture of wrought iron, both from the blast furnace and the puddling furnace. John Urpeth Rastrick (1780–1856) addressed this issue. He was born in Northumberland and in 1816 became a partner in the Stourbridge iron founders, Bradley, Foster and Rastrick. He is better known to us as a railway engineer and at Stourbridge he built the 'Stourbridge Lion' which, when exported to the USA became the first locomotive in that country. While at Stourbridge, he designed a new boiler and heated it with waste heat from the puddling furnace, one boiler heated by waste heat from four puddling furnaces. Rastrick was also responsible for designing the Chillington Iron Works in Wolverhampton and the Shut End Works at Stourbridge.[26,27]

James Beaumont Neilson and E.A. Cowper

In 1828, the Scotsman, James Beaumont Neilson, took out a patent whereby the blast of air to the tuyers (the removable pipe conveying the air blast to the furnace) was first heated in a separate coal fired chamber. The so called 'hot blast' furnace had many advantages: the increased temperature enabled sulphur to be taken up as calcium sulphate and removed with the slag, melting was speeded up, less fuel used and an increased output of pig iron achieved.[28,29] But it was slow to establish itself, many being convinced that since blast furnaces tended to operate better in winter than summer, it followed that cold blast should be preferred to hot blast. In the Black Country, locally designed ovens were used at first to heat the blast, but they were eventually surpassed by the Cowper Stove, patented by E.A. Cowper in 1857.[30]. In Cowper's process, a tall metal tower was almost completely filled with bricks. Hot exhaust gas from the blast furnace was directed through the bricks to raise their temperature. Air was then passed through, and the bricks gave up their heat to the air which was hot blasted to the furnace. Cowper stoves usually worked in pairs – as one gave up its heat, the other was heated by furnace waste gas. The Cowper Stove eventually became accepted throughout the world but only to a limited extent in the Black Country.[31]

In other parts of the country, attempts were made to utilise the waste heat from the furnace to heat boiler plant or hot-blast stoves. The practice was largely ignored in the Black Country (there were plentiful supplies of coal slack for heating), but some works experimented successfully, including Samuel Lloyd at Old Park Works at Wednesbury.[32]

By the mid-nineteenth century, the Black Country was the most important iron-making centre in the world. Most blast furnaces were of a similar design and a typical works had two or three. Steam engines powered the blast; their boilers, apart from a few heated by furnace waste gas, were fired with slack coal. Steam engines also provided the power to lift the iron ore in wagons up an inclined plane to the top of the furnace. By the mid-nineteenth century, the Black Country was producing 500,000 tons of pig iron every year.

Many works had a forge adjacent to the furnace plant – Barrows and Hall eventually had one hundred puddling furnaces at their three works at Bloomfield, Tipton Green and Factory. The forge usually contained a tilt hammer, a heavy hammer fixed to a wooden arm (or helve) which tilted about a pivot. A series of cams were attached to a revolving wheel near to the other side of the beam – powered originally by a water mill and later by steam power – which acted on the beam so that the hammer fell by gravity in a uniform way onto the object to be worked. The tilt hammer was eventually superseded by James Nasmyth's Steam Hammer. Here, the hammer is attached to the end of a steam engine's piston. The hammer rises and falls within vertical guides above the anvil and in sync with the piston's stroke to give a series of blows whose force is dependent on the steam supply. Nasmyth's hammer had a definite advantage over the tilt hammer. With the latter, which gives regular blows applied by gravity, the larger the block of iron to be forged the smaller is the blow, which could be insufficient to hammer the iron into shape.

The Mid-Nineteenth Century and Beyond

In the mid-nineteenth century, Black Country iron production was at its peak. The finished wrought iron was used as sheet for boilers and ship building, as bar iron for cables and chains and to make nails. The number of blast furnaces had increased from fourteen in 1796 to 170 by the 1860s. Jones lists them.[33] The numbers quoted are blast furnaces built, not all of which were in blast. They were: Barber's Field, Bilston (two), Birchills, Walsall (two), New Birchills, Walsall (five), Bloxwich, Walsall (two), Bradley, Bilston (two), Brettell Lane, Stourbridge (two), Broadwaters, Wednesbury (three), Borverux, Bilston (seven), Bilston Brook, Bilston (three), Chillington, Wolverhampton (four), Moseley Hole (three), Bentley, Walsall (two), Capponfield, Bilston (three), Gold's Hill, West Bromwich (two), Coneygree, Dudley (three), New Level, Brierley Hill (three), Cape, Smethwick (one), Corbyn's Hall, Dudley (four), Corbyn's Hall New, Dudley (four), Corngreaves, Birmingham (six), Coseley Hall, Bilston (two), Crookhay, West Bromwich (four), The Lays, Stourbridge (three), Darlaston Green, Wednesbury (three), Deepfields, Bilston (three), Dudley Port, Tipton (two), Dixon's Green Dudley (one), Park Lane, Tipton (two), Dudley Wood, Dudley (three), Groveland, Tipton (one), Hallfields, Bilston (one), Hatherton, Bloxwich (two), Herbert's Park, Bilston (one), Horseley, Tipton (two), Ketley's Dudley (four), Old Level, Brierley Hill (two), Millfields, Bilston (four), Netherton, Dudley (two), Netherton New, Dudley (two), Stour Valley, Tipton (two), Oak Farm, Kingswinford (two), Oldbury (four), Old Hill, Dudley (two), Old Park, Wednesbury (three), Osier Bed, Bilston (three), Parkhead, Dudley (two), Parkfield, Wolverhampton (five), Pelsall, Walsall (two), Priestfield, Wolverhampton (three), Priestfield New, Wolverhampton (two), Priors's Field, Bilston (three), Rough Hay, Darlaston (three), Russell's Hall, Dudley (five), Shut End, Kingswinford (four), Spring Vale, Bilston (three), Stonefield, Bilston (one), Stow Heath, Bilston (four), Tipton (two), Tipton Green (four), Wednesbury Oak, Tipton (three), Union, West Bromwich (three), Willenhall (three), Willingsworth, Tipton (three), Wolverhampton (three), Woodside, Dudley (three), Withymoor, Dudley (two), Windmill End, Dudley (three).

Despite the apparent vibrancy of the industry, there were problems ahead. Although more than half of the iron used by Black Country ironmasters came from local sources, considerable quantities were imported from outside the area.

George Adams Priestfield Iron Works, Wolverhampton (Samuel Griffiths, 1873)

Coal stocks were also in decline. Upwards of 750,000 tons of iron was produced every year but it was still insufficient for local needs, necessitating the import of 300,000 tons of pig iron every year.

In many respects, the Black Country iron masters were behind the times. Jones[34] summed it up when he wrote 'In respect of its forges and mills, as well as its blast furnaces, it bears ample internal evidence that it is rather old fashioned.' Then, in 1856, in a groundbreaking lecture at the British Association, Henry Bessemer announced to the world that he was able to manufacture malleable iron and steel without fuel. So began the advent of the age of steel and the decline of the wrought-iron industry, on which so much Black Country prosperity was based.

Steel

Henry Bessemer (1813–1891) was born in the small village of Charlton in Hertfordshire. His father, Anthony, came from a Huguenot family and was a prolific inventor; Henry followed in his father's footsteps. Henry Bessemer owned a factory, Baxter House, near London's St Pancras and made bronze powder which was used as a constituent of gold paint. It was a lucrative business and Bessemer made enough money to enable him to follow other interests. One of these was an attempt to make wrought iron which could be melted and then cast to make gun barrels. This he achieved by blasting air through molten pig iron to remove the carbon by oxidising it to carbon dioxide. Significantly, he did not heat the molten pig iron. It was the renowned engineer, George Rennie, who persuaded Bessemer to publish and patent his invention. Hence the paper he read at the British Association in 1856: *The Manufacture of Iron without Fuel*.

Bessemer granted licences to several iron works to use his process, including the Dowlais and Ebbw Vale Ironworks in South Wales. When the firm tried out Bessemer's convertor, it failed completely, and the metal produced turned out to be 'cold short' (brittle when cold). The problem was caused by phosphorus in the pig iron and because the convertor was lined with a siliceous material. There was another difficulty: too much oxygen was being absorbed in the process leading to iron of low quality. To avoid this, the Forest of Dean ironmaster, Robert Forrester Mushet, added a substance known as spiegeleisen to the mix. It is high in manganese and, given the affinity of manganese for oxygen, it solved the problem of excess oxygen. Therefore, provided an ore low in phosphorus was used and the converter was lined with a non-siliceous material, the Bessemer Convertor proved fully capable of producing mild steel.

The news did not go down well in certain parts of the Black Country, particularly with Joseph Hall, pioneer of wet puddling. Hall decided to do something about it. He set off for London to attend a lecture on Bessemer's process at the Polytechnic Institution. He also attempted to meet Henry Bessemer and challenge him to test his system in competition with the puddling furnace. The competition was to be either in London or the Black Country, with competent judges awarding £500 to the winner; this sum to be provided by the loser. Henry Bessemer declined the challenge. Hall responded by writing, 'the age has not yet arrived to dispense with the puddling furnace'[35]. Regrettably for many in South Staffordshire the age had arrived, for in time the Bessemer Convertor was able to produce steel of the highest quality.

The Bessemer Convertor and the high-quality mild steel it supplied sounded the death knell of the Black Country wrought-iron trade. From the 1860s onwards, wrought-iron production declined. In 1860 there were two hundred blast furnaces in the district, within three years the number had fallen to 170.[36] Furthermore those still in blast did not have the capacity to meet local demand, added to which iron ore deposits were being depleted forcing supplies to be imported from other areas. Efforts to automate the wet-puddling process proved fruitless; it was a skilled job, much dependent of the expertise of the puddler, built up over many years. First in the Black Country to install a Bessemer Converter was Lloyds, Foster & Co. of Wednesbury at their Old Park Works. They were followed in 1882 by Alfred Hickman, both companies making steel.[37]

A further innovation was to threaten the wrought-iron industry. This was the Open-Hearth Furnace developed by the German, Carl Wilhelm Siemens (1823–1883). He granted a licence to Pierre Emile Martin, who used the technique of regenerative preheating to refine steel. Decarbonisation is achieved in a reverberatory furnace by the oxygen in iron oxide. Iron ore can also be added to supplement the oxygen levels. The technique involves passing the hot exhaust gases from the furnace through a chamber containing bricks. Heat is transferred to the bricks and then the flow reversed, whereby heat from the bricks is passed to the incoming flow of fuel and air. By this means, a sufficiently high temperature can be attained to rid the pig iron or scrap metal of carbon and other impurities. In practice, there are a pair of brick columns as one passes its heat to the furnace the other receives heat from the furnace waste gases. The process is then reversed. The Open-Hearth Process is a batch process. In contrast to the Bessemer process, it has the advantage of not exposing the steel to large amounts of nitrogen which would otherwise cause brittleness. It also enables scrap iron to be recycled. The Old Park Works at Wednesbury installed an open-hearth furnace, as did the New British Iron Co. at Cradley Heath. In 1891, an open-hearth furnace was commissioned at the Earl of Dudley's Round Oak Steel Works at Brierley Hill.[38] The fact that the considerable expansion at the Round Oak works was at the expense of its iron works emphasises the extent to which mild steel had supplanted wrought iron.

Well-Known Ironworks

A brief description is given below of prominent iron works in the Black Country. There are many more. Others are described in *Griffiths' Guide to the Iron Trade of Great Britain*, first published in 1873 and reprinted by David and Charles in 1967. There are also excellent web sites – Bev Parker's www.historywebsite.co.uk and www.blackcountrymuse.com.

The Netherton Ironworks of M. & W. Grazebrook[39]

Grazebrook's can date their history back to 1641 when Michael Grazebrook was working at a glassworks at Stourbridge. In 1800, a descendent, again named Michael, leased land at the Netherton Hall estate to mine the ten-yard seam of coal. He also opened an ironworks and in 1806 connected it to the Dudley Canal. A Boulton & Watt steam engine was installed in 1817 to power the bellows of the blast furnace. It did sterling service and was still going strong right up to the time when the furnace was finally taken out of service in 1946. Grazebrook's got into financial difficulty in the 1870s but were rescued by the diligence of Francis Grazebrook who joined the firm in 1878, aged 22. In 1888, Grazebrook's was connected to the railway.

The company diversified in the twentieth century and in the Second World War was commissioned to build gigantic bombs. The company's minute book records:

> Early in 1941, Air Commodore P. Huskinson of Bomber Command and his designated staff put into our hands the blueprints of the 8000

lb. Bomb. A trial explosion at Shoeburyness in August 1941 led to improvements. In 1942, the first bomb was dropped by specially equipped Lancasters on the Gnome Works, Limoges.

Another vast bomb of 12,000lb soon followed. Models of these bombs were later made for Sir Winston Churchill, Arthur Harris of Bomber Command and King George VI.

In 1960, Grazebrooks merged with N. Hingley and Sons and later with F. H. Lloyd.

Bromford Ironworks[40]

Bromford Ironworks began in 1780 and made iron wire in West Bromwich by the Birmingham Canal Navigation near Spon Lane. In 1800, they were bought by Wright and Jesson (see the section on John Wilkinson), later, in 1809, to be joined by Samuel Dawes and now operating under the name of Jesson and Dawes. William Henry Dawes took control in 1850 and soon Bromfords become one of the foremost ironworks in the Black Country. By 1881, they had two forges, sixty-five puddling furnaces and seven mills making six hundred tons of iron per week with seven hundred employees. William Henry Dawes died in 1878, after which the firm faced financial difficulty and closed in 1886. Two years later, they were sold for £17,000, becoming known as the Bromford Iron Company and diversified in the twentieth century as makers of hot and cold steel strip.

Ironworks Associated with the Lloyd Family[41,42,43]

Samuel Lloyd (1768–1849), a banker born in Birmingham, had twelve children, two of whom became important Black Country ironmasters. (Samuel Lloyd was descended from the Quaker ironmonger Sampson Lloyd (1699–1779), who in 1765, with John Taylor, founded Birmingham's first bank. It went on to become the present-day Lloyds Bank.) The two brothers were Samuel Lloyd (1795–1862) and Sampson Lloyd (1808–1874).

Samuel Lloyd was living in Wednesbury in 1818 and set about exploiting land owned there by the Lloyd family for coal mining. The colliery was known as

Old Park Colliery. In 1819, Samuel and his brother George went into business with the Middlesex-born brothers, Joseph Talwin Foster and Sampson Foster. A forty-two-year lease was obtained on the land and the firm of **Lloyds Fosters & Co.** was born. The business was run by Samuel Lloyd and by 1828 a Wednesbury directory described the **Old Park Works** as iron founders. In the mid-1830's, George Lloyd left, by which time the brother Sampson Lloyd had joined with a one-quarter share. Lloyds Fosters then began an association with John Joseph Bramah (1798–1846), nephew of the famous Joseph Bramah of hydraulic-power fame. John Joseph was well acquainted with railway engineering, having worked at his uncle's Pimlico works with George and Robert Stephenson. The railway boom was about to explode and with Sampson Lloyd, Bramah enabled Lloyds Fosters to go into the business of making railway materials. The Old Park works were therefore one of the first companies to make railway wheels, axles and related materials. In 1854, the **Monway Axle and Tyre Works** were formed to make iron plates for boilers and bridges, axles and tyres. (Locomotive tyres were that part of the wheel which came into contact with and ran on the railway line.)

Samuel Lloyd died in 1862 and was succeeded by his son Wilson Lloyd (1835–1908). Two years later, Lloyds Fosters entered into a contract with the London firm of P.A. Thorn & Co. to provide wrought iron for a new bridge in London over the Thames at Blackfriars. It was to prove costly! The first Blackfriars Bridge was designed by Robert Mylne in 1760. It was a fine bridge, completed in 1770, but problems began to arise with its foundations. Joseph Cubitt was commissioned to design a new bridge and Thorns were to pay for iron purchased on a 'on receipt' basis. The problem was that Thorn's did not honour their side of the contract; payment was not received, leaving Lloyds Fosters with a loss of £250,000, forcing them into liquidation. By this time, they had also installed a Bessemer Converter with the intention of making steel. The company was then sold to the **Patent Shaft & Axletree Co.**, Mr Sampson Lloyd becoming vice chairman.

In the early nineteenth century, a gun lock maker called Richard Bills established a furnace and foundry at Furnace Lane, Lower Green, in Darlaston. In 1826, he was joined by his stepson, Samuel Mills and the partnership of **Bills and Mills** was formed. It soon became known as the **Darlaston Green Iron Works.** By the mid-nineteenth century, the firm was operating from a fifty-five-acre site, had three blast furnaces, puddling furnaces and rolling mills. All sizes and shapes of iron plates and bars were made for boiler plates, rails, wire rods as well as steel by the cementation process. In 1849, the partnership

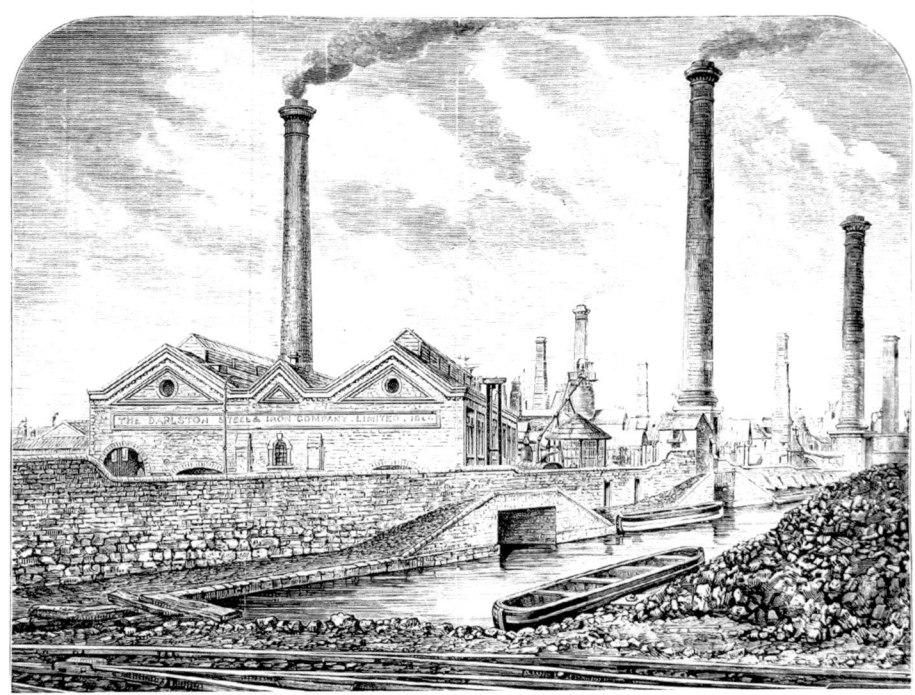
Darlaston Steel & Iron Company (Samuel Griffiths, 1873)

was dissolved, and Samuel Bills carried on alone until 1865 when he sold out to the Lloyd family for £250,000, by which time the firm was employing two thousand men. The firm then became known as the **Darlaston Iron and Steel Company.** Sampson Lloyd (1808–1874) was chairman and his son, Francis H. Lloyd (1845–1916) became the managing director.

The company expanded to some considerable size, situated on both sides of the Walsall Canal, with three blast furnaces, forty-three puddling furnaces, sixty-three steam engines and rolling mills and was served by the railway. There was a further plant at King's Hill. In 1877, because of the depression in the iron trade and in common with many Black Country iron works, the Darlaston Green works went into liquidation. The works on the south side of the canal passed to the bolt and nut manufacturer, **Charles Richards,** which according to the 1881 census was employing 130 men. (By 1890, a Charles Richards had started the Beau Ideal Cycle Company of Wolverhampton.) But iron making was reborn when the Bradley family took over the works on the north side of the canal. In 1900, a new steel blast furnace was built, and two Cowper stoves installed. W.J Foster joined the firm in 1910 and became works director in 1914.

The recession of the early 1920s hit the company, which went into liquidation. **Bradley and Foster** were then formed, a cupola furnace was installed, and the company began making refined iron.

After the Darlaston Iron and Steel Company folded, Francis Lloyd purchased a redundant timber yard at James Bridge. It became the **James Bridge Steel Works of F. H. Lloyd.** In its early days, the steel was refined in gas-fired open-hearth furnaces. An article written in about 1900 describes how James Bridge Steel Works had been commissioned to supply steel castings for Queen Victoria's new yacht. By this time, F.H. Lloyd were specialising in the manufacture of steel castings. The works extended from the Walsall Road to the London and North Western Railway from which private sidings ran into the premises. During the First World War, F.H. Lloyds concentrated on producing cast steel shells. The firm's history in the twentieth century can be found on Bev Parker's web site, describing how the company grew to become the largest steel foundry in Europe[44].

The **Patent Shaft & Axletree Company**[45] had its origins in a partnership between two Wednesbury men: Rev. James Hardy, a nonconformist minster and Samuel Hodgetts, a grocer. Hardy had taken out a patent for making iron axles for horse-drawn carts. He got his idea, so the story goes, by observing an orange and noticing how it is made up of segments. He reasoned that this would be a better method of making a shaft than welding square iron bars together. Hodgetts financed him and in the early 1830s the two went into business and purchased a forge at Leabrook. By the 1840s, both men had left to be replaced by Thomas Walker and Charles Geach, the business now known as the Patent Shaft & Axletree Company. Geach was a Birmingham banker with connections with the burgeoning railway industry and the company set about making railway axles. By 1844, it had ten puddling furnaces, a forge and rolling mill. The nearby iron works of Fletcher, Rose & Co. at Victoria Iron Works were acquired, and by 1854 the company had expanded to employ eight hundred men. A limited company was formed in 1864 with £300,000 capital, and three years later Lloyds Fosters were taken over together with all their plant (Old Park and Monway Works) and collieries. By 1870, Patent Shaft was the largest company of its kind in the Midlands and employed four thousand workers at three works; the original site of Hardy and Hodgetts (Brunswick), Monway and Old Park. The company's history in the twentieth century is included on Bev Parker's site.[44] Other axle makers in Wednesbury were Edwin Richards of the Portway Works, John Rigby & Sons and Richard Disturnal & Co. .

Horseley Coal and Iron Company[46,47]

The iron works and coal mines at Horseley were founded by Edward Dixon and Joseph Amphlett, both of Dudley, and a Birmingham solicitor, William Bedford. In 1792, they paid £10,000 for land at the Horseley Estate with the intention of sinking coal mines. By this time, the Birmingham Canal Company had cut a branch to Broadwaters. It had six collateral cuts, one of which was to the Horseley Company's land. Anxious to exploit the benefits of the canal, the company was prepared to pay one-fifth of the cost of erecting locks. Newcomen atmospheric steam engines were installed to rid the mines of floodwater and in 1809 a blast furnace was commissioned, blown by a Boulton and Watt steam engine. By 1813, the works had expanded with two blast furnaces, a puddling furnace, finery, three cupolas, seven engines, six pits, a house and an office. It was at this time that Aaron Manby joined the Horseley Company and with Joseph Smith an engineering works was built adjacent to the iron works.

Manby was a man of considerable talent. He was born at Shifnal in Shropshire and immediately after joining the Tipton works set about expanding the engineering side of the business. He lobbied the president of the Board of Trade for ordnance orders and took out a patent for making bricks with furnace slag. But his real claim to fame came about after his patent for the construction of an oscillating marine steam engine. The first vessel so powered was the *Prince Coburg*. Its potential was quickly seen by Sir (later Admiral) Charles Napier who, recognising that Manby 'had more talent than money', sponsored his work and with him, formed a French company with the intention of running a steam packet service on the Seine. Marine steam engines were provided for the three timber ships plying their trade on the Seine – the Ville de Rouen, the Duc de Bordeaux and the Génie du Commerce. But Manby had ambitions to build a ship of iron, and in 1821 he set about the task at Horseley. The ship Manby built was appropriately named the *Aaron Manby*. It was 106ft in length and 17ft wide, powered by a thirty-two-horsepower steam engine and equipped with revolving paddles. The vessel was then despatched in parts by canal to London and reassembled on the Grand Surrey Canal in Rotherhithe, under the supervision of Aaron's son, Charles Manby.

Trials were held on the 9th of May 1822 between Blackfriars and Battersea bridges. *The Morning Chronicle* reported on the 14th of May that 'a large party of distinguished naval officers, engineers and savants embarked at Parliament Stairs' and concluded that 'she is the most complete piece of workmanship in the iron way that has ever been witnessed'. Aaron Manby then set off for France to work on the Seine. A second ship was built for Napier and Manby at Horseley, the *Commerce de Paris*, and reassembled as before at Rotherhithe.

But Manby's time at Tipton was coming to an end. He became a partner at a foundry in Paris, La Fonderie de Charenton, and much to the displeasure of the Horseley works took many Tipton iron workers with him. And it seems that the Black Country men enjoyed the sophistication of French life, the *Quarterly Review* reporting:

'The Englishmen abroad, though able workmen, are in general, persons of extremely bad character, continually drunk… they drink nothing but the most expensive wines… and never leave the cabarets till the whole of their wages are exhausted.'

The *Aaron Manby* ended her days working on the Loire and was finally broken up in 1855. Manby himself died in 1850 on the Isle of Wight.

Iron making and coal mining continued at Horseley, despite a mining strike in 1822 which severely affected iron production. The men were enticed back to work with a promise of 3s per day plus two quarts of good drink for six days. The firm ran into financial difficulty in 1846. In 1865, new works were constructed about a half mile away and the old works pulled down.

In 1832, the Horseley Company made three railway engines for the St Helens and Runcorn Gap Railway, the Greenall, the St Helens and the Runcorn. But the railway company was less than satisfied: 'We have seldom had more than one out of three at work together – the others laid up for repairs.' Engines were also supplied to the Liverpool and Manchester Railway and the Dublin and Kingstown Railway. The company also built bridges, including one for the East India Dock in 1816, the Grand Union Canal at Brentford in 1824 and, most famously, in 1829, the Galton Bridge over the Birmingham Canal at Smethwick, designed by Thomas Telford and at the time the highest bridge in the world.

In 1846, the Horseley Works went into liquidation. In 1864, under new management, a new engineering factory was built which specialised in the manufacture of gas holders. Ten years later, a limited company was formed, and the company continued with its policy of building bridges and plant for the gas industry, including the Gas Light and Coke Company in Westminster and Beckton Gas Works. The company thrived throughout the twentieth century but, like so many others, declined and failed in the 1980s.

Round Oak Iron and Steel Works[48,49]

The first mention of iron making was in 1806, when Benjamin Gibbons worked three blast furnaces at a site called the Level, on land owned by the Dudley family. Each furnace produced about thirty-five tons of iron per week. The furnaces were charged in a unique way; they were set against an immense slag heap on top of which was a plateau along which a railway line ran to discharge coal and ironstone to bunkers and thence to the furnace top. In 1823, four furnaces were recorded, each operating by cold blast, but by 1839, of the three furnaces in blast, two were by hot blast each producing eighty-five tons per week. The plant was one of the most productive in the Black Country; only Chillington, Shut End and Gold's Green could compare. By 1842, Gibbons

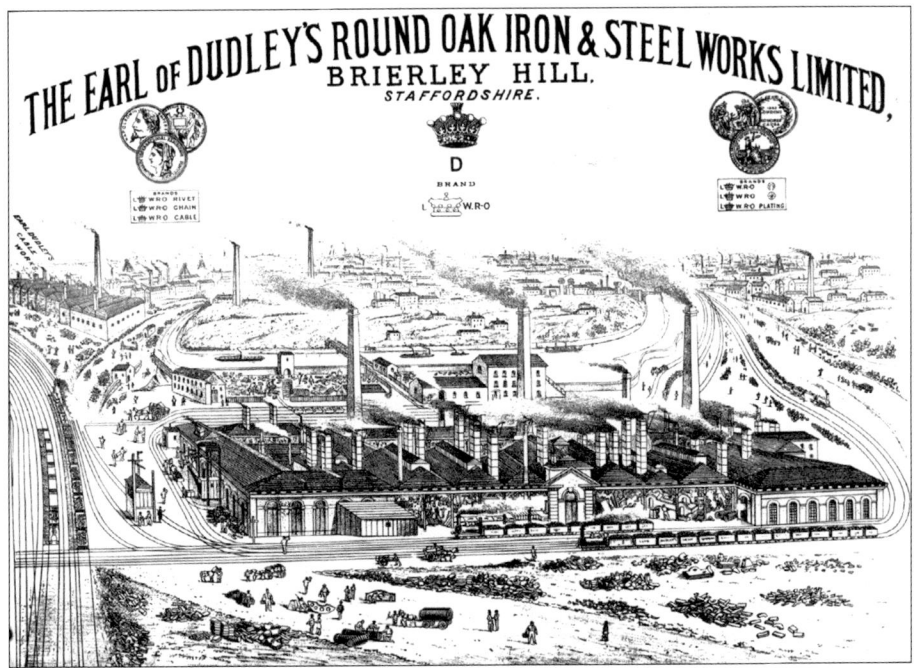

Round Oak Iron & Steel Works

had left for Corbyn's Hall and the plant was taken over by the Earl of Dudley.

Richard Smith was the Earl of Dudley's agent, and a decision was taken to modernise the Level furnaces; two were taken down and replaced by larger ones. The private railway owned by Lord Dudley (the Pensnett Railway) was also extended to cross the canal to feed the furnaces. Then, on the opposite side of the canal, a forge and mills were built, soon to be the Round Oak Iron Works. Round Oak opened in 1857, with six hundred employees, twenty-eight puddling furnaces, five mills and two hammers. The new plant was fed with pig iron from the Level furnaces and from the Earl of Dudley's other works at Coneygree in Tipton. In 1868, the firm could produce 550 tons of iron per week. It made fine iron, winning prizes at the International Exhibition of 1862, its iron described as 'a fine collection of iron of good quality'. It also sold iron to William Barrows & Son, well known for the quality of their products.

Things looked set fair; a fifth furnace was added at the New Level and an observer was quoted as writing: 'His lordship has still great stores in the crust of his large domains of all kinds of the best argillaceous ironstone and his thick coal in this Eldorado is inexhaustible.'

In 1894, steel making came to Round Oak. To supply it two brick-built furnaces were demolished and replaced by two steel-cased furnaces. A new engine was also installed, a Lilleshall vertical compound blowing engine. Mild steel was produced from three open-hearth furnaces. At the same time, the Round Oak works were sold to Lancashire Trust and Mortgage Company for £110,000 with a mortgage from the Dudley Estate. Facing financial difficulty, the company then went into liquidation and was repossessed by the Dudley family, becoming the Earl of Dudley's Round Oak Works Ltd.

Once more the company looked forward with confidence to the future with the works 'bang in the middle of the best scrap in the world, with Lord Dudley's superb coal at the end of our own railway and most of our customers on the doorstep'. Apart from a significant downturn in the 1920s, the company did thrive. It was modernised after the Second World War and nationalised when the steel industry became government owned. It was later jointly owned by Tube Investments Ltd, and the British Steel Corporation. Round Oak finally closed in 1982.

Chillington Iron Company

Chillington Iron Company was established in 1822 when a partnership was formed between the banker James Foster of Stourbridge, and John Barker and George Jones of Wolverhampton. Land was leased at Chillington Park in Wolverhampton from a Mr Gifford and an iron works built to the design of James Rastrick, who was soon to become a well-known civil engineer, specialising in railways. The original works had four blast furnaces. In 1852, John Barker died, leaving his share in the business to his two sons, George and Thomas, who then purchased the interests of the other partners. The firm then expanded by acquiring the Capponfield Works at Bilston and the Lea Brook Works at Wednesbury. Works were also opened in Walsall at Bentley. In 1872, Chillington's became a joint stock company at which time it had about ninety-five puddling furnaces. The company was badly hit by a depression in trade in the 1870s and diversified to concentrate on making edge tools. The tools were sold under the 'Crocodile' brand[50].

Shrubbery Iron Works (Thorneycrofts)

George Thorneycroft was born in Tipton in 1791. He moved with his parents to Leeds but returned to work at the Moorcroft Iron Works in Bilston, where he rose to become superintendent. He went into business for a short while in Willenhall but in 1824, together with his brother, Edward, opened the Shrubbery Iron Works on the Birmingham Canal Navigation on each side of Walsall Street in Horseley Fields. Edward left the partnership in 1841, after which George carried on alone. George fell victim to a dreadful accident in 1848 when he was seriously scalded after a boiler exploded. He became Wolverhampton's first Mayor but never really recovered from his injuries, dying in 1851. For a while Thorneycrofts thrived, making shells and armoured plate to be used in the Crimean War, but the firm fared badly in the recession of the 1870s, and closed in 1877. The Corrugated Iron Company took over the site and remained there until moving to Ellesmere Port.[51]

Woodside Iron Works and Foundry

Alexander Brodie Cochrane (1786–1853) was born in Scotland. He became furnace manager at the Netherton Ironworks of M. & W. Grazebrook. His son worked under him, also Alexander Brodie (1813–1863). In 1840, father and son went into partnership with John Joseph Bramah (nephew of the Bramah of lock making and hydraulic-power fame) and opened the Woodside Ironworks. At the end of 1853, Cochrane senior died, and the partnership was dissolved. Cochrane junior then joined Charles Geach and Archibald Slate, the firm becoming **Cochrane & Co**. The company built structural iron work for the Crystal Palace, after which employees spent four days in London at the Great Exhibition, a special train being provided. The company were involved in many well-known construction projects, including dock gates for the Royal Victoria Dock, Holborn Viaduct, Westminster Bridge, Cannon Street Railway Bridge and Station and Rochester Bridge, spanning the River Medway. They removed iron from the redundant Hungerford Bridge and re-erected parts of it for the Clifton Suspension Bridge. The company was also well known for its post boxes and in 1859 manufactured the first national standard design of the letter box. The company built a further ironworks in Middlesbrough, managed by Alexander junior's son, Charles Cochrane. Cochrane's were excellent employers – there were excursions to London and also to see the Clifton Suspension Bridge, but the rules, which every employee was given, were strict:

> 'No workman to bring a dog into the premises, no smoking allowed in working hours, and no workman should bring any kind of liquor or beer into the premises and any man using violent language or swearing shall be fined six-pence which shall go into the poor box.'

There is an excellent article in Graces Guide describing what seems to be a sort of open day in 1856.[52,53].

Alfred Hickman Ltd.[54]

Alfred Hickman was born in Tipton on the 3rd of July 1830. His father managed Moat Colliery in Tipton and after attending Edward VI Grammar School in

Birmingham, Hickman went to work with his father at the Bilston Brook furnaces and later the Groveland Ironworks in Tipton. In the 1860s, Hickman purchased the Spring Vale blast furnaces at Ettingshall from John Jones. (The first blast furnace was built at Spring Vale in 1780.) Hickman then set about modernising the plant, adding further furnaces and installed puddling furnaces and mills. First, the three old brick furnaces he inherited were dismantled and replaced by iron-clad ones. In 1873, a fourth furnace was added, followed by furnaces five and six in 1889. In 1895, visitors from the Iron and Steel Institute noted that 'the blast furnaces which are in two groups, are among the largest in the district, being 65ft high, 18ft in the boshes and 9ft in the hearth, working with closed tops and Cowper hot-blast stoves'. Half of its iron ore was mined locally, and the firm also owned ironstone quarries in Northamptonshire. In 1884, the steel works were started, and Hickman set up the **Staffordshire Steel & Ingot Iron Co. Ltd**.

In 1882, Gilchrist and Thomas read a paper at the Society of Arts describing the manufacture of steel from pig iron containing phosphorus. In this process, the Bessemer Converter is lined with dolomite or limestone to counteract the presence of phosphorus. The paper was based on experiments directed by Alfred Hickman and conducted by Gilchrist and Thomas. Pig iron, containing between 3–4% phosphorus and between 1–2% silicon and manganese, was used in the Bessemer Converter to form steel. Based on these experiments, Alfred Hickman could see the advantages of the Bessemer process over the traditional puddling furnaces and went ahead and purchased four converters from a company in Liverpool which had gone into liquidation.

In 1887, a Batho Open Hearth furnace was installed at the plant. The Batho furnace was pioneered by William Fothergill Batho (1828–1886). It differed from the Siemens furnace in that the regenerators for heating the gas and air were placed outside and separate from the main furnace. By these means, the installation costs of the furnace were reduced. The main advantage of the open-hearth process over the Bessemer Process was that any kind of pig iron and scrap iron could be used. In 1897, the two companies amalgamated to form Alfred Hickman Ltd. At the turn of the century, 1,500 were employed. In 1920, the company was acquired by **Stewarts & Lloyds**. Alfred Hickman was MP for Wolverhampton West. He was knighted in 1891 and elevated to a baronetcy in 1903.

Corngreaves Iron Works (Keith Hodgkins Collection)

Corngreaves Works

The Attwood family were prominent landowners in Cradley. In the early nineteenth century, they built blast furnaces which were purchased, in 1825, by three London-based investors, John Taylor, James Henry Shears and Robert Small, directors of the **British Iron Company**. This was at a time when demand for iron had fallen caused by the end of the French wars. Problems arose when the directors accused Attwood of deception by charging an excessive amount for the sale. The matter went to court and dragged on until 1838 when the House of Lords finally came down in Attwood's favour. Corngreaves was the British Iron Company's largest works. It was situated at Cradley and had sidings connecting with the Great Western Railway. The company also acquired the Brierley Hill Iron Works, situated above the nine locks on the Dudley canal and also works at Dudley Wood, Netherton and Withymoor. But another recession exacerbated the company's difficulties forcing them to liquidate and begin again, in 1843, as the **New British Iron Company**. The Corngreaves works became the company's most important site. It began with only two furnaces, increasing to six by 1860. Steel making began in 1884 but in 1894 the New British Iron Company went into liquidation. At this time, it was served by six collieries and linked with the Great Western Railway. Corngreaves continued, however, under the direction of a former manager until 1912.[55,56]

Gospel Oak Iron Works

John Read was making iron at the Gospel Oak works in 1801. He went bankrupt in 1817, after which Gospel Oak was taken over by Samuel Walker and his cousin, William Yates. (Walker was grandson of Samuel Walker of Rotherham, who made cannon at Conisbrough Foundry used in the Peninsula War.) A couple of years later, equipment was transferred from South Yorkshire to Gospel Oak, where cannon making was begun. Gospel Oak provided iron for the construction of Hammersmith Bridge in London and the cast-iron columns for the fire-resistant warehouses at Albert Dock and Gladstone Dock in Liverpool. By 1848, the works were owned by John and Edward Walker who were making tin plate. They also made cannon, described as 'brought to such perfection as probably to supersede brass cannon, from their possessing more tenacity, when hot, than those of brass, and not being heavier, a great desideratum with artillery-men'. But in 1860 the works were demolished, and the equipment purchased by three former employees who established Hope & Co. Walter Robinson is then recorded as operating the Gospel Oak works. In its later days, galvanised iron was made at Gospel Oak by first cleaning in an acid bath and then submerging in a bath of molten zinc. Sometime before the end of the nineteenth century, the firm came into the hands of the east-London-based **Blackwall Galvanised Iron Company**, who themselves were taken over by the Swansea based **Baldwin's Ltd**. By 1902, operations at Gospel Oak had ceased.[57,58]

John Bradley & Company

John Bradley (1769–1816) founded the Stourbridge Iron Works in 1798. It was situated on the Stourbridge Town branch of the Stourbridge Canal and connected to it by two basins. Pig iron was imported, and the works was equipped with a slitting mill and forge. Bradley died in 1816 and his widow married Henry Foster. The works then passed to Henry's son, James Foster. The firm expanded and Foster added a foundry and rolling mills. He entered partnership with John Urpeth Rastrick and began to make steam engines. It was an ideal partnership. Foster was an astute businessman and Rastrick an accomplished engineer. The latter was a colleague and advisor to Richard Trevithick and eventually, after leaving Foster, became a civil engineer, working on various railway projects, including the London to Brighton line.

The Foster and Rastrick partnership is best known for the design and manufacture of the locomotive *Agenoria*, which worked on the Shut End (Pensnett) Railway which opened up collieries and furnaces that Foster had established at Brockmoor and Shut End. Orders were also obtained from America, most famously from the Delaware and Hudson Canal Company for the 'Stourbridge Lion' the first locomotive to run in the United States. John Urpeth Rastrick was to leave Foster, after which Foster and Rastrick and Co. was wound up. The firm continued and thrived as John Bradley and Co. and by 1843 was employing five thousand workers. In the late nineteenth century, with the advent of steel and the decline in the iron industry, the company's production fell away.[59,60]

Social Conditions

Writing in 1866, John Jones gives us his own impression of the social conditions of ironworkers. He tells us the 'nature of their employment induces a generally rude external appearance, and the strain upon physical energies leads them as a rule to live expensively, and to drink excessive quantities of stimulants. They are singularly improvident as a class, and although they obtain good wages, they have a remarkable genius for spending all they earn, while they devote but little attention to their home comforts. They are vivacious pleasure seekers, and hence Saint Monday is observed as a general district holiday'. (Saint Monday is a reference to the absenteeism that was rife on Mondays throughout the Black Country as a whole – caused inevitably by the excesses of the previous weekend.) Jones continues: 'Their general bearing is calculated to give an unfavourable impression, as their language and manners are unpleasantly uncouth." He does nevertheless find some redeeming features finding that "they are extremely hospitable and kind to each other, and if anyone is unfortunate enough, they willingly assist him out of his difficulties – not by loans, but by gifts outright' [61]

Industry was booming in the Black Country, but safety procedures were a far cry from what would be acceptable today. Accidents were common. In 1875, a massive explosion occurred at the Green Lane Iron Works of Messrs. Jones & Co. in Walsall, when a tuyere, blowing hot air to the blast furnace, split open. Molten iron flooded out in every direction. Several men leapt into the canal to escape the molten iron and seventeen men suffered terrible burns, eleven of whom were to die. The injured were conveyed to the Walsall Cottage Hospital where they were nursed by Dorothy Wyndlow Pattison, better known in Walsall as Sister Dora. She was to leave an indelible mark on hospital care in Walsall, with her cheerful sense of humour and a quick sense of the ridiculous. She had pet names for many of her patients – Darkey, Everlasting, King Charles, Head, Burnt, Hand and so on. She died in 1878 and the whole town turned out when her coffin was carried to Queen Street cemetery by eighteen railway workers. In all, Sister Dora spent fourteen years in Walsall. She is commemorated by a stained-glass window in St Matthew's Church and a statue in the town centre. The statue is, apart from royalty, the first ever for a woman. The accident at the iron works is depicted in relief at the base of her statue.[62]

References

1. Robert Plot, The Natural History of Staffordshire, 1686
2. Geoff Marshall, Walsall, an Illustrated History, History Press, 2008, p 66
3. W.H.B. Court, The Rise of the Midland Industries, 1600-1838, p 84
4. Andrew Yarranton, England's Improvement by Sea and Land, 1677-1681, p56
5. G.C. Allen, The Industrial Development of Birmingham and the Black Country, 1860-1927, London, Cass, p 15
6. Dud Dudley, Metallum Martis, 1665
7. R.A. Mott, Dud Dudley and the Early Coal-Iron Industry, Trans. Newcomen Society, XV, 1934/5, p 17.
8. P.W. King, Dictionary of National Biography, Vol. 17, Oxford University Press, 2004, p 65.
9. John Jones, Report on the Iron Trade of South Staffordshire, in The Resources, Products, and Industrial History of Birmingham and the Midland Hardware District, ed. Samuel Timmins, 1866, p 54.
10. H R Schubert, The Truth about Dud Dudley, Journal of Iron and Steel Institute, 1950, CLXVI, p184
11. Nancy Cox, Dictionary of National Biography, Vol. 15, Oxford University Press, 2004, p 108.

12. W.H. Chaloner, John Wilkinson, Iron Master, History Today, May 1951, p 63.
13. J.R. Harris, in Dictionary of National Biography, Vol., 58, Oxford University Press, 2004, p 1010.
14. H.W. Dickinson, John Wilkinson, Iron Master, Ulverston, 1914.
15. G. R Morton and W. A .Smith, The Bradley Iron Works of John Wilkinson, Journal of the Iron and Steel Institute, CCIV, 1966, p. 661
16. www.gracesguide.co.uk/Richard_Jesson
17. W.K.V. Gale, The British Iron and Steel Industry, David and Charles, 1967, p 44.
18. Chris Evans, Dictionary of National Biography, Vol., 13, Oxford University Press, 2004, p 513.
19. Gale, 1967, p. 62
20. John W. Hall, Notes on the Life and Work of Joseph Hall, Proceedings of Staffordshire Iron and Steel Institute, Session 1915-16, p. 5-10.
21. ibid, p.15-18.
22. Chris Evans, Dictionary of National Biography, Vol., XX, Oxford University Press, 2004, p 21
23. John Gibbons, Practical Remarks on the Construction of the Staffordshire Blast Furnace, Wrightson and Webb, Birmingham, 1839
24. John Gibbons, Practical Remarks on the Use of Cinder Pig in the Puddling Furnace and the Management of the Forge and Mill, Simpkin, Marshall &Co., 1844
25. Gale, op.cit. p. 59-60
26. W.K.V Gale, The Black Country Iron Industry, a Technical History, The Metals Society, 1979, p. 69
27. G.C. Boase and M.W.Kirby, Dictionary of National Biography, Vol., 46, Oxford University Press, 2004, p 85.
28. Francis Espinasse and Ian Donnachie, Dictionary of National Biography, Vol. 40, p. 372.
29. Gale, 1967, p. 55-58.
30. Ronald M. Birse, Dictionary of National Biography, vol. 13, p.801.
31. W.K.V Gale, 1979, p. 88.
32. ibid., p.86
33. John Jones, op cit, p.58.
34. ibid. p.68
35. John W. Hall, op-cit p, 18-20.
36. John Jones, op.cit., p. 68.
37. W.K.V. Gale, 1979, p.108

38. T. M. Hoskison, The Earl of Dudley's Level New Furnaces, Transaction of Newcomen Society, XXVIII, 1951-3, p. 153-61.
39. Primrose Rostron, M. & W. Grazebrook's Netherton Ironwork, Blackcountryman, 1979, XII, (2) p.47.
40. W. K. V. Gale, Bromford Ironworks, Blackcountryman, 1980, Vol., XIII(3), p. 11
41. L. Holden, Bradley and Foster, Blackcountryman, 1972, V, (2), 11-15.
42. G.R. Morton, The Industrial History of Darlaston, West Midlands Studies, 1972, 5, 11
43. www.gracesguide.co.uk and links
44. Bev Parker, www.historywebsite.co.uk and links
45. Keith Gale, Patent Shaft Steel Works 1835-1980, Blackcountryman, XIV (2), 1981, p 18-22
46. J.S. Allen, The History of the Horseley Company to 1865, Transactions of Newcomen Society, 1987, p. 113
47. W.H. Chaloner and W.O Henderson, Aaron Manby, Builder of the First Iron Steamship, Transactions Newcomen Society, XXIX, 1954, p77
48. T.M. Hoskison, The Earl of Dudley's Level New Furnaces, Transactions Newcomen Society, XXVIII, p. 153.
49. C. Knox, Steel at Brierley Hill: The Story of Round Oak Steel Works, 1857-1957, Newman Neame, 1957.
50. www.gracesguide.co.uk and Chillington links
51. Bev Parker, www.historywebsite.co.uk
52. A.T.C.and E.M. Lavender, The Woodside Ironworks, Blackcountryman, 1984, Vol., 17(2), p 47-50
53. www.gracesguide.co.uk
54. G.R. Morton and M Le Guillou, Alfred Hickman Ltd., 1866-1932, Journal of West Midlands Regional Studies, 1969, Vol 3, p. 1-30
55. www.gracesguide.co.uk
56. Ray Shill, Birmingham and the Black Country's Canalside Industries, Tempus, 2005, p. 56-7.
57. ibid., p. 93.
58. www.gracesguide.co.uk
59. J. Ian Langford, A Towpath Guide to the Stourbridge Canal, Lapal Publications, 1992, p. 25-6.
60. www.gracesguide.co.uk
61. John Jones op.cit. p. 75.
62. Geoff Marshall, p. 90-2

THREE

Glass

Glass in its simplest form is a mixture of sand (silica), soda ash (sodium carbonate) and limestone (calcium carbonate) fused and then cooled to form a non-crystalline and transparent material. Silica is the main ingredient. It requires very high temperatures for it to fuse (1700°C) and when cooled, quartz is formed. If soda ash is added as an alkaline flux, the mixture melts at a much lower temperature (800°C) but the resulting water glass, as the name implies, is soluble in water. This is overcome by adding limestone as a stabiliser. The product is soda-lime glass (or commercial glass, as it is sometimes known), with composition typically silica (55%), soda ash (25%) and limestone (20%).

Early History

The ancient Mesopotamians and Egyptians were familiar with glass and used it to glaze beads. Glass probably came to Britain with the Romans. In the Middle Ages, glass making was a rural industry concentrated in the Weald of Sussex and Kent. Glass makers were attracted to this area because it was heavily wooded and wood ash provided the alkaline flux, with wood also used as fuel for the furnace. Samuel Winbolt has investigated glass making sites in Surrey and Sussex.[1] Many were located in the Chiddingfold area and others at Wisborough Green in Sussex, where there is a window of old glass of about 1600 in the church, commemorating the glass-making industry which thrived in this area. It is in the south aisle and tells of the Bongars and Caquerays from Normandy and the Hennezels and Thietrys from Lorraine. But Wealden wood was a valuable commodity, used extensively in ship building, and this prompted James I, in 1615, to issue a Royal Proclamation forbidding its use as fuel in glass making: 'Of late yeers the wast of wood and timber hath been exceeding great and intolerable by the glass-houses and glass works of late in divers parts erected.' Coal had to be employed instead and this posed real problems for the ancient Wealden glass industry and effectively brought about its demise.

The Weald's problem was an opportunity for Stourbridge. There was a plentiful supply of coal from the Black Country's mines and fire clay was readily available for making the melting pots. As Plot noted: 'The goodness of which clay and cheapness of coal hereabouts, no doubt has drawn the glass-houses to these parts.'[2] The first mention of clay at Stourbridge was in a charter of 1566 granting permission 'for getting and digging glasshouse clay.'[3] Clay occurs in a relatively small area, centred in the valley of the river Stour, and was also used for the manufacture of bricks. Before the Staffordshire and Worcestershire Canal opened, clay was taken by pack horse to Stourport-on-Severn and thence to Bristol and elsewhere. The best clay for making glasshouse pots was the so called 'Old Mine Clay,' found in the Hungary Hill district at a depth of about 42 yards. Beneath it there were successive beds at depths of up to 100 yards known as 'New Mine Clay'.[4] Writing in 1866, Harrison describes its treatment:

> 'In summary, the clay is first broken into small pieces and finely ground by heavy edged punners (a tool for ramming), mixed with water, tempered by the feet and allowed to stand for at least five to six weeks. The pots are built up by hand, layer by layer, and before use left to dry very gradually for nine to twelve months. Their sizes vary according to the type of glass to be made. Flint glass (see later) pots weigh about 12cwt and have a lifetime of up to nine months, while those for bottle works weigh as much as 28cwt and last for four to seven weeks. As much as two thousand tons of clay was raised every week, giving employment to 1,500 to 1600 hands, who in the mid-nineteenth century earned about twenty-three shillings per week.'[3]

The glass workers who were drawn to Stourbridge came from Lorraine; many were Protestants, escaping religious persecution. The first we have information about was Paul Tyzack, who is recorded as baptising his son, John, at St Mary's parish church in Kingswinford, in 1612. Another was Joshua Henzey, who integrated into the neighbourhood so well that in 1651 he became a governor of the Free Grammar School of King Edward VI in Stourbridge. During the next 150 years, names which originated in Lorraine crop up repeatedly.[5] They may have worked under licence to Sir Robert Mansell (1573–1656) who, at the time, had a monopoly on glass making with his patent for making 'all sorts of glass with pit coal'. Mansell was an admiral in the Royal Navy and Member of Parliament. He opened a glass works in Newcastle and owned the famous Vauxhall Glassworks in Lambeth. In 1624, because of public protests, monopolies came under attack, resulting in the 'Statute of Monopolies'. It decreed that, apart from genuinely new inventions, 'monopolies are and shall be utterly void and no effect'. This prompted Lord Dudley, who held considerable amounts of land in Kingswinford, to appeal to the House of Commons, asserting that Mansell's invention was not new and therefore a patent should not have been granted. Dudley claimed that 'two years before this pretence of a new invention, or any patent granted there was glass made with coal upon his grounds by glassmakers'.

A major advance in glass technology came when George Ravenscroft (1632–1683) improved the clarity and brilliance of glass by adding lead oxide to the starting materials. By so doing, the brown/greenish colour of soda-lime glass caused by the presence of iron impurity was removed. Ravenscroft was

Stourbridge Canal and Glass House Kiln (Dudley Achives)

originally intended for the priesthood but instead went into business and spent time in Venice, then a centre of glass technology, where he may have formulated his ideas. His lead crystal glass or flint glass had a high refractive index and therefore was much clearer than soda glass and more easily cut, manipulated and engraved.

As time progressed, the popularity of glass increased – particularly for window glass and bottles – and glass cones became a prominent feature at Stourbridge and other glassmaking centres. They were large brick-built structures, about 80ft (24m) in height and 40ft (12m) across. The furnace was in the centre and the glassworkers worked in the annular space within the cone in teams of men called 'chairs'. The team leader was the 'gaffer', the first use of this now well-known term. He was assisted by the servitor, and then came the footmaker who was responsible for the initial gathering of the glass and blowing; finally there was the taker in, often a boy, who took pieces to the lehr for annealing.[6]

There were two techniques for making window glass. The first was the Crown method. It originated in Normandy and was pioneered in London by the Bankside glassmaker, John Bowles. The skilled glassblower would blow a hollow glass globe at the end of a metal rod or pontil. The glass was then reheated and the pontil rapidly spun so that the glass collapsed about the pontil by centrifugal force into a flat disc. After further heat treatment to strengthen them, the panes of glass were cut from the disc. The blemish in the centre, where the pontil was attached, became the 'bull's eye' pane often seen in old windows. Window glass panes were restricted in size: the maximum was only 24x15 inches. (60x40cm), explaining why windows in old buildings are so small. The name 'Crown Glass' comes from Bowles' trademark – a crown that he embossed at the centre of each pane.[7]

The method of making window glass favoured by the Lorrainers in Stourbridge was the Broad glass method. The glassblower would blow a paraison (gob) of glass into a long cylinder of required length. While still hot it was opened longitudinally by shears, reheated and laid on a marver (table) sprinkled with sand. Broad glass, so formed, was duller than Crown glass but had the advantage that much larger planes could be formed.[8]

Jason Ellis has written a comprehensive study of the glasshouses of Stourbridge and Dudley. He makes the point that most of Stourbridge's glass cones were north of the town in the hamlets of Wordsley and Amblecote. Paul Tyzack opened **Coleman's**, the first glasshouse to be established in the Stourbridge area, at Lye, south of the River Stour and north of Bott Lane,

Glass Cones at Wordsley (Keith Hodgkins/Jack Haden)

sometime between 1610 and 1614. Very soon afterwards, a glasshouse was founded by Joshua Henzey in Hungary Hill Lane, not far from the junction with Halfpenny Lane, 0.7 miles east of Stourbridge and 285 yards south of the present day Stambermill railway viaduct.[9]

By the end of the seventeenth century, there were seventeen glasshouses in the town: seven making window glass, five making bottles and five making flint glass.[10] Bottles and windows were made with commercial sodalime glass. Potash was obtained by burning bracken or fern; limestone and silica were gathered locally. It was the usual practice to add cullet (broken or scrap glass) to the mix and there were 'many hundreds of poor families who kept themselves from the Parish (Poor Law) by picking broken glass of all sorts and sell to the maker'. Lead for flint glass came from Derbyshire and the finest sand from King's Lynn or the Isle of Wight.[11]

Excise Duty

Much to the discomfort of the Stourbridge glassmakers, in 1695 the government imposed an Excise Duty on glass. The purpose of the tax was to provide money for William III and his wars. It didn't go down well. A pamphleteer wrote, 'Tis very strange that all other manufacturers should be under noli me tangere and this of glass and earthenware should be singled out for ruin.' A 20% duty was placed on flint glass and one shilling per dozen on bottles. By 1698, 'four bottle houses had not worked since the duty while others had kept open for only 7 or 8 weeks of the usual 40 in the year'. Some, like Thomas Bachelor, tried to get out of paying. He was to regret it when all his bottles were seized.[12] So distressed were the Stourbridge glassmakers that they petitioned Parliament. One complained that he had 'not one day's work and if the duty should be continued the petitioners and their families must starve or be maintained by their parishes.'. In 1699, a Committee of Enquiry was set up which found the duties were 'of little advantage to the king and there was a danger of the glass industry being lost to the kingdom'. The petitioners were successful, and the duty was withdrawn but the glassmakers were still left to the vicissitudes of the market. By 1712, the price of window glass had fallen from twenty-six shillings to twenty-two shillings per case. There were bankruptcies including Samuel Tyzack of Kingswinford.[13]

It was in the mid-eighteenth century that Stourbridge's glassmakers began to specialise in the manufacture of decorated flint glassware. In the early part of that century, London was the centre of the flint glass trade but in 1751, Dr Pocock, in his *Travels Through England*, published by the Camden Society, wrote: 'Came to Stourbridge, famous for its glass manufacturers, especially the coloured glass with which they make painted windows in their several shades and if I am mistaken not, it is a secret which they have here.'.[14]

Glass excise duty was imposed once more in 1745. Glass was taxed on the weight of raw materials and – much to the annoyance of the glassmakers – excise officers were stationed at every glassworks to make sure it was collected. A glassmaker complained 'it is astonishing how flint glassworks exist at all under such a concentration of commercial and manufacturing hindrances as are imposed by the excise regulation'.[15]. Windowglass manufacturers had every reason to complain about the Window Tax, first introduced in 1696. The government reasoned that the more windows in a house the bigger the house and hence the richer the owner. In 1776, seven or more windows incurred a tax, reducing to a duty on eight or more in 1828. It is easy to see why people bricked up their windows. The medical journal, *The Lancet*, saw it as a 'tax against fresh air', or to quote an enduring expression, 'daylight robbery'. The tax was eventually abolished in 1851, as was the glass tax in 1845.[16]

Well-Known Glassworks

Several authors have outlined the history of the glasshouses in Stourbridge and Dudley.[17, 18,19,20,21]

The **Amblecote or Holloway End Glassworks**[18] was founded in the seventeenth century by Thomas Rogers, who married a daughter of a member of the Huguenot Tyltery family. It was here in 1771 that James Keir (see chapter: The Chemicals Industry) worked when he took a lease of the works from Thomas Rogers IV. Keir took up residence at Holloway End House and as well as making glass carried out many experiments on alkalis, which he put to good use later in his career. He was an active member of the Lunar Society and corresponded with Josiah Wedgwood on the techniques of annealing (slow cooling) to alleviate problems of cording, a sort of wavy imperfection found in flint glass. Keir opened his alkali works in Tipton in 1780 but remained a partner at Stourbridge, the firm operating as **Scott, Keir, Jones & Co**. The firm then went through various hands until it closed in the 1930s.[17]

By the Stourbridge Canal at Wordsley there were three glass works. The **White House Glassworks** was still operating in the 1930s and was connected to the **Wordsley House Glassworks** by a wooden footbridge over the canal. Nearby was the **Red House Glassworks.** They had many owners over the years, all detailed by Ellis.[17]

Red House Glassworks

Thomas Webb was a well-known glassmaker in Stourbridge. He was born in 1804 and at the age of twenty-five joined the Wordsley Flint Glassworks. It was sometimes known as the London House, referring to the fact that it supplied the London market. Thomas later moved to the White House Glassworks and then, in 1834, built new works at Amblecote, on a site adjacent to Platts House. While at

Platts, Webb's work was described as 'in clearness and purity he is confessedly unsurpassed in Europe. Hence much of his produce goes to the creation of chandeliers, candelabras, and objects in which the quality alluded to is of the highest importance'. The firm exhibited at the Great Exhibition in Hyde Park in 1851 and four years later expanded to new works to the rear of Dennis Hall. In 1864, Thomas Webb retired and left the firm in the capable hands of his son, Thomas Wilkes Webb. It went from strength to strength, exhibited at the Paris International Exhibition of 1878, was awarded the Grand Prix for glass and was described in the French catalogue as the 'best makers of glass in the world'. In recognition of his work, Thomas Webb was awarded the prestigious Chevalier of the Legion of Honour. In 1908, Webbs displayed their glassware at the Franco-British Exhibition and built a small glasshouse at the exhibition to enable the public to witness the glassmaking process. In the Second World War, Webbs made glass for radar and X-ray machines. But by this time, they had amalgamated with others and closed in 1990 due to the collapse of their parent company, Coloroll.[22] Wakefield and Ellis have described many other glasshouses. Wakefield's paper was published in the Stour Gazette in 1934 and can be obtained from/in the British Library.[18] Jason Ellis' book was published by himself. It is also available from the British Library.[9]

The Portland Vase

'Anyone who reproduced that vase faithfully in glass could command £1000 for it.' So said Benjamin Richardson of the White House and Wordsley houses, often styled the 'father of English glassmaking'. He was referring to the Portland Vase. The original is now in the British Museum and takes its name from a former owner, the Duchess of Portland. It is a cameo vessel made about two thousand years ago and shows scenes from Greek mythology. It was made by taking a mass of pure cobalt glass and blowing it into a crucible of white glass, thereby forming two layers. The skilled gem cutter then cut away the white layer to form the design. It came into the hands of Sir William Hamilton (of Lord Nelson and Lady Hamilton fame) who sold it to the Duchess of Portland and is now one of the British Museum's most prized possessions.

John Northwood stepped forward to make a copy of the famous Portland Vase. He was born in 1836, the son of a grocer, and for a time worked for Ben Richardson. He was encouraged in his endeavours by P. Pargeter, a glass manufacturer at the Red House Glassworks. A glass blank was made at the Red House by Daniel Hancock and Pargeter commissioned Northwood to complete the work for £1,000. John was given a room dedicated to his work and separate from the rest of the workshop. It was vital that no mistakes were made; for instance, if a portion of white glass were removed from the wrong place the whole vase would be invalidated and not be a faithful replica. The engraving wheel was used by John only for less delicate work; precise work was done with hand carving tools. Frequent visits were made to the British Museum to compare with the original and ensure accuracy. When the vase was finally completed disaster struck; it broke into two pieces. Pargeter and Northwood were not deterred. The two pieces were successfully united and after careful polishing the Portland Vase was born again, two thousand years after the original.[23]

Chance Brothers [24, 25, 26, 27, 28, 29]

Glass making began in Smethwick in 1814, when Thomas Shutt set up in business on land on part of Blakeley Hall Farm, Spon Lane, on the banks of the Birmingham Canal Navigation. He made Crown glass, and the firm was known as the **British Crown Glass Company**. Shutt's company was bought by Robert Lucas Chance in 1824 for £24,000, Chance exclaiming, 'I have every reason for thinking that the concern will realise the most sanguine expectations I have form'd', and it presents a scope for the exercise of my acquirements as a man of business.'[24] He was right, the 'concern' developed to become Chance Brothers.

Chance Brothers became the largest glass makers in the country. In the nineteenth century, the American Consul in Birmingham, Elihu Burritt, wrote of the company: as 'in no other establishment in the world can one get such a full idea of the infinite uses which glass is made to serve as in these immense works'.

The story of the Chance family and glass making began at the Nailsea Glassworks, near Bristol. The small works were started in 1788 by John Lucas, brother-in-law to William Chance. He sold his beer and cider business and put the money into the glassworks. William joined the business in 1793 and by 1810 it was managed by William's son, Robert Lucas Chance. Lucas (as he was always known) was an ambitious man. He established himself as a merchant in

London and travelled to France to expand his knowledge of glass making. After he acquired the Spon Lane works he was joined by John Hartley, recognised as a leading expert on Crown glass.[25]

But it was sheet glass that captured Lucas Chance's interest. In 1830, he visited the works of Georges Bontemps at Choisy-le-Roi in France to see sheet glass being manufactured for himself. Sheet glass, described by Guttery as broad glass writ large, was made by gathering 20 to 40lbs of molten glass on a blowing iron about 5ft in length. The hot glass was then swung in a tunnel about 10ft deep, to form a cylinder. Cylinders were usually 12 to 20 inches. in diameter and 50 to 70 inches in length. The cylinders were then slit lengthways and when reheated in a flattening kiln or 'lear' allowed to collapse and fall into a flat sheet. By this means, much larger panes of glass could be made than were possible with Crown glass. Following Lucas's visit to Bontemps, many French glass workers were recruited to Spon Lane to make sheet glass. [26]

Soon, Lucas's brother, William Chance, joined the company and invested money to strengthen it. John Hartley died in 1833 and was replaced in the business by his two sons, the firm now known as 'Chances & Hartleys'. But, like their father, they were never in favour of the French sheet glass, preferring the traditional Crown glass. They were soon to leave to start up on their own at Sunderland. It was at about this time that the firm began to make its own alkali (see chapter: The Chemicals Industry).

In November 1836, William's son, James Timmins Chance, joined the company. He had been educated at University College in London and Trinity College Cambridge and was an accomplished mathematician. His first achievement was to enable the grinding and polishing of sheet glass to give it the transparency of plate glass.

In 1837, Chance Brothers & Co. (as they were now known) purchased Georges Bontemp's manufacturing techniques for optical glass. Optical glass is made by allowing molten glass to cool very slowly and thereby to obtain homogeneity. It is used to make lens for lighthouses and was pioneered, between 1768 and 1775, by the Swiss woodcarver, Pierre Louis Guinard. He used flint glass with a special stirring technique to prevent striations. Guinard left records of his technique to his son, which George Bontemps purchased for three thousand francs in the mid-1820s.

The manufacture of optical glass proved elusive to achieve in England. The Royal Society appointed Michael Faraday to find a method of manufacture but even the great experimental scientist was thwarted, writing to the Royal

Society: 'I may lay the glass aside for a while, that I may enjoy the pleasure of working out my own thoughts on other subjects.' Then, following the European Revolution of 1848, George Bontemps fled from France and joined Chance Brothers. Bontemps, about whom it was said, 'no one alive knew more than he about every branch of glass manufacture, whether in theory or practice' was put in charge of the 'Coloured and Ornamental Department'. It was also the opportunity for Chance Brothers to begin making optical glassware. A special department was placed under his direction. Until 1914, Chance Brothers was the only British firm making optical glass. Bontemps was paid £500 per year, five-twelfths of the net profits of the optical department and one-tenth of the Ornamental department.[28,29]

Demand for glass increased dramatically when excise duties were repealed in 1845. The price of Crown glass fell from £12 per crate in 1844 to £2 8s in 1863. There was a similar fall in the price of sheet glass from 1s 2d per foot to 2d per foot. At this time, Chance Brothers had six glasshouses making sheet glass. Lucas was an astute businessman and the company thrived. He also had a philanthropic side to his character. He looked after his workers well and, in 1845, built a school for their children. Chance Brothers also employed children, but none below twelve years of age. They were expected to attend school, at least three times every week, on pain of a sixpence fine.[26,27]

By the late 1840s, plans were well advanced for the Great Exhibition, due to be held in Hyde Park in 1851 in London. The centrepiece was Joseph Paxton's Crystal Palace and, despite being cynically written off by *The Times* newspaper as a 'monstrous greenhouse', plans went ahead. Chance Brothers supplied all the glass. Employing about 1,200 people, many of whom were recruited in France, they were the only glass manufacturers capable of fulfilling such a large contract. Rolled plate glass was used. This is made by pouring molten glass onto a flat surface and spreading it evenly by rollers. It is then ground and polished. An astonishing 950,000 square feet of glass was supplied as forty-nine by ten-inch panes, all transported along the Grand Union Canal to London.[27, 28] Chance Brothers exhibited at the Great Exhibition, as did other Black Country concerns – Richardson's of Wordsley, Davis Greathead and Green of Brettell Lane Stourbridge and Thomas Webb of Amblecote. Chance Brothers also received high-profile contracts to supply glass for Sir Charles Barry's Houses of Parliament, the four faces of the clock face of Big Ben and for the White House in America.

The glassmaking skills of Georges Bontemps, and later M. Tabouret, who had worked with Augustin-Jean Fresnel, combined with the mathematical and engineering expertise of James Timmins Chance, enabled Chance Brothers to enter the field of lighthouse manufacture and exploit the dioptric lens pioneered by Augustin Fresnel. An effective lighthouse needs a powerful illuminating lamp mounted in a tall tower to give a concentrated parallel beam of light. The beam is provided by a series of Fresnel lenses positioned around the light. The Fresnel lens works by the principle of the refraction of light, not, as in existing lighthouses, by the reflection of light. In effect, the Fresnel lens is a series of concentric rings (steps or thick ridges) positioned around the central light. Each step refracts the light slightly more than the one beneath to give a parallel beam of light capable of being seen from far away. A number of them would be positioned around the powerful light so that when the light was rotated the beam would be directed in different directions. It would also flash in sync with the speed of rotations of the light and hence be more noticeable.

In 1849, there was a crucial meeting between Robert Chance (son of Lucas) and officials from Trinity House in London. The meeting facilitated an introduction to Robert Wilkins who supplied Trinity House with lighthouse equipment, purchased from the firm of Letourneau in Paris. Chance Brothers decided to build their own lighthouses and set their sights on building a lens to demonstrate it at the 1851 Great Exhibition. Orders were received from Trinity House; the first was for a lighthouse at Bardsey Island off the coast of North Wales. More orders followed, including ones for Lundy, Galway and Whitby. Between 1857 and 1867, Chance Brothers acquired more land for the lighthouse division and an 80-ft tower was built to test the optics and the light. As well as optical equipment, the firm built the carriages, burners lanterns and cast-iron towers. As the century progressed, Chance Brothers supplied lighthouses to countries throughout the world. James Timmins Chance was awarded a baronetcy in 1900. There is a memorial to him in West Smethwick Park.[28,29]

Glassmaking is kept alive today at the **Red House Cone**, the only glass cone still standing in the Stourbridge. The cone stands on the Stourbridge Canal at Wordsley and is 90ft in height with a diameter at its base of 60ft. It is open to the public and hosts many activities associated with the glass industry. The cone dates from about 1788–1794 and was built by Richard Bradley. It passed through many hands before it closed in 1936, by then worked by Stuart Crystal. Nearby is the Broadfield House Glass Museum which houses a collection of British glass from the seventeenth century to the present day.[30]

References

1. Samuel Edward Winbolt, Wealden Glass, the Surrey Sussex Glass Industry, AD1226-1615, Hove Combridges, 1933
2. Plot, Natural History of Staffordshire, Oxford, The Theatre, 1686
3. George Harrison, The Stourbridge Fire Clay, in The Resources, Products and Industrial History of Birmingham and the Midland Hardware District, ed. Samuel Timmins, Robert Hardwick, 1866, p133
4. M.H.Edwards, Stourbridge Fireclay and the Manufacture of Glasshouse Pots, Journal Society of Glass Technology, 1927, XXXI, p.400
5. H.J. Haden, Notes on the Stourbridge Glass Trade, Library Arts Committee, Brierley Hill, 1949.
6. Graham Fisher, Jewels on the Cut, Sparrow Publishing, 2010, p. 48.
7. Leonard Riley and Geoff Marshall, The Story of Bankside, London Borough of Southwark, 2001, p28
8. D.R Guttery, From Broad Glass to Cut Crystal, Leonard Hill, 1956, p45.
9. Jason Ellis, Glasshouses of Stourbridge and Dudley, 1612-2002, Harrogate, 2002
10. H.J.Haden, op.cit
11. D.R.Guttery, p39
12. Ibid, p34
13. H.J.Haden, op.cit
14. D.N.Sandilands, The Early History of Glass Making in the Stourbridge District, Journal Society of Glass Technology, 1931, XIX, 219.
15. D.R.Guttery, op.cit
16. Graham Fisher, op cit., p.44
17. Jason Ellis, op.cit..
18. R. Wakefield, The Old Glass-Houses of Stourbridge and Dudley, Reprinted from Stour Gazette, 1934.
19. Francis Buckley, Notes on the Glasshouses of Stourbridge, 1700-1830, Journal Society Glass Technology, 1927, XI, 106
20. ibid, The Birmingham Glass Trade, 1740-1833, 1927, XI,374
21. H.J. Haden,op.cit
22. H.W. Woodward, Art, Feat and Mystery, The Story of Thomas Webb and Sons, Glassmakers, Mark and Moody, 1978
23. John Northwood II, John Northwood, his Contributions to the Stourbridge Glass Industry, 1850-1902, Mark and Moody, 1958
24. Chance Brothers, Mirror for Chance, p. 6-9.

25. David C.Encill, Chance Expressions, Cortex Deign, 2007, p. 2
26. D.N.Sandilands, The Spon Lane Works , J. Society of Glass Technology, XXII, 1931,p. 245
27. www.gracesguide.co.uk
28. Toby Chance and Peter Williams, Lighthouses, the Race to Illuminate the World, New Holland, 2008
29. James Frederick Chance, A History of the Firm of Chance Brothers & Co.
30. Paul Grove, Red House Glass Cone, Guide Booklet.

FOUR
Chains

Chains have been made for well over two thousand years. In the Old Testament, at the time of King David, mention is made of 'bars of iron and fetters of iron'. In 322 BC, at the siege of Tyre, 'Greek ships were anchored with iron chains'. In this country, an iron chain was found, dating to 150 BC, at Bigbury near Canterbury. In 1216, the Justicier of England, Hubert de Burgh, after he fell from grace, was ordered to be fettered in chains. But because of de Burgh's loyalty and heroism in resisting a French invasion, it was an order the smith refused, insisting 'no iron of mine shall ever fetter such noble hands'. Apart from a means of restraint, chains have found many other uses such as preventing enemy ships from entering a river or harbour; in 1553 a chain was strung across the river Medway from Upnor to Gillingham to deter invasion.[1]

Chains have been made in the Black Country for well over two hundred years. Ron Moss has written a comprehensive account of chain and anchor making with special reference to the Black Country.[2] He notes that the area's underlying geology of iron ore and coal deposits are well suited for the production of good-quality wrought iron, which enabled generations of men to become skilled in iron working. The industry was concentrated in Cradley, Cradley Heath, Netherton, Old Hill, Quarry Bank and Brierley Hill. Chain making developed from the nailing industry and began in a very small way in out-houses of domestic premises. There would be a small forge and anvil in the back yard of a dwelling house and all the family – husband, wife and children – would play their part. Typical was 'Purser's Yard', also known as 'Anvil Yard', in present-day Colley Lane, Cradley. Working conditions could be and often were appalling; a Government Board of Trade report complained of 'squalor and dirt far surpassing anything I have yet seen – little domestic workshops, built onto the houses, so that occupants can step at once from kitchen to anvil'. Ninety-two workers are recorded as making chains there in 1881, but Purser's Yard was demolished in 1930; it is now a pleasant memorial garden.³

Chain Making (Dudley Archives)

The Chain Makers' Life

Life for the chain maker was far from easy; it was hard, relentless, physical work. The hours of work were particularly exacting. For unknown reasons, chain makers would begin work at 5.30am (winter included) and knock off at about 12.30pm. The only explanation they gave is that 'it was always like that'. Particularly if they were out-workers, chain makers were frequently open to exploitation by middlemen who both supplied them with wrought iron and also purchased the finished product. Middlemen often owned 'Tommy Shops' and were in the habit of paying the chain maker with tokens which could only be exchanged for food and provisions at high prices in the 'Tommy Shop.'⁴ Robert Peel Blatchford (1851–1943) the socialist campaigner and journalist, wrote vividly in an article, *Chains and Slavery*, of life as a Black Country chain maker:⁵

> 'At Cradley I saw a white-haired old woman carry half a hundred-weight of chain to the fogger's round her shoulders; at Cradley I saw women making chain with babies suckling at their breasts; at Cradley I spoke to a married couple who had worked 120 hours in one week and had earned 18s by their united labour; at Cradley I saw heavy-chain strikers who were worn out old men at thirty-five; at Cradley I found women on strike for a price which would enable them to earn two pence an hour by dint of labour which is to work what the Battle of Inkerman was to a Bank

Holiday review. At Cradley the men and the women are literally being worked to death for a living that no gentlemen would offer his dogs.'

Chain Cables

The chain industry was given a significant boost in 1784 by the pioneering work of Henry Cort (1740–1800) at his forge in Fontley, Hampshire. Not only did he invent the puddling furnace, to enable good quality wrought iron to be made in bulk from pig iron (see chapter: Iron), but he also introduced a groundbreaking rolling mill to produce round bar iron. An elementary sort of rolling mill had been used in the iron industry since about 1590. It was a development of the slitting mill and produced strip iron. Cort incorporated grooved rolls, by which means round bar iron could be made, ideal for the chain industry.[6]

Until the beginning of the nineteenth century, hemp was used as cable in the shipping industry. In 1808, the first iron chain cable was employed on a 221-ton vessel, built at Berwick-on-Tweed, called the *Ann and Isabella*. The chain was made by Robert Flinn, who worked as a blacksmith at Ford Forge on the River Till in Northumberland and later at his own chain-making shop in Bell Street, North Shields. Flinn is credited with making the first reliable chain cables but in the same year of 1808, a patent was taken out by Samuel Brown (1776–1852) for twisted link chains. Brown had been born in London, was a captain in the Royal Navy and was later knighted. Flinn was acquainted with Brown and disputed the patent. It is Brown, however, who became better known. He claimed to have invented the stud link (a short stud across the centre of the link), which both strengthens the chain cable and prevents it from becoming tangled. Brown started in business near Waterloo Bridge in London, later moving to Limehouse and then in 1812, as Brown Lennox & Co., to Millwall on the Isle of Dogs. Brown used South Staffordshire wrought iron for his chain cables and for a time was successful in gaining a contract as sole supplier to the Royal Navy.[7]

Well-Known Black Country Chain Makers

Noah Hingley (1796–1877) was born in Cradley and worked with his father as a chain maker in premises by the River Stour. In the 1840s, he began making anchors, small ones at first and then, after using the Nasmyth hammer, up to

74cwt in weight. In 1832, he founded **Noah Hingley and Sons** and set up beside the Dudley No 2 Canal at Netherton. Coal mines were acquired by the firm at Dudley Wood, Old Hill and Gawn. He began working his own iron, purchased from the New British Iron Company, at Netherton and Dudley Wood. He had furnaces at Old Hill, previously worked by T and I Badger and later David Rose. Also more at Harts Hill Iron Works.

In 1820, Hingley made the first chain cable in the Black Country It was of 1½ inch diameter. (Chain size is always expressed in terms of the diameter of the material forming the link, i.e. a 1½-inch chain is made from 1½-inch diameter iron bar.)[8] Trail tells of how Hingley travelled to Liverpool, either on horseback or by stagecoach, where he sealed a contract with a Liverpool ship owner to supply chain cable. The success of the venture set in trail the Netherton area of the Black Country, becoming the foremost chain-making centre in the country, if not the world. The 1½-inch chain cable of fifteen fathom length (One fathom = 6ft) was end welded and made from bar iron by two strikers, with two boys to blow the bellows. The studs were of cast iron, made hollow, the ends being made to fit the sides of the link. When a chain of such size was completed (90ft), people came from far and wide to see it – so much so that a day's holiday was granted to celebrate the occasion.[9] Thereafter, Noah Hingley's works expanded at Netherton on Dudley No. 2 Canal between Bishton's Bridge and Primrose Bridge. The company benefitted when the Old Hill to Netherton Railway opened; the GWR built sidings at the Old Hill Works and a goods station and interchange basin at Withymoor to serve the main works. As well as chains the company also made anchors; the most famous for the ill-fated *Titanic*.

Noah Hingley went on, in 1869, to be Mayor of Dudley. He also stood unsuccessfully for parliament in 1874. He was a resolute philanthropist and promoted ragged schools in Cradley. On his death, the firm passed to his son, Benjamin and in 1885 Hingley's were employing three thousand workers.[10,11]

In 1817, **Harry Pershouse Parkes** began making chains at Pit Hole, near Dudley. In 1837, he moved to Tipton at the **Tipton Green Chain & Anchor Works**; three years later he pioneered the technique of side welding in the manufacture of his chain cables, which he considered better than the previous practice of end welding. The firm exhibited at both the 1851 Great Exhibition and the 1862 Paris Exhibition. It made what was then the largest anchor in the world for Brunel's *Great Eastern*, launched in 1857. The anchor was vast, weighing eight tons and 26ft in length. The business eventually passed to his

Anchor for the Titanic *Being Hauled through Netherton (Dudley Archives)*

son, Harry P. Parkes, the firm's name changing in 1870 to Harry P. Parkes and Ross.[12] The firm came under the control of N. Hingley in 1906.

There were many other chain cable manufacturers in the Black Country. They are listed by Traill[13], who outlines the situation as he recorded it in the 1880s. Gideon Billingham were established in 1784 and operated from the **Cradley Heath Chain and Anchor Works**. In 1845, Jesse Billingham &Son were founded at **Maritime Works**, Cradley Heath. Connop Brothers commenced business in 1883 at **Great Western Works**, Cradley Heath. John Green was at the **Crown Chain Cable, Anchor and Iron Works** at Old Hill from 1872. Geo Hartshorne & Co were founded by Geo Hartshorne in 1856. He was joined by a Mr Ward, the firm becoming **Hartshorne &. Ward**, and operated from Old Hill. They moved to the canalside in Netherton in 1869. Brazillai Hingley & Sons was established in 1815 at the **Lion Chain Works,** Cradley Heath. The more famous Noah Hingley was at the **Netherton Iron, Chain Cable and Anchor Works**. The firm was later carried on by Noah's son Benjamin, and grandsons. In addition to works at Netherton they had premises at Old Hill. Thomas P Jones was at Rowley and before that at Cradley. Joseph and William Rock founded what was to become the largest chain works in Cradley in 1837; they became **Jones and Lloyd** at Top Shop, Scotia Works, near

Intended Street, Cradley. They had other premises, Lower Shop, nearby at Lyde Green. They ceased trading in 1970 and Top Shop was dismantled, brick by brick, to be re-erected at Avoncroft Open Air Museum in Bromsgrove. Thomas Mills & Son was an old established firm at **Crescent Works**, Pleck Road, Walsall. **Mountford & Co.** came into business in 1773 with many changes since then. It is now in the hands of Richard Mountford at Marine Works, Netherton. **Benjamin Priest** was founded in 1854 in Old Hill. It traded for a time as Priest & Johnson but in 1876 reverted to its original name when Johnson left. S Taylor & Sons were at the **Thorns Works** in Brierley Hill and were founded in 1879. Whitehouse & Co. were established in 1881 at **Tipton Hall Iron and Chain Works** in Tipton. In 1841, **David Willetts** were founded at Cradley Heath. Willetts died in 1883 and the business carried on at Bowling Green and Canal Wharf, Netherton. **Henry Wood & Co.** was first at Stourbridge in 1780 and had works at Chester and Liverpool, Cradley and Wolverhampton. In 1790, the Wood brothers started at Stour Works in Stourbridge. The firm was known as **J. Wood Aston & Co.** Joseph Wright & Co. was founded by Theophilus Tinsley in 1851 at **Neptune Forge, Chain, Anchor, Engine and Boiler Works**. Neptune Works stood alongside the canal at the southern end of Sedgley Road West in Tipton. All of these works were involved in other manufacturing work such as rigging, cranes, pulley blocks, etc.

Although Cradley was recognised as the centre of chain making in the Black Country, chains were also made in Walsall. There were all sorts, ranging from those used to haul ploughs to dog chains. Chains were also used with hames (the curved bars of a draught-horse collar) in the cart gearing trade. **Job Wheway and Son** of Birchills, founded in 1790, was a prominent firm in this branch of industry.

Gale[8] has classified chains into three categories – heavy chains, medium chains and small chains. Heavy chains were made by teams of three men and range in size from 1¼ inch diameter to 6 inches or more. Medium chains were from $3/_8$ inch to 1 inch diameter and were usually made by one man working alone, often in a domestic workshop. Small chains range from $13/_{125}$ inch to $11/_{32}$ inch diameter and were often made by women.

It was very common for Cradley girls to go into the chain-making trade. Examination of census returns enables the number of males and females in the industry to be compared: in 1861 there were 2,324 males and 572 females employed in the chain-making industry; 1871 it was 2,845 men and 892 women and in 1891, 3,567 men and 1,587 women. The most famous lady was

Women Chain Makers (Dudley Archives)

Lucy Woodall who spent sixty years as a chain maker. She was born in 1899 and despite the advice of her headmistress, at the age of thirteen signed on as an apprentice. 'It was what I wanted and the money was needed at home,' Lucy remarked. She worked for many chain makers, including Harry Stevens of Old Hill for thirty-five years. Lucy eventually retired at age seventy-three; her work being recognised when she was made an honorary vice president of the Black Country Society.[14]

Chain Making

Chain making is a highly skilled job. A series of articles published in Iron and Coal Trades Review describe the process, from which the following is taken.[15] Hand-welded chains are often made in small workshops, containing as many as twenty-three forges, each one employing one smith. The process consists of first cutting bar iron to the requisite length with shears. The bar is then heated in the fire and bent into a U shape. At the next heating, the ends to be welded are scarfed and bent round to form the link. (A scarf is a joint connecting two pieces of metal in which the ends are bevelled or notched so that they fit over or into

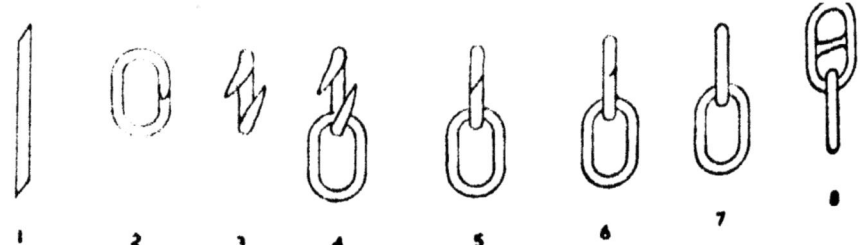

Stages in manufacture of chain cables.
1. Cut from Bar with Scarfed End. 2. Bend in Machine. 3. Open. 4. Thread. 5. Close. 6. Half Weld. 7. Finish Weld. 8. Set Stud. (With Permission of Newcomen Society)

each other.) The final operation is welding which is done with a hand hammer on the anvil and finally finished with an 'Oliver', the simplest and oldest form of power hammer, which is worked by depressing a treadle with the foot, so keeping both hands free to work the metal.

Chain slings are lifting components connected to a hoisting device such as a crane. On the end of the chain is a hook (or similar) fixed onto the load to be lifted. For heavy loads, chains can be as large as 8 inches. Smaller ones for lighter work are typically $^5/_8$ inch to $^3/_4$ inch.

Heavy and Chain Cable making is usually performed by side welding with a three-man chain-making team, helped by assistants. The process has been described in detail by Gale[8] from which the following is taken and illustrated by reference to the figure above.

The assistants cut wrought-iron bars to the required total length of the link. The shear blades are set at an angle of 30° so that the ends of the bar, once cut, are ready scarfed for welding. The bars are heated to red heat in a reverberatory furnace, removed and bent to the shape of the link. They are then reheated to red heat in the furnace once more, all these operations being carried out by assistants. The chain-making team consists of the chain maker, the first hammer and the second hammer. The second hammer removes the link from the furnace and drags it along the floor to the hearth with a hook. The first hammer, with tongs, then lifts the link onto the anvil with the join upwards. The second hammer then separates the scarfed ends with the 'opener', a 14lb sledgehammer with a tapered head. The link (with scarfed ends open) is returned to the fire by the first hammer. The chain maker then takes over and, with tongs, removes the link from the fire and places it on the stake, while the first hammer threads the previous link onto it. With the chain maker still holding the link with his tongs the link is closed by the first and second hammers using a 'johnny', a two-handled 28lb sledgehammer. It is then returned to the fire by the chain maker and second hammer and raised to welding heat. The chain maker and the first hammer remove the link and place it on the stake after which the chain maker applies the 'squabber' a hollow-faced tool, to the top of the scarf, while both hammers strike it with the 'johnny'. Half the weld is now made. The process is repeated to make the second half of the weld, the technique going by the name of 'shutting', a name in chain making meaning welding. The chain maker takes the 'runner', a hollow-faced tool similar to the 'squabber', and places it on the weld. Both hammers then strike it with 7lb sledgehammers whereby it is 'runnered'. It is now finished and there are no hammer marks. The final stage of the process is the insertion of the cast-iron stud. The first hammer places it in position with the link lying horizontal. The chain maker then turns the link on its side and holds the stud with tongs while both hammers close the link with the 'johnny'. Another hollow faced tool, the 'setter', is used to finish the stud setting by being struck with the 'johnny', worked by the hammers, while the chain maker holds it in place. In the same paper[8], Gale also describes end welding, medium chain making and slight chain making, to which the reader is referred.

Testing

Noah Hingley, who had pioneered the manufacture of chain cables in the Black Country in 1820, was also the first to develop very rudimentary testing in 1830. His method consisted of nothing more than parallel timbers of length equivalent to the chain to be tested, to which a ram and hydraulic cylinder at the end applied the strain. The indicator was a weighted valve from which water was supposed to escape when the desired strain had been applied.[15]

By the mid-nineteenth century, chain cables were replacing those made of hemp. In 1846, Lloyds Register required their surveyors to ensure that all new chains supplied to classed vessels were tested and that the test applied was marked on each length.[16] Its rules were amended in 1853 to mandate that before a vessel is classed, a certificate of chain cable testing should be produced. Five years later, Lloyds Register stipulated the length and size

Lloyds Proving House Certificate (Thomas William Traill, 1885)

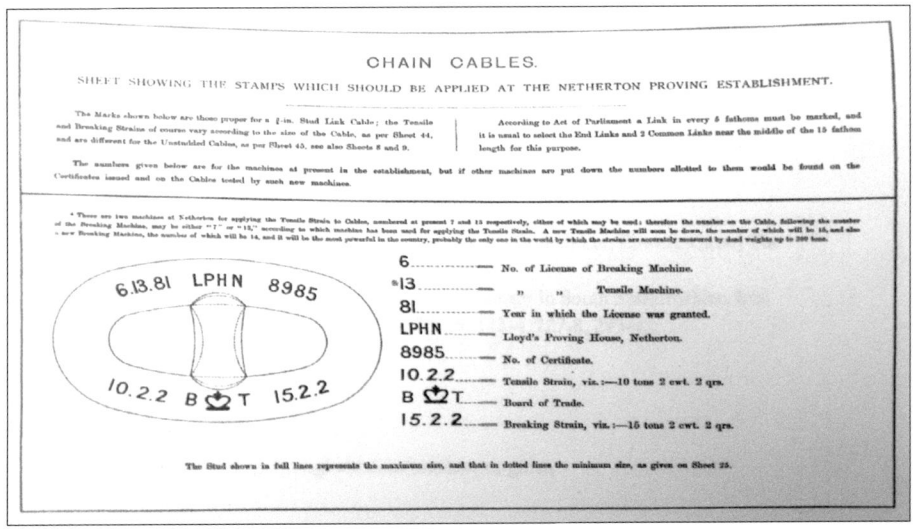

Chain Cable Stamp (Thomas William Traill, 1885)

of cable. Then, in 1862, that testing should be done by a public machine. Two years later, it strengthened its regulations by insisting that a certificate would not be recognised unless it came from an establishment that was under a corporation or open to inspection by an inspector approved by its committee.[17]

In 1864 the government stepped in, and in that year, the first Act of Parliament came onto the statute book for regulating and proving the sale of chain cables and anchors. The Act was amended in 1871 and again in 1874.[18] There was a Proving House in Tipton to the west of Bloomfield Road, between the canal and the railway, where Bloomfield Park industrial estate stands today. It was owned by Lloyd's Public Proving House Company Ltd, with machines that were licensed by the Board of Trade.

Traill outlines in great detail statutory tensile strain and breaking strain that chain cables of various diameters are to be subjected to by superintendents of proving establishments. As well as Tipton there were proving establishments in the Black Country at Netherton, where chains had to be stamped as appropriate to signify it had been tested.[19] (see figure above.)

There is no better way of getting a real 'hands-on' experience of chain making than by visiting the Mushroom Green Chain Shop operated by Industrial Heritage Stronghold.[20]

References

1. P. Jump, Historical Notes on Chains and Chain-Making, Proceedings of the Staffordshire Iron and Steel Institute, 1928/9, Vol. XLIV, p. 6-12.
2. Ron Moss, Chain and Anchor Making in the Black Country, Sutton, 2006.
3. www.cradleylinks.co.uk
4. A.F.Moseley, Black Country Chain makers, West Midland Studies, 1970/1, Vol. 4, p. 56.
5. C.J.L Elwell, Robert Blatchford on the Cradley Heath Chainmakers, Blackcountryman, 1975, vol 8 (3), p. 12.
6. W.K.V.Gale, The British Iron and Steel Industry, David and Charles, Newton Abbot, 1967, p. 43-7.
7. Thomas William Traill, Chain Cable and Chains, Crosby Lockwood & Co (London), 1885, p. 16-19.
8. W.K.V Gale, Hand Wrought Chains, Transactions of the Newcomen Society, 1953/55, Vol. XXIX, p. 195-204
9. Traill, p. 30
10. www.gracesguide.co.uk and links therein
11. Ray Shill, Birmingham and the Black Country's Canalside Industries, Tempus, 2005, p. 118-20
12. Traill., p. 37-8

13. Ibid., p. 47-8
14. Rob Wooley, Gi it sum'ommer, [Epwell] [Underlea Church La., Epwell, Oxon] The Author, 1979.
15. Anonymous Author, Wrought Iron and Chain Industry in South Staffordshire, Iron and Coal Trades Review, 1942, Vol. CXLV, p. 183-4, 227-8, 273-4.
16. Traill, , p. 38
17. Ibid., p.38-41.
18. P.Jump, p. 16-7.
19. Traill, op.cit., sheets 8-9
20. www.industrialheritagestronghold.com/mushroom-green

FIVE

Nails

Nail making has a long history. Nails have been used in this country since at least Roman times. A vast quantity of 875,000 were discovered during excavations in 1960 at the Roman Legionary fortress of Inchtuthil in Perthshire, Scotland.[1]

Handmade Nails

Leland was in Birmingham in the 1540s and wrote that there were 'many smithes in the towne that used to make knives and all manner of cuttynge tooles, and many loriners that made bytes and a great many naylors. So that a great part of the towne is mayntayned by smiths'. But by the sixteenth century, the trade had moved to the Black Country, largely because nail making was a poorly paid job, and more money could be made in Birmingham in other work.[2]

Nails have been made in the Black Country for many centuries, mainly because the area's underlying geology of iron ore and coal deposits are well suited for the production of good-quality wrought iron. It was also an easy trade to learn and often taken up in a part-time capacity by workers in other occupations, such as farm labourers. The industry developed from very small beginnings in out-houses of domestic premises. There would be a small forge and anvil in the backyard of a dwelling house and all the family, husband, wife and children would play their part. The nineteenth-century Black Country historian, Frederick Hackwood, describes one such – probably from personal experience – in vivid terms as typically 'a small dirty shanty, about 10 foot by 12 foot, ventilated only through the door and lighted by one or two unglazed apertures'.[3]

Before the invention of the slitting mill, there was only one way to make iron rod nails. A bloom of iron, perhaps 15kg to 29kg in weight, would be hammered into a sheet of the same thickness as the finished nails and then cut into rods with a sort of chisel, similar to everyday hand shears. The appropriate length was then cut off, heated in a charcoal fire and struck with a hammer to make a point. The head was made by securing the pointed rod in a vice and hammering the blunt end so that it spread out.[4] Early in the seventeenth century, the slitting mill was introduced to this country, where waterpower was used to hammer heated iron into strips. It was then cut or slit into rods for nail making.

Richard Foley

Local legend has it that the slitting mill was introduced to South Staffordshire by Richard Foley (1580–1657), son of a Dudley nail maker. There are a series of fantastic and lengthy stories concerning Richard Foley, so fantastic they are worth telling. First, from the pen of Samuel Taylor Coleridge, a saga of industrial espionage:[5]

> 'The most extraordinary and best attested instance of enthusiasm existing, in conjunction with perseverance, is related to the founder of the Foley family. This man who was a fiddler, living near Stourbridge, was often witness of the immense labour and loss of time caused by dividing the bars of iron, necessary in the process of making nail rods. The discovery of the process of slitting was first made in Sweden, and the consequences of this advance in art were most disastrous to the manufactures of iron about Stourbridge. Foley, the fiddler, was shortly missed from his accustomed rounds and was not again seen for many years. He had mentally resolved to ascertain by what means the process of rod slitting was accomplished; and without communicating his intention to a single human being, he processed to Hull, and thence

without funds worked his passage to the Swedish iron port. Arrived in Sweden, he begged and fiddled his way to the ironworks where, after a long time, he became a favourite with all the workmen; and from the apparent entire absence of intelligence, or anything like ultimate object, he was received into the works, to every part of which he had free access. He took the advantage thus offered, and having stored his mind with observations and all the combinations, he disappeared from amongst his kind friends, as he had appeared, no one knew whence or whither. On his return to England he communicated his voyage and its results to Mr Knight and another person in the neighbourhood with whom he was associated, and by whom the necessary buildings were erected and machinery prepared. When at length everything was prepared, it was found that the machinery would not act; at all events it did not answer the sole end of its erection, viz., slitting bars into rods. Foley disappeared again, and it was concluded that shame and mortification at his failure had driven him away forever. Not so; again, though somewhat more speedily, he found his way to the Swedish iron works where he was received most joyfully, and to make sure of their fiddler he was lodged in the rod mill itself. Here was the very end and aim of his life attained beyond his utmost hope. He examined the works and very soon discovered the cause of failure. He now made drawings or rude tracings; and having abided an ample time to verify his observations, and to impress them clearly and vividly upon his mind, he made his way to the port and once more returned to England. This time he was completely successful, and, by the results of his experience, enriched himself and greatly benefited his countrymen.'

Samuel Taylor Coleridge's tale is just one of three about our hero, Richard Foley. In a second story, we read that Foley was fond of both ale and the alehouse. One day, his wife, in some distress, rushed in to tell Foley their cow had been seized in lieu of the rent. Not a man to shirk his responsibilities, he at once set off for Holland, flute in hand, where he remained for three years learning the intricacies of the slitting mill. Back home he came, but as before was forced to return to Holland to appreciate it was necessary to cool the cutters with a flowing stream of water. In the third story it was a man called Brindley who, after a sojourn in Germany, brought the slitting mill to South Staffordshire.[6]

The Slitting Mill

In actual fact, the slitting mill was introduced into this country from Liege, then a thriving nail-making centre. The first record of a slitting mill in England was at Dartford, Kent, in the late sixteenth century. It was here, in 1588, that Bevis Bulmer (1536–1615) – otherwise known as the builder of the waterworks at London Bridge – who was granted a patent for a water-powered nail-making machine and was given licence for twelve years 'to make and cut iron into small pieces to work out nails'. The patent was later transferred to Clement Dawbeney, who eventually extended it in 1618 for twenty-one years. It was during this time that, on the 4th of April 1627, Richard Foley leased Hyde House at Kinver where he said 'he hath erected and built an Engine and Slitting Mill for the use and benefit for a greate part of this Kingdome'. Dawbeney insisted his patent had been infringed and had it ratified with the statement, 'no one is to make or use the machine patented by Bulmer and Dawbeney or any other like engine'[7] It would be Foley who was in his sights.

Slitting mills[8,9] are made up of two iron shafts mounted one above the other. Both are equipped along their length with a series of sharp-edged cutters that

Slitting Mill (Swedenborg's Regnum Subterraneum, 1734)
(With permission of The Engineer.)

intersect with each other. Waterpower rotates the shafts in opposite directions, so that a sheet of iron which is passed between the shafts would be cut into strips of iron of width determined by the spacing between the cutters on the shafts. In addition, two plain cast-iron shafts, one above the other, would be similarly rotated in opposite directions by a water mill. These would be used first to flatten a bloom of heated iron into a strip (sheet) of iron ready for slitting. Thus a ¼-inch strip of iron passed between ¼-inch cutters would produce square ended rods, ¼ inch by ¼ inch.[10]

The introduction of the slitting mill into South Staffordshire had a major influence in establishing the nailing industry in the area. Slitting mills were built on the banks of the Black Country's small rivers, the Stour and the Tame; indeed, at the end of the eighteenth century the river Stour was said to have on its banks a greater number of works than any river in England of the same length, and slitting mills formed a considerable proportion.[11] A traveller, walking from Birmingham to Wolverhampton in 1795, commented that 'for five or six miles it was one continuous village of nailers'. There were four slitting mils on the Stour and two on the Tame, with about 40,000 nailers converting 10,000 tons or iron rods into nails.[12]

Working conditions

Life for the nail maker was hard. In a publication of 1713, entitled, *An Essay to Enable the Necessitous Poor to Pay Taxes*, nailers were said to work from 4am on Monday to late on Saturday to earn three shillings per week. Later in the mid-nineteenth century, Parliamentary Commissioners 'disclosed the melancholy facts that the lapse of 150 years had neither improved the dwellings, workshops, nor the habits of a male or female nailer; and that the education of their children has continued, till now, to be neglected'.[13] A poem by Sir Frank Short is more illuminating:

> *By the sweat of their brow they exist.*
> *Sunrise to them is over late, and sun down but a lighting of their work-lamp.*
> *As little sleep to them as may be, and not much, save smoke to swallow.*
> *Simple and sturdy hearts, man and women that work and make a nation.*
> *Where is your reward?*
> *Great God! That there be nail shops down in hell for other folk to try.*[14]

Many women worked in the nail trade and in 1888 their conditions came to the attention of the Board of Trade:[15]

'Women are to be seen engaged on spike nails as large as 6-inch and 8-inch on which they will be required to push down the treadle of the heavy oliver some 1300 or 1400 times in addition to blowing the bellows and using the hand hammer… many of them look pale and thin, although their arms are wiry and muscular… average earnings seldom reach a higher figure than from 2s.6d. to 5s per week… many take their children to the shop with them, where they seat them on the hearth, sling them in chairs suspended from the rafters, or lay them to sleep on the bellows… these women (work) side by side with men, and during very hot weather in a state of semi-nudity, not only indecent, but is conducive to immorality… in many cases they are the chief breadwinners of the households, many men taking advantage by being comparatively idle themselves.'

The way the trade worked was that nail masters, centred at Dudley, would meet to regulate nail makers' wages. The nail masters would operate from warehouses and hold supplies of nail rod which would be provided for the nailmaker and his family, enough for one week's work. The finished nails would then be delivered back to the warehouse and the nail maker would get paid.[16] The system was open to abuse, with the poor uneducated nailers at the mercy of unscrupulous masters, known as 'foggers'. The fogger would weigh out iron rods on faulty scales to undersell the nailer, only to cheat again when the finished nails were returned to him for weighing once more. He would also operate the 'tommy shop' system whereby the nailer would be paid in tokens to spend in a shop owned by the fogger.[17]

Such was life for the handmade nailer and by the early nineteenth century as many as 50,000 were employed in the trade. But then, in about 1830 'cut' or 'machine-made' nails began to be made. Bodey has outlined their manufacture: strips of iron are rolled and slit so that they are the thickness of the finished nail and as wide as the nails would be long. The strips are then heated and held against a powerful guillotine, worked by overhead shafting, moved by water or steam power.[18] Nails made by machinery are clearly a factory-based undertaking and it spelled the death knell of the domestic handmade nail trade which went into terminal decline.

Before 1830, all the London Dock Companies had contacts for handmade nails. The East India Dock Company contracted for 110 tons per year, ninety tons of which were for tea chests. Machine made nails were $1/5$ the cost of hand – made and in consequence the wages of nailers fell by 35%. The handmade nail industry was never to recover. Many former nail makers entered the chain-making trade.

References

1. Austin Moseley, The Nailmakers, Blackcountryman, 1971, Vol. IV (1), p. 47-56.
2. Hugh Bodey, Nailmaking, Shire, 2008, p. 11.
3. F. W. Hackwood, Wednesbury Workshops: Some Accounts of the Industries of a Black Country Town, Horton Press, 1897, p.20.
4. Bodey, 2008, p. 7-8.
5. Hackwood, p. 21-2
6. W. H. B. Court, The Rise of the Midland Industries, Oxford University Press, 1965, p. 104
7. ibid., p. 105-7.
8. Rhys Jenkins, Links in the History of Engineering, The Engineer, 1918, vol. 125, p. 488
9. H. R. Schubert, History of British Iron and Steel Industry, 1957, p. 304-12
10. W. K. V. Gale, The British Iron and Steel Industry, David & Charles, 1967, p. 26-27.
11. Court, p. 113.
12. Bodey p. 14.
13. Hackwood, p. 21.
14. F.W.Hackwood, Oldbury and Round About in the Worcestershire Corner of the Black Country, Brewin Books, 2002.
15. Board of Trade Report on the Conditions of Nail Makers and Small Chain Makers in South Staffordshire and East Worcestershire,1888
16. Ephraim Ball, The Hand Made Nail Trade, in The Resource, Products and Industrial History of Birmingham and the Midland Hardware District, ed., Samuel Timmins, Robert Hardwicke, 1866, p. 110-16.
17. Austin Moseley, p. 55
18. Bodey p.21

SIX
Locks and Keys

The history of locks and keys can be traced back to the Egyptian era. In 1850, John Chubb (1816–1872), son of Charles Chubb (1779–1846), founder of the famous Wolverhampton Company of Chubb and Son, read a paper at the Institute of Civil Engineers, where he described how a lock is depicted on the carved reliefs of the Great Temple at Karnack in Egypt.[1] Locks are also mentioned in the Bible, in Judges, Chapter 4, Verse 23–25: 'Ehud went forth through the porch, and shut the doors of the parlour upon him, and locked them… and behold he opened not the doors of his parlour; therefore they (his servants) took a key and opened them, and behold their lord was fallen down dead on the earth.'

Chubb identified four types of ancient lock from which most, if not all, modern locks are derived. These are: 1. The Egyptian Lock. 2. The Warded Lock. 3. The Letter Lock. 4. Locks having a Single Tumbler in addition to Fixed Wards.

For his groundbreaking paper, in 1850, John Chubb was awarded the Telford Medal by the Institute of Civil Engineers. (The Telford Medal was made possible by a bequest from Thomas Telford.)

Egyptian Pin Tumbler Lock[1]

Egyptian locks work by moveable pins dropping into and securing the bolt. To unfasten the bolt, the pins are raised by corresponding pins in a key.

Ancient Egyptian locks were made of wood. An Egyptian Lock (also known as a pin tumbler lock) is shown in the figure below. Chubb described its operation as follows:

> 'A staple A is fixed to the outside of the door, into the upper part of which three loose pins BBB are fitted; these three pins drop into three corresponding holes in the bolt C, so as to fasten the door when the bolt is pushed in to its full extent. The key D is a straight piece of wood. At one end there are three pegs EEE corresponding in position with the pins in the lock. The key is inserted lengthways through a slot F, formed in the bolt, and then the pins in the key, corresponding to the vertical holes in the bolt C, into which the pins have dropped, lift up the pins, raising them flush with the top side of the bolt, thus disengaging the moveable pins from the bolt, and allowing it to be moved backwards and forwards.'

The principle of operation of Egyptian pin tumbler locks is still the same as in locks made today, albeit with intricate modifications.

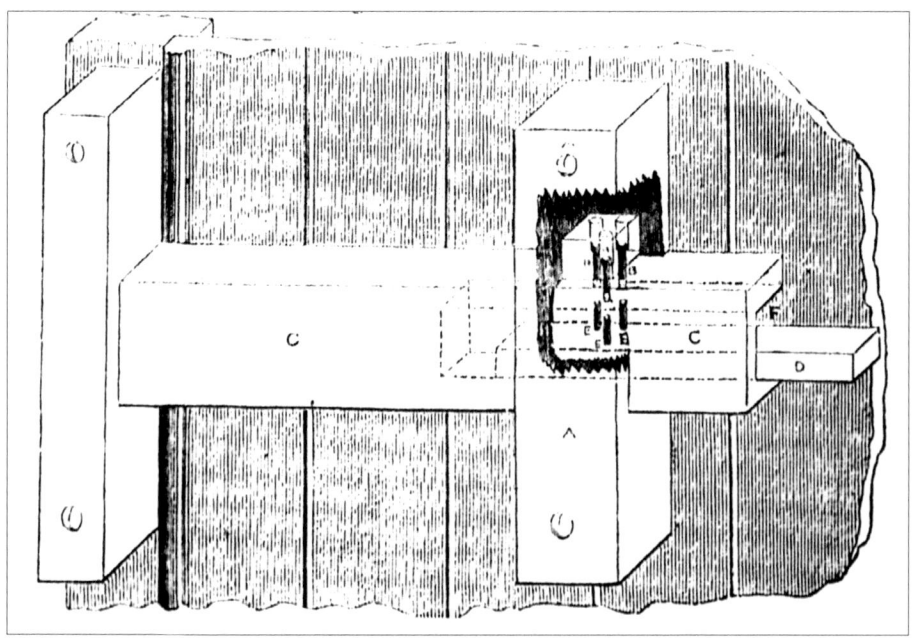

Egyptian Lock (John Chubb, 1850)

Warded Lock

An alternative to the Egyptian Lock and of similar antiquity is the warded lock. Warded locks predominated throughout the medieval era and beyond. They are made of metal and contain fixed wards to act as obstructions to any but the valid key. The web of the key is cut to pass the wards and so open the bolt. Chubb[1] noted that warded locks are easy to pick and even – perhaps with a wry smile – went to the length of illustrating picks commonly used by burglars. The figure below shows a warded lock, complete with keys and picks. A shows the wards of the lock; B, the original key, with the cuts in the web exactly corresponding to the wards in the lock; C is a burglar's instrument, made of tin, having a composition of wax and yellow soap fitted on one side of the bit, so that on its being inserted into the keyhole, a perfect impression of the wards is taken. To make a picklock, it is only necessary to preserve the end of the web which moves the bolt; this is accomplished by the instrument D, which is made so as to escape the wards, and will open or shut the lock, as well as the original key. The picklock E, also by passing round the wards, will easily open the lock.

As if to emphasise his dislike of warded locks, Chubb makes the point that twenty skeleton keys might be made which would open the majority of street

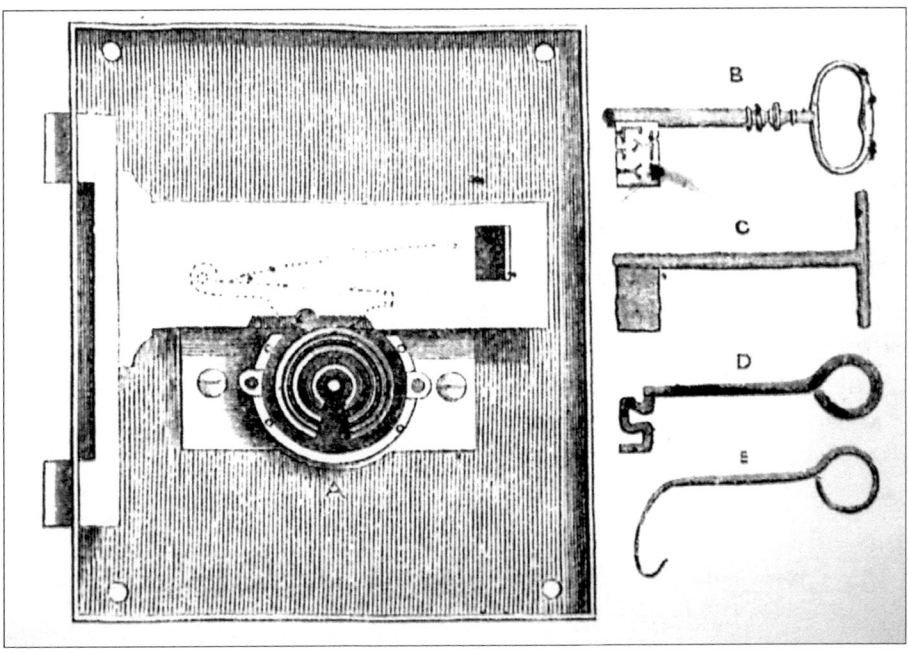

Warded Lock (John Chubb, 1850)

The Making of the Black Country

doors in London. Egyptian locks (or pin tumbler locks) work by moveable pins dropping into and securing the bolt. To unfasten the bolt, the pins are raised by corresponding pins in a key.

Letter Lock

The combination padlock or letter lock is of similar antiquity. Chubb described and illustrated it in his 1850 paper thus:

'AA are the ends of the lock, to one of which the shackle B is hinged and a barrel C is fixed. D is the spindle which screws into the opposite end of the lock; it has four projections and fits inside the barrel C. E is one of four rings (side view FF) having grooves on the inside, so as to fit over the barrel C, and small projecting nibs on the outside, just over the grooves. G is one of the four external rings, which fit over the ring E; they are marked on the outside with letters of the alphabet, and on the inside, under each letter, there is a groove as shown by the side view, H, of one of these rings. The rings E are riveted to the barrels C, the inner edge of the end ring being bevelled for that purpose, but they are left to revolve freely. The external rings G are then put on, at any combination of letters that may be required, taking care that the groove under each particular letter shall be exactly over the projection on the inner ring. When these letters are brought into a line with the notches on the ends of the

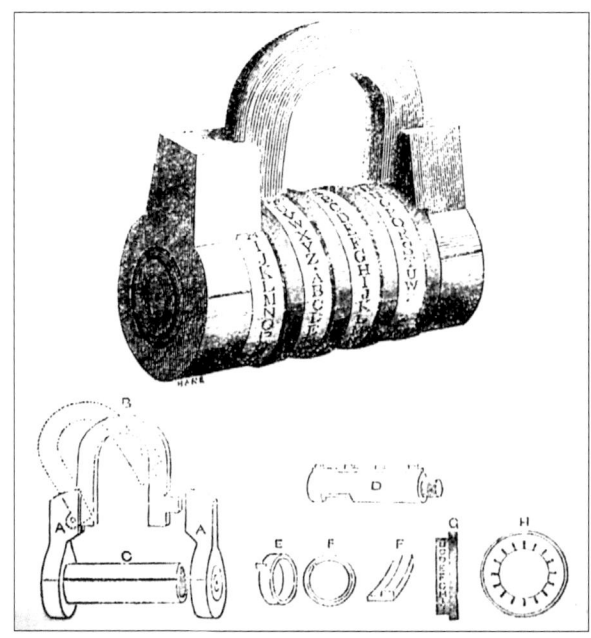

Letter Lock (John Chubb, 1850)

lock, the grooves in the inner rings and the barrel will also be in a line and the spindle D will slide backwards and forwards. By shutting down the shackle, pushing the end of the lock up close, and turning the rings the interior flanges prevent the withdrawal of the spindle until the same letters are in line again.'

* * *

Lock making in the Black Country was centred at Wolverhampton and Willenhall. According to Dr Wilkes, a Willenhall vicar, the industry came to the district in the reign of Elizabeth 1.[2] There were many locksmiths, and each individual concern was small in scale; typically each locksmith would employ about eight to ten men or children, working in his own house or in a small outbuilding. Locks were made of locally produced wrought iron; a square or round blank would be hammered into a rough form on the anvil and then filed down into the correct shape. It was back-breaking work. Filing was often done by children, requiring them to bend down for long periods, giving them life-long hump backs. The seats in public houses even had hollows at the back so that humped-backed regulars could sit upright. This led to Willenhall often being called 'Humpshire'. The locksmith would sell his locks to a middleman, known as a chapman, who would journey from place to place on a packhorse to sell them on to the end user. By the eighteenth century, storerooms were opened at Birmingham and Wolverhampton. The old established wareroom of Messrs Tarratt & Sons was still operating at Townwell Fold, in Wolverhampton, in the mid-nineteenth century.[3] In 1770, 134 locksmiths were working in Wolverhampton, with 148 in Willenhall. By 1855, the number in Willenhall had increased to 340, while those at Wolverhampton stood at 110.[4]

Working conditions were appalling and hours were long: 6am to 7pm in summer and 7am to 8pm in winter. At the beginning of the nineteenth century, children were paid 3s per week and adults about 10s. By the mid-nineteenth century, men were earning 18s to 25s per week. Wages were a little higher in Wolverhampton, where better-quality locks were made. A report by the Children's Employment Commission of 1843 describes workshops as 'regular menageries, dogs being tied up under the bellows, bird cages hung in the window, rabbit pens constructed under the workbench and pigeons kept outside on the roof, a pigsty under the workshop window… with the accumulated dust and dirt of the floor, form the enchantment of a locksmith's shop'. The same report emphasised the dreadful treatment of children: 'In Willenhall the children are shamefully and most cruelly beaten with whatever tool is most near at hand.'[5] Towards the end of the nineteenth century, conditions improved, and a degree of mechanisation was introduced.

Individual Lock-Making Firms

Carpenter and Tildesley[6,7]

In 1830, James Carpenter and John Young made a door-rim lock with perpendicular action. (Rim locks are locks which attach to the surface of a door.) It developed into the modern mortice lock. (A mortice lock has a pocket, the mortice, in the edge of the door into which the lock is fitted.) The pair held a joint patent with Young making mortice locks and Carpenter perpendicular rim locks. The lock became known as 'Carpenter's Lift up Lock.' Carpenter opened a factory in New Road, Willenhall, called Summerford Works. James Tildesley married Carpenter's daughter and in 1851 the business was known as Carpenter and Tildesley. In time, James Tildesley became the sole owner of the company.

Josiah Parkes & Sons [8,9,10]

One of the largest lock-making firms in the Black Country was founded in 1840 by the brothers Josiah, Richard and William Parkes at 28, 29 and 30 Doctor's Piece in Willenhall. The family came from Gornal and Josiah, the youngest brother, born in 1824, was apprenticed at Hickman's Iron Works in Bilston. To begin with, he continued working at Hickmans and helped his brothers out in the evenings. As well as locks made from wrought iron blanks, the brothers produced a variety of other metal goods. By 1852, the firm had acquired new premises in Union Street. They acted as factors by supplying iron to the many locksmiths in Willenhall and then buying back their locks and selling them on to chapmen.

In 1868, William left (Richard had left some years before) and Josiah was joined by his son, William Edmund and later by a younger son, James Harry, the firm now known as Josiah Parkes & Sons. Other members of the family joined in succeeding years and additional premises were obtained in Wood Street. Josiah Parkes senior retired in 1887 and three years later, the firm, now just concentrating on lock making, sold Doctor's Piece. The Union Street firm began manufacturing cylinder locks (an adaptation and modern version of the traditional Egyptian lock) in the early twentieth century by which time, in 1906, Parkes & Sons were employing thirty-five people, rising to one hundred in 1913. During the First World War, the firm produced a variety of munitions and became a limited company. After the war, land was acquired at Portobello for a sports ground and in 1936 Josiah Parkes became a public company, employing over five hundred people.

Munitions were produced again in the Second World War, after which the company diversified to make doorknobs, window fasteners, stays, hinges and other related articles. Foundry production began at Portobello and a company was also started in South Africa.

The company was now of considerable size. It took over Edwin Showell of Stirchley in Birmingham and by 1958 employed 1,300, rising to 2,000 in 1961, exporting its locks all over the world. In 1965, Josiah Parkes merged with Chubb. In 1971, a £500,000 metal finishing factory opened at Portobello with an automatic chrome plating plant and associated effluent treatment plant. In 1984, Parkes became members of the Racal Group of Companies.

John Harper & Co. Ltd, Albion Works[11]

The firm was founded in 1790 by William Harper and Samuel Tildesley. It was mentioned in a directory of Wolverhampton in 1849, located at the Albion Works, Somerford, near to the brook and owned by James Tildesley. At the time, Willenhall did not have a bank and so James Tildesley had to borrow money from his suppliers, including his cousin, Matthew Tildesley, an iron seller. James got himself into serious debt, only relieved by handing over the business to Matthew. It was valued at the considerable sum of £2,350 and included a range of buildings comprising an engine house, boiler house, engineer's house, warehousing, a casting shop, varnish house, annealing oven and stable. A number of other concerns joined in 1851, including James Lockett of Somerford (screw maker), John Fox of Willenhall (lock maker) and Thomas Bruerton of Mount Pleasant, Bilston (bag-lock maker). Apart from making locks and keys, the firm also made castings of malleable iron.

The Albion Works moved to Walsall Road in 1855, now becoming the New Albion Works. The firm manufactured and exported the malleable tumbler lock, patented by James Tildesley. The new works was well equipped with a beam engine to drive machinery and a Nasmyth hammer for forging bolts.

The firm was one of the four Willenhall lock makers which protested that locks supplied to the Admiralty from America, had mostly been produced in Willenhall and sold to the Admiralty at higher prices than that charged by the makers.[12]

But the temperaments of John Harper and Matthew Tildesley were incompatible. Harper had business sense and oversaw the office. He had a prickly nature and clashed with Matthew, who, with his easy-going nature, was in charge of manufacture. The result was bankruptcy and a plague of legal wrangles. Nevertheless, a new firm rose from the ashes and thrived in the twentieth century. It employed 764 people in 1914, became a public company and was described as general- and malleable-iron founders and manufacturers of finished hardware of all kinds.[11]

Enoch Tonks & Sons[13,14]

Enoch Tonks was a prominent lock maker in the Little London area of Willenhall. He was born in 1827 and spent the early part of his life making padlocks all day long, so much so that he resolved never to make them again when he set up on his own, now making rim locks. He was joined by his father and brothers and the family set up at Temple Bar. The company thrived and made locks under the trade name ETAS, including penny-in-the-slot locks for public lavatories, from which the expression 'spend a penny' derives. The firm was taken over by Yale and Towne in the mid-twentieth century.

Yale & Towne [15,16]

In 1868, Linus Yale Junior adapted and patented a pin-tumbler lock, that had been invented by his father, and went into business with Henry Towne, a mechanical engineer. So was born, in October 1868, at Stamford, Connecticut, the Yale & Towne Manufacturing Company. In 1904, the company had expanded and opened a subsidiary in London at 17 to 20, West Smithfield. For the next twenty-five years, locks were imported into this country from America. Then, in 1929, Yale decided to open a lock-making facility in the UK. It was logical for them to look for the acknowledged centre of the lock-making industry and it was to Willenhall that they looked. In consequence, they acquired the old established firm of **H. & T. Vaughan** of Wood Street.

H. & T. Vaughan were established by Henry William and Thomas Vaughan, son of the lock maker, Abel Vaughan. It had built an excellent reputation making cylinder locks, padlocks and lever locks. In 1872, a second factory was acquired in Union Street. They were well known as the manufacturer of keys for the Automobile Association's call boxes and when taken over employed about five hundred workers. They had been one of the four Willenhall firms objecting to the purchasing practices of the Admiralty, as mentioned above.

Chubb[17,18]

The famous firm of Chubb was founded by Charles Chubb (1779–1846). Charles had been born in Fordingbridge (Hampshire), trained as a blacksmith and moved to Portsmouth, where he worked as a ship's ironmonger. It was his brother, Jeremiah, however, who first patented the celebrated detector lock in 1818. There had been a break-in at Portsmouth Dockyard; as a result, the authorities offered a reward of £100 to anyone who could make a 'burglar-proof' lock. Jeremiah took up the challenge and the detector lock was the outcome. He challenged a prisoner on one of the prison hulks in Portsmouth harbour – well known for his lock-picking skill – to pick the lock. After many months of trying, the convict gave in and Jeremiah was duly awarded the prize.

The detector lock has up to six separate double-acing tumblers and a detector which comes into action if the lock is tampered with. It then jams and so gives the owner notice that this has happened and can only be released with the appropriate regulating key.

Chubb set up in England in Wolverhampton in Temple Street, later St James Square and then in 1838 at the junction of Horseley Fields with Mill Street. Meanwhile, a London office had been opened at 57 St Paul's Churchyard.

It is said that the fame of the detector locks rests on the fact that George IV sat down on it. Whether true or not, the firm had many well-known customers, including the Duke of Wellington. He used it to secure his London residence at Apsley House. The Bank of England was another customer. The company also became sole suppliers to the General Post Office and the newly introduced post-boxes were all secured with Chubb locks. In 1851, the Koh-I-Noor diamond was displayed at the Great Exhibition in Hyde Park; a Chubb detector lock secured its cabinet. Contracts were similarly secured from H.M. Prison Service.

There were scores of other lock-making firms in Willenhall[19]. They included Henry Squire & Sons Ltd, founded in 1780; J. Legge & Co. Ltd, who made door locks; and Enoch Pinson, founded in 1870. Many were located at The Crescent.[20] They included Charles Adams, Edward Burns, Joseph Dunn and Joseph Smith. In 1815, Charles Harthill was making padlocks in a cottage in The Crescent. It later became part of the well-known firm of John Worrall & Sons, which was founded in about 1895, styling themselves general lock-and-key manufacturers and suppliers to the Ministry of Public Buildings and Works.

Willenhall is the centre of the lock-making industry but locks were also made in Walsall, particularly padlocks. **Walsall Locks and Cart Gear** was set up by a group of workers as a cooperative in 1873 and had premises in Birchills. They made locks for a range of purposes varying in size from locks weighing 7lbs, suitable for securing warehouse doors, to miniature specimens to attach to watch chains.

References

1. John Chubb, On the Construction of Locks and Keys, Paper Presented at Institute of Civil Engineers, April 9, 1850.
2. S. Mould, The Lock Industry of the West Midlands, Blackcountryman, 1971, IV, (3), p. 12-14
3. J.C.Tildesley, Locks and Lock-Making, in Samuel Timmins (ed.) The Resources, Products and Industrial History of Birmingham and the Midland Hardware District, Robert Hardwicke, 1866, p. 77
4. George Price, A Treatise on Fire and Thief-Proof Depositories and Locks and Keys, London (Wolverhampton), 1856.
5. G.Varndell, A Short History of Lock Making in Willenhall, Walsall Metropolitan Borough Council Library and Museum Services, March 1978.
6. Bev Parker, Willenhall Through the Ages, in www.historywebsite.co.uk
7. www.gracesguide.co.uk and link
8. Harold Parsons, Josiah Parkes & Sons, A Company History, Blackcountryman, 1973, VI, (1), p. 39-43.
9. Anon., Keys by the Million, Blackcountryman, 1975, VIII, (2), p. 31-4.
10. www.gracesguide.co.uk and link
11. N.W.Tildesley , The Early History of the Albion Works, Willenhall, 1790-1880, Journal of West Midland Studies, 1970/1, 4, p.32-45.
12. The Times Newspaper, 24 February 1879.
13. www.historywebsire.co.uk (Enoch Tonks)
14. Horace Davis, in Alan Godfrey Old Ordnance Survey Maps, Willenhall (NW), 1901

15. www.gracesguide.co.uk and link
16. Harold Parsons, A Half Century of Yale at Willenhall. Blackcountryman, 1979, XII, (3), p. 33-40.
17. www.gracesguide.co.uk and appropriate links.
18. www.chubbarchive.org.uk
19. Deirdre Wilkes and Sarah Elson, Lock Making in Willenhall, Industrial Archaeology, 1983, 16 (4), p. 345.
20. G. Stevens, The Crescent Lock Makers, Blackcountryman, 1971, IV, (1), p.33- 5

SEVEN

The Chemical Industry

Although the Black Country cannot really be thought of as a centre of the chemical industry, there were, beginning in the eighteenth century, a number of significant men who came to the area and founded important chemical industries. Foremost amongst these were James Keir and Arthur Albright.

James Keir

James Keir was born in Stirlingshire on the 20th of September 1735, the eighteenth and youngest child of his parents. He studied medicine at the University of Edinburgh and there formed a lasting friendship with Erasmus Darwin. Keir joined the army after Edinburgh and served in Canada, the West Indies and Ireland. He narrowly escaped death while in the West Indies but having requested antimony – presumably on the basis of his chemical and medical knowledge – recovered. James Keir found himself in the Black Country in 1768. He renewed his friendship with Erasmus Darwin, now practising as a doctor in Lichfield, and probably on Darwin's advice decided to settle in the Black Country.

Keir leased a glass works at Holloway End in Amblecote and remained for eight years making glass with Samuel Skey, who also made vitriol (sulphuric acid) at Bewdley. But all the while he was occupying himself with private research into the production and properties of alkalis. Keir also spent a short while at the works of Boulton and Watt but declined a partnership, preferring instead to set up an alkali works with Alexander Blair, an old friend from army days. The works was in Tipton, adjacent to the canal at Bloomsmithy and Soap Factory Road (now Factory Road).[1,2]

An alkali, in eighteenth century terms, was either sodium carbonate or potassium carbonate. From it, lye, a general name for either sodium hydroxide or potassium hydroxide, could be produced and this in turn enabled Keir and Blair to begin making soap. Soaps are salts of fatty acids and are produced by a process called saponification. Vegetable oils or fats are boiled in alkaline solutions. In the reaction, triglycerides (an ester of glycerol and an acid) are broken down by the lye to form a fatty salt (soap) and glycerol. According to Barbara Smith[1], Keir's and Blair's twenty-acre factory was the first soap factory in the world.

Keir and Blair also made red lead and white lead. Red lead is the oxide of lead and is used in the glass-making industry to make flint glass. White lead, the carbonate, was supplied to Josiah Wedgwood and the potters of North Staffordshire. Stebbing Shaw[3] tells us that at their factory there were two water wheels, and two fire engines (steam engines). In 1794, Keir and Blair purchased Tividale Colliery to supply their thriving works with coal. The firm also made metal sashes for windows and supplied them to Windsor Castle and the Prince Regent's Carlton House. As well as working in his soap factory, Keir found time for more fundamental scientific studies. He composed a dictionary of chemistry and synthesised an alloy of copper, zinc and iron, very similar to Munz metal. In 1779, he took out a patent for his alloy, which could be forged hot or cold. It was used for metal window sashes. Keir also published many scientific papers.

James Keir was a fine scientist. He was an active member of the Lunar Society, an informal society of scientists who lived in the Birmingham area between 1765 and 1813. Members included Erasmus Darwin, James Watt, Matthew Boulton, Josiah Wedgwood and Joseph Priestley. The Lunar Society was so-called because members (who called themselves lunaticks, a pun on lunatics) met when the moon was full, thereby, in an age without street lighting, making their journey home safe. Keir was elected a fellow of the Royal Society in 1785. James Keir was sympathetic to the causes espoused by the French Revolution. On Bastille Day in 1791, he presided over a dinner to celebrate the revolution; it resulted in Joseph Priestley's house being burnt to the ground by the mob. James Keir died in West Bromwich in 1820 and was buried at All Saints' Church.

After James Keir died, the firm continued under Alexander Blair and John Stephenson, with a Mr Boyle as manager. Boyle left in 1817 and the firm finally closed in the late 1830s or early 1840s.

Adkins and Co.

Henry Adkins published a paper in 1866[4] in which he wrote that at the beginning of the nineteenth century there were three types of hard soap: white soap, mottled soap and brown soap. White soap was made from soda (sodium hydroxide) and tallow (beef and mutton fat); mottled soap from soda, tallow and kitchen grease; and brown soap from soda, palm oil and resin. But palm oil is red in colour and proved to be unpopular. To remove the colour, the oil was treated with potassium dichromate and hydrochloric acid, but before that, Mr Boyle of Messrs Blair of Tipton (James Keir's company) removed the colour simply by heating to 430°C.

In 1817, Boyle joined the firm which had been founded by Thomas Adkins and John Nock on the bank of the Birmingham Canal at Smethwick. He brought his expertise with him and soon the Smethwick firm was making red lead as well as soap. When the Tipton Chemical Works founded by James Keir closed, Adkins and Co. became the leading manufacturer of red lead in the area. Red lead was produced by heating metallic lead in a reverberatory furnace for twelve hours. Litharge was formed which was removed from the furnace with a rake[5]. Any residual metallic lead is separated out and lead oxide, red lead, is formed. In 1887, Adkins was purchased by Henry Wiggin and Co. Ltd, the well-known Birmingham nickel company.[6]

Robinson Brothers

William Leckie Robinson was born in London, but by 1869, together with his brothers, John Henry and Charles, had founded a chemical works on the bank of the canal at Ryders Green in West Bromwich. The brothers had

The Chemical Industry

Robinson Brothers, West Bromwich

family connections with owners of the gas works at Coventry, Leamington and Leicester. Robinsons therefore had ready access to a plentiful supply of coal tar and became manufacturers of its distillation products. (In a gas works, coal is heated in the absence of air and town gas, or coal gas is given off. Many impurities are produced which must be removed before the gas is sold. First, the gas is passed through pipes surrounded by cold water to condense out tars, which as a by-product can be sold to coal tar companies.)

Throughout the nineteenth century, creosote for preserving wood, and pitch, used as a binder in patented fuel, were important products of Robinsons. Benzene was formed in lighter fractions and was used in the manufacture of aniline and dyestuffs. The coming of the motor car highlighted the need for improved road surfaces and Robinsons exploited this new market by obtaining a license to manufacture 'Tarvia', a tar-like substance used in road making and road maintenance. In 1825, John Bethell built a tar works in West Bromwich, part of which was later bought by Robinson Brothers.

Major and Co. was founded in 1856 by John Clarkson Major and E.L. Turner. One of their employees was Lewis Demuth, a young German. He left to set up on his own in Oldbury in 1866 and, such was the quality of his benzene and toluene, he was awarded a silver medal at the Paris Exhibition of 1867.[7] Lewis Demuth operated the **Springfield Chemical Works** on the Birmingham Canal Navigation at Tat Bank. In 1921, Herbert Robinson got wind of the likely sale of Lewis Demuth's coal tar business to **British Cyanides.** Despite the information being gained from a canal boatman (perhaps not the most dependable of sources), Robinson immediately bought all Lewis Demuth's shares and formed **The Midland Tar Distillers Ltd.** The latter company took over the tar-distilling interests of Robinson Brothers and acquired the tar distillers, **Major and Co.** of Wolverhampton as well. All tar distilling was now carried at Oldbury.

In 1894, Robinsons became a private limited company and expanded to produce a large range of organic chemicals. They are still based in West Bromwich.[8]

Oldbury Chemical Works (Chance and Hunt) [9, 10]

Chance Brothers are better known to us as glass manufacturers. In 1834, they took into partnership the brothers James and John Hartley and the firm became known as **Chance and Hartley.** In 1835, they bought land at Park House Lane in Oldbury and started to make saltcake (sodium sulphate), a starting product in the manufacture of soda ash (sodium carbonate) by the Leblanc Process. The process, devised by the French chemist Nicolas Leblanc in the late nineteenth century, enabled the production of soda ash from common salt. In the first stage, salt is heated with sulphuric acid to form saltcake:

$$2NaCl + H_2SO_4 = Na_2SO_4 + 2HCl$$

The saltcake is then heated in a furnace with limestone and coke:

$$Na_2SO_4 + CaCO_3 + 2C = Na_2CO_3 + CaS + 2CO_2$$

The soda ash is then leached with water and crystallised. It will be noticed that hydrogen chloride is evolved in the process. It was also noticed by local people living nearby, when it fell as hydrochloric acid, forcing the company to absorb it in water at source. Many other chemicals were made at the Oldbury Works, including sulphuric acid by the lead-chamber process, pioneered by Birmingham man, John Roebuck.

The Hartley brothers left after one year to set up in Sunderland and the Oldbury firm became known as **Chance Brothers and Company.** Alexander Macomb Chance joined the company in 1852 and headed it for many years, also providing many humanitarian initiatives, both for employees and the local community, such as financing schools, libraries and houses. Together with J.F. Chance, he patented a process for recovering sulphur from the waste product of the Leblanc process.

In the 1880s, new gold deposits were discovered in South Africa – but they tended to be of low-grade ore. Working at Tennant's Chemical Works in Glasgow, John MacArthur and the brothers Robert and William Forrest exploited Carl Wilhelme Scheele's discovery that gold can form a complex ion with cyanide. The crushed ore is combined with a cyanide solution and the complex ion Au $(CN)_2$ is formed. This is then brought into contact with zinc to form a stronger complex with cyanide and so release pure gold. In 1894, excited by this development, Chance Brothers, their chemical works now a separate company known as **The Oldbury Alkali Company Ltd**, formed a subsidiary company, **British Cyanides Co. Ltd**, with their near neighbours **Albright and Wilson** and began making cyanides. They built a plant on land by the Birmingham Canal; Albright & Wilson were one side and the GWR railway between Langley Green and Oldbury on the other. British Cyanides met with mixed success in producing ammonium sulpho-cyanide and subsequently converted it to prussiate (sodium ferro-cyanide), which had a wider market. They were also hindered by the outbreak of the South African Boer War, which significantly reduced the demand for cyanides. Later, the company was successful in converting ammonium sulpho-cyanide into thiourea. By reacting thiourea with formaldehyde a synthetic resin was formed, which became the basis of the company's plastics industry. In 1936, the company became **British Industrial Plastics**.[11]

William Hunt learnt his trade at the Stoke Prior Works of the British Alkali Works with William Gossage. When Gossage set up on his own at Widnes, Hunt did likewise at Leabrook in Wednesbury and began to make alkali and sulphuric acid. He also had works at Castleford in Yorkshire. In 1898, **W. Hunt and Sons** amalgamated with the Oldbury Alkali Company, the new company becoming known as **Chance and Hunt**.[12]

Albright and Wilson [13]

Arthur Albright was born in Charlbury in Oxfordshire on the 3rd of March 1811. He was brought up as a Quaker and, like so many Quakers, had an eye for business. Arthur was trained as a chemist, first in Bristol, then Birmingham and Stourbridge, before travelling in Europe. In 1840, he joined the firm of manufacturing chemists J & E Sturge of Birmingham. The manufacture of white phosphorus and potassium chlorate (the constituents of matches), were amongst the chemicals made by the Sturges. In 1840, Albright moved to a site described as a 'ploughed field' near the Birmingham Canal at Tat Bank in Oldbury. The site was purchased for £1,182 from Chance Brothers and was chosen to be near Chance's alkali works (manufacturers of sulphuric acid) and the South Staffordshire coalfield. Arthur Albright built premises at a cost of £1,957 and began making phosphorus and potassium chlorate.

Phosphorus was first made from bone ash (calcium phosphate) by the German, C.W. Scheele, in 1769. White phosphorus was formed, then the only form of phosphorus. It is inflammable and was used to coat the heads of matches. Regrettably, it is also extremely poisonous and gives rise to a dreadful condition called phossy jaw, literally a collapsed jaw, to those unfortunate enough to be exposed to it. Or as an eyewitness described one such afflicted, 'you could take his chin and shove it all in his mouth'.

In 1856, Albright, now joined by John Edward Wilson, set up making white phosphorus. First, bone ash was softened and degreased with hydrochloric acid. It was then decomposed by sulphuric acid to yield phosphoric acid. The syrupy phosphoric acid was mixed with coal or charcoal, dried, ground and placed in bottle-shaped retorts, 48 inches long and 8 inches in diameter. Twenty-four of these were then placed in a coal fired furnace.

$$4HPO_3 + 12C = P_4 + 12CO$$

Phosphorus was vapourised, condensed, treated with oxidising agents and dilute sulphuric acid and cast into blocks.

Two chemical works, therefore, stood side by side in Oldbury. One can only feel sorry for those who lived nearby. The Oldbury historian, F.W. Hackwood, captures the scene vividly:

> 'Corroding chemicals emitted from chemical works in the heart of the town so completed the blight that even grass of the hardiest of plants failed not to succumb. Nor by incessant labour could Oldbury housewives keep fire irons, or the utensils of bright steel in any desirable condition of cleanliness. They are tarnished in a single night and in the process of time faded away as they had been petals of a fading flower.'[14].

In 1872, Albright and Wilson built their famous 251ft-high chimney – seen from near and far – in an attempt to disperse effluent gases over a wide area and thereby reduce ground-level concentrations to negligible levels. After the chimney at Stoke Prior, it was the largest in the country. An obvious landmark for German bombers, it was demolished in 1941. The traitor, William Joyce (Lord Haw Haw) mocked, 'Albright and Wilson, you can pull your chimney down, but we shall find you.'

Arthur Albright – a religious man – had misgivings about making white phosphorus: 'With the strongest reasons for believing the very best I possibly could do of the great merits of common phosphorus matches for millions, I had no right to shut my eyes to the dangers and risks to health and property which attended their use.' In 1849, the Viennese chemist, Anton Schrotter, discovered red phosphorus, an allotrope of white phosphorus. Albright and Wilson immediately bought Schrotter's patent and began making red phosphorus by heating white phosphorus in closed cast-iron pots. Schrotter's process caused explosions, but Albright and Wilson avoided them by inserting safety valves in their furnaces.

The production of red phosphorus heralded the invention of the safety match. The 'safety' was due to separating the combustible materials on the match head from the special striking surface on the box, as well as replacing toxic white phosphorus with red phosphorus. The safety matches' striking surface was composed of 25% powdered glass, 50% red phosphorus, 5% neutraliser (calcium carbonate), 4% carbon black and 16% binder. The match head consisted of 45–55% potassium chlorate, sulphur, starch, antimony sulphide and 20–40% siliceous filler and glue. At that time, the market leader in safety match production was the Swedish firm run by Carl and John Lundstrom in Jonkoping. They placed a large order with Albright and Wilson but, at first, Arthur was reluctant to supply them because phosphorus was also used in the manufacture of incendiary bombs.

He replied to Lundstrom:

'Gentlemen, Amorphous phosphorus in such quantities as stated in your letter, can to the best of my judgement, only be used for purposes of war. As I, who belong to the Society of Friends, disapprove of war, I beg respectfully to decline your order.'

The Lundstroms replied that their order was to enable them to make matches, or, in other words, 'not for war of destruction, but for peace and the enlightenment of mankind' – this reply inspiring Albright and Wilson's to design their seal as 'the torch of life'. Arthur was moved to write a poem:

> *The safety match, the safety match,*
> *Oh, that's the match for me;*
> *Let others praise the common sort.*
> *With them I can't agree*

In the early 1880s, the Siemens regenerative furnace replaced direct firing. Coal was converted first to hot gases which then passed to the furnace. But electricity was soon to supplant gas. In 1888, John Readman, Tom 'Honest' Parker, and A.E. Robinson of Wolverhampton were granted a patent whereby heat was supplied to phosphate in a closed vessel via an electric current passing between two electrodes. It was exploited by the **Electric Construction Co. of** Wolverhampton who, in 1890, formed **The Phosphate Co.** in nearby Wednesfield. Albright and Wilson were quick to purchase the Wednesfield plant for £16,000 which worked for two years before new plant was built at Oldbury. This method is now the only large-scale method for the production of phosphorus. In the process, a mixture of phosphate, silica and carbon is introduced to the furnace. When current is passed via massive carbon electrodes, decomposition of phosphate is completed at 1,400°C to 1,500°C.

$$2Ca_3(PO_4)_2 + 6SiO_2 + 10C = P_4 + 10CO + 6CaSiO_3$$

Albright and Wilson diversified and expanded in the twentieth century to produce phosphorus-based chemicals with many applications.

References

1. Barbara M D Smith, Dictionary of National Biography, Volume 31, (no31), p50
2. C.J.L Elwell, The Ingenious Mr Keir of West Bromwich, The Blackcountryman, 1979, Vol 12, (4) p. 11-20.
3. Stebbing Shaw, History and Antiquities of Staffordshire, 1798.
4. Henry Adkins, On the Manufacture of Soap, in Samuel Timmins (ed.) The Resources, Products, and Industrial History of Birmingham and the Midland Hardware District, 1866, p. 168-76
5. Ibid., p. 177-8
6. www.british-history.ac.uk/vch/staffs/vol17/p107-118

7. www.blackcountryhistory.org/collections/getrecord/GB146_BS-MY
8. Robinson Brothers, The Chemistry of Progress, Newman Neame, 1969.
9. www.gracesguide.co.uk
10. J. Elliot Hornby, The Alkali Works of Chance Brothers, Blackcountryman, 1981, XIV, (3), 6-7.
11. C.S.Dingley, A History of B.I.P. in The Blackcountryman's View of B.I.P., Blackcountryman, 1975, Vol. 8 (3), p. 32-6
12. www.gracesguide.co.uk
13. R.E.Threlfall, 100 Years of Phosphorus Making, 1851-1951, Albright and Wilson, 1951.
14. F.W.Hackwood, Oldbury and Round About, Cornish Bros., Birmingham, 1915.

EIGHT

A Multitude of Industries

Awls[1,2,3]

The manufacture of awls (a pointed instrument for boring small holes) was a trade confined almost exclusively to Bloxwich. Homeshaw tells us a Bloxwich man could make as many as two gross every day and his market was typically to the shoemaker, saddler and carpenter. Pearce records that, in 1813, there were fourteen firms making awl blades in Bloxwich. By 1834 the number had increased to forty and White in his History Gazetteer and Directory of Staffordshire of that year noted 'the inhabitants of Great Bloxwich are chiefly employed in the manufacture of saddlers ironmongery and awl blades, for which the latter the village is more celebrated than any other in the kingdom'. As well as awls, Bloxwich awl makers also made tacks.

In common with their neighbouring Walsall bit and buckle makers, Bloxwich awl makers worked in the smallest of workshops, employing at most only a handful of workers, situated at the rear of, or even within, their own homes. Middlemen were therefore essential to enable the individual awl blade maker to sell his wares as widely as possible. George Stokes was one such. He travelled to Birmingham three times every week to sell Bloxwich awls to the manufacturers of Birmingham. The trade in awls eventually declined when stitching machinery was introduced in the leather industry.

References

1. Geoff Marshall, Walsall, An Illustrated History, Tempus, 2008, p.54,73
2. Ernest James Homeshaw, The story of Bloxwich, Geoff J. Clark Ltd., 1955, p.149–158
3. Thomas Pearce, The History and Directory of Walsall, 1813

Brick making[1,2,3,4]

There are ample deposits of clay in the Black Country, particularly in the Stourbridge area. Etruria marl is found as well. Both Geoff Stevens and Jack Haden have written about brick making in the *Blackcountryman* magazine. Bricks were made by mixing clay with sand. The mixture is then ground to a powder and water added. It is then moulded to shape and dried in a kiln. Manufacture was a batch process. A continuous process was invented by Friedrich Hoffman in 1858 but was slow to be taken up in the Black Country. In the eighteenth century, the industry was small in scale but expanded dramatically as the Black Country itself rose in importance and population, Staffordshire becoming second only to Lancashire in the manufacture of bricks.

There was an insatiable demand for bricks when the Black Country's canals were first dug in the late eighteenth century. Bricks were needed for both building bridges and for locks. Brick making would be carried out on land adjacent to the canal itself, with the proviso that once the canal had been completed the site would be returned to its original condition. Bricks were produced by the million, typically from November to March, but the extent to which the land was returned to nature is perhaps a moot point.

In 1834, there were forty-three firms operating in the Black Country, twenty-one of which were in the Kingswinford/Sedgley area. In 1836, 119 million bricks were produced. By 1854, the number of firms had increased to eighty-nine. **Timmis & Co**. were a well-known firm in Lye, founded in 1871. They mined clay, blasting it from the seams. Women would then take over, picking the clay out by hand and breaking it into small pieces. The

American consul, Elihu Burritt, wrote of 'visiting brick yards near Old Hill station where Staffordshire Blues were made at a rate of 100,000 per week. The work was carried out by women of all ages. Young girls would carry heavy weights of cold sodden clay to the bench for older women to work into shape'.

Seven firms were operating in West Bromwich in the 1890s. One of the largest was **Hamblet's Blue Brick Company**, making 400,000 to 500,000 bricks every week. Intense heat at the top of the kiln formed blue bricks; at the cooler base, red bricks were produced. Hamblets became a public limited company in 1898 with capital of £180,000. It was situated near Albion Road by the Birmingham Canal.

Francis Tongue Rufford was born in Stourbridge in 1822, son of Francis Rufford who opened a fireclay brick works in 1802. The latter made glazed bricks, sinks and troughs and was MP for Worcester and chairman of the Oxford, Worcester and Wolverhampton Railway Company, going bankrupt along the way. The firm passed to his son Francis Tongue Rufford, who opened new works in 1880. **Ruffords** had their own coal and clay mines, the products of which were brought to the works by tramway. The company had ten kilns, each holding 12,000 bricks, and so designed by a Mr Holcroft that the flame does not come into contact with the bricks.

The famous pottery manufacturers, Doulton and Co. Ltd., owned the **Springfield Brick & Tile Works** in Rowley Regis. It stood on the Dudley No. Two Canal opposite another of Doulton's works making piping. Doulton's made terracotta and engineering bricks; red terracotta being provided to construct the Birmingham General Hospital in Steelhouse Lane. The company's main product was glazed sanitary ware. By the late nineteenth century they were in possession of the Yew Tree Colliery in Netherton from where coal and fireclay were extracted.

Life was tough for those working in the brick-making industry, including the many women. In April 1913, the women asked for a minimum wage of 10s per week. It was put to the employers in a letter, which they ignored. In May, a mass meeting was organised at the Temperance Hall in Lye and strike action threatened. The strike continued into its fourth week but ended in victory. A 10% advance on all piece day-work was awarded to both male and female workers engaged in the preparation of materials, making, finishing, burning, handling and loading bricks. Women got their 10s per week minimum wage. The victory was celebrated with a cricket match between Mrs Lowin's XI and

Bethel C.C. Bethel scored seventy-eight to win the match against only thirteen runs by Mrs Lowin's team, four of which were extras!

References

1. Geoff Stevens, Staffordshire Blues Quarries and Half-Enders, Blackcountryman, 1973, Vol.6, (1), p.60–5
2. H. Jack Haden, The Brickmakers' Battle, Blackcountryman, 1978, Vol.11, (2), p.24–31
3. www.gracesguide.co.uk (Francis Rufford)
4. Dudley Archives, p.2189
5. Elizabeth Thomson, Brickmaking and the Development of Canals in the Black Country, Black Country History Conference, July 2023

Buckles[1]

The manufacture of buckles was an important trade in eighteenth-century Walsall. There were buckles made for shoes but also for saddle straps, bridles and spurs indicating that the trade grew out of the lorinery industry. By the mid-eighteenth century, buckle making became Walsall's foremost trade and Sketchley and Adams in their directory of 1770 recorded 278 workshops in the town. There was a thriving export trade, and buckles were exported throughout Europe but then someone (somewhere else) produced the idea of securing shoes with string laces. The trade slumped but Walsall's buckle makers were unwilling to take this unwelcome development lying down and quickly sent a deputation to London in 1792 to lobby that well-known arbiter of taste, the Prince of Wales. They were introduced by Sheridan and pleaded 'that if the stagnation of trade caused by the patronage of shoe strings and slippers continued, miseries, emigrations, and other horrible consequences must inevitably ensue'.

It seems that Walsall's plight did not fall on deaf ears, for the prince at once ordered all members of his court, including the Dukes of York and Clarence, to discard shoe strings and at once return to fastening their shoes with buckles and 'never offend him by disusing so important an article of British manufacture as buckles'. The townsmen were overjoyed and celebrated by inviting members of the court to a fine dinner. Unfortunately, their success was temporary, as the prince's father, George III, was later to favour shoelaces.

Although ruination was predicted, Walsall's buckle makers realised there were many other uses for their product and the trade continued, albeit at a reduced level. **Eyland and Sons** were well-known manufacturers, who as well as making buckles for shoes also made them for braces, belts, straps, leggings, garters, bags, surgical appliances and dog collars. They also specialised in the manufacture of spectacles. Eyland's were based in Lower Rushall Street and their premises, now converted to flats, are still there today.

References

1. Geoff Marshall, Walsall, An Illustrated History, Tempus, 2008, p.71,73

Edge Tools

Edward Elwell made edge tools at the Wednesbury Forge. (An edge tool is any cutting tool with a sharp cutting edge, such as a chisel, axe, or knife, etc.) It all began with his father, William Elwell, sometime mayor of Walsall, who set up making edge tools at Sparrow's Forge, Wednesbury. His son, Edward, had been an army surgeon in the French wars but after the peace of 1815 returned to work in Wednesbury. In 1817, he leased land at Wednesbury Forge, situated on the river Tame near Bescot and began making edge tools himself. By 1839, he was making spades, shovels and hoes as well. Edward's son predeceased his father and so the firm was continued by his grandson, Alfred Elwell. During the American Civil War, edge tools were exported to America and by the late nineteenth century the firm was employing two hundred people. Edward Elwell Ltd were great benefactors in Wednesbury, building St Paul's Church, converting old workshops to workmen's houses and opening football pitches and bowling greens.[1,2]

The Brades Steel Works was situated by the Birmingham Canal (Wolverhampton level) at Brades Village, Oldbury. It was founded in 1782 by William Hunt and made edge tools such as trowels, knives, hoes, axes, etc. By 1803, Hunt was making crucible steel by the cementation process. Crucible steelmaking was pioneered by Benjamin Huntsman (1704–1776) in Sheffield by a process of repeated experimentation. First, wrought iron must be carburised by the cementation process by packing bars of it with charcoal and heating in a closed vessel for seven to ten days. Blister steel is formed, so called because it is covered in blisters. The blister steel is then broken into small pieces and melted in a clay crucible to form a uniform distribution of carbon after slag is removed. Sharp-edged tools can now be made from the crucible steel.[3,4]

References

1. Bev Parker, www.historywebsite.co.uk/aricles/Wednesbury/industries
2. C.J.L Elwell, The Workers of Wednesbury Forge, Blackcountryman, 1987, Vol.20 (4), p.6–15
3. Ray Shill, Birmingham and the Black Country's Canalside Industries, Tempus, 2005, p. 58–9
4. www.madeinoldbury.co.uk/articles/brades-works

Enamelwork and Japanning[1,2,3,4,5,6]

Enamelling was first recorded in the Bilston Parish Register of 1718. The craftsmen were William Smith, Joseph Allen and Samuel Stone. It is an ancient art whereby metal is decorated by a coating of a vitreous glaze, fused to its surface by the application of heat. A hard, durable surface is formed. Enamel is a soft glass containing flint or sand, red lead and soda ash or potash. It melts to produce a clear glass and metal oxides can be added to give colour. Rather than gold or silver, Bilston enamellers used thin sheets of copper, which would be scrupulously cleaned before application of the enamel. A layer of enamel would be applied, and the metal object (typically a snuff box) then placed in a muffle furnace at high temperature to allow the enamel to fuse on the surface. It could then be painted by transfer printing or, for more expensive work, by hand.

Primrose Rostron writes that Bilston enamelwork could often be identified and dated by its ground colours. Dark blue was fashionable in 1755, to reflect the '*bleu-de-roi*' of Sèvres.

In 1780, James Ross pioneered a tint which he called 'English Pink', after the Rose Pompadour of Sèvres.

Enamellers were often known as toymakers, in other words, makers of small decorative objects. Matthew Boulton was in partnership with John Fothergill and the firm sent a salesman to St Petersburg to introduce Bilston enamels to Empress Catherine. She was so impressed that he came back with a large order. Every year, thousands of Bilston snuff boxes were produced, decorated with designs based on French artists such as Boucher, Fragonard, and Watteau. Many were made for the wedding, in 1761, of George III with Charlotte of Mecklenburg-Strelitz. There would be a picture of George on the lid, with Charlotte on the inside. Many other objects were enamelled, such as needle cases, candlesticks, scent bottles, medallions and etui. Examples of Bilston enamelwork can be seen in London's Victoria and Albert Museum.

Tin plating is a process in which a corrosion-resistant surface of tin is applied to a surface of sheet iron. As well as in Bilston, it was carried out in Wolverhampton, as was japanning. Timmins records that in 1866, there were 2000 employed in the japanning industry. Japanning is so called because its practice originated in the Far East. A lacquer of a resin-based varnish is applied to metal (or wood) to produce, after heating, a hard, black glossy finish which can then be decorated. Typical japanned articles were tea trays, small boxes, and candlesticks. The trade declined in the late nineteenth century after the introduction of the technique of electroplating.

An early firm of Wolverhampton japanners was the **Old Hall Japan Works**, in the 1770s occupying a converted Elizabethan mansion and worked by Jones and Taylor. It went through a number of hands before closing in the nineteenth century.

Benjamin Mander was born in 1752. He worked as a baker and maltster and in 1792 went into partnership with Thomas Shepherd, opening a japan shop in John Street, Wolverhampton. In 1754, his brother John Mander was born, who operated next door as a chemist, druggist and varnish maker. The brothers combined and went into business as japanners in the late eighteenth century. Many articles were produced including fire screens, trays and boxes. At the beginning of the nineteenth century, they began making varnish. Benjamin Mander was a staunch non-conformist; each day ending in hymns and prayers. Workers were fined if they did not take part. By 1817, Manders were employing thirty people and as the century progressed, they diversified to make paint and printing ink. Mander Brothers expanded in the twentieth century to become one of Wolverhampton's largest companies. Latterly it specialised in printing ink.

Henry Ferncombe came to Wolverhampton from Taunton and set up in Walsall Street as a japanner; later moving to larger premises at the Phoenix Works in Dudley Road. The firm japanned on tinplate and exhibited at the Great Exhibition in 1851.

Edward Perry was educated at Wolverhampton Grammar School and set up in the tinplate and japanning trade at Queen Street and later in Paul Street.

He was mayor of Wolverhampton in 1855 and one year later founded the Wolverhampton Chamber of Commerce. He died childless and his business was carried on by his nephews, who then combined with the firm of Richard Perry and his son, George. The firm produced beautifully designed pieces such as jugs and tankards, some by Christopher Dresser, the well-known Scottish proponent of the aesthetic movement.

The Great Tinplate Strike of 1850

Edward Perry is renowned as the man who resisted the great tin plate strike of 1850. It began when delegates from the National Trades Association in London arrived at Wolverhampton to inform tinplating firms that their workers were unhappy with their rates of pay. The delegates (Messrs Peel and Green), finding there were substantial variations in pay, attempted to impose a standard rate for all firms. Many firms agreed but Edward Perry declined. Furthermore, he sacked an employee, a man called Preston, who was encouraging other workers to resist the firm's intransience. The delegates insisted that Preston should be reinstated. He wasn't and a strike was called. A strike committee was formed with the Swan with Two Necks pub as its headquarters, conveniently placed in Paul Street, a stone's throw from Perry's Jeddo Works. The committee's members were George Duffield, John Gaunt, Thomas Woodnorth, Charles Piat and Henry Rowland. Perry's works were picketed and astonishingly, apprentices – who would otherwise break the strike – were 'spirited away' (I assume this means kidnapped) to London and other distant towns. Others were plied with drink and sent to Scotland, Ireland and other faraway places, with promises that their families would be looked after. Perry at once counteracted by placing his nephew, George Winn, as a mole at the Swan with Two Necks. Winn would laugh and joke with the committee, join with them in drinking sessions and so learn their secrets and the whereabouts of the 'spirited off' men. Armed with this information Perry then issued warrants for their apprehension. Outraged, the committee intensified the campaign; a coffin was placed in front of the Jeddo Works, inscribed with the words 'E. Perry, prepare to meet thy God' and a strike breaker, Tom Jones, was roughed up. Edward Perry was not to be daunted. He sent George Winn to France to recruit French workers. They duly came, but not speaking a word of English, or realising what they had got themselves into, were soon encouraged to return home after the committee engaged a French soldier, taken prisoner at Waterloo and still living in Wolverhampton, to act as interpreter. Still Perry persisted. His next move was to despatch Winn to Germany. Winn returned with thirty men who were given contracts for twelve months work and, to prevent intimidation, housed within the factory premises where all their needs were met. The committee responded with a crowded gathering at the Theatre Royal in Cleveland Street, where rousing speeches were delivered, highlighting the workers' grievances. But Perry produced the trump card. All the committee and the delegates were indicted for conspiracy, the trial taking place in August 1851 at Stafford Assizes. Although the committee claimed that Perry was paying less than the agreed rate, he countered by asserting that, because he had automated his plant, more articles were being produced and so the men were being paid proportionally more. A verdict of guilty was returned, confirmed on appeal. Most of the strike leaders were given prison sentences with hard labour. After they were released, they found themselves liable to costs but penniless. An appeal was raised in Wolverhampton for the men, but not enough was collected. Then help came from an unlikely source. It was none other than Edward Perry, who paid the remaining deficit.

John Marston was born in 1836 in Ludlow and in 1851 was apprenticed to the japanner, Richard Perry and Son. After he had completed his apprenticeship, he set up on his own as John Marston Ltd in Bilston as a producer of japanned ware. When the trade declined, he diversified to make bicycles in the late nineteenth century, soon moving to Wolverhampton to make the famous Sunbeam motorcycle.

Joseph Sankey was born in Bilston in 1827. He was apprenticed to John Duncalfe who made tray blanks to sell to japanners. By 1861, he was in business making trays stamped from tinplate to be sold on to be japanned. In 1862, a rolling mill and iron works were purchased at Stonefield, known as the Bilston Iron Company. By the end of the 1860s, Sankey was making all sorts of hollowware – dish covers, lamps, lanterns, milk churns, tin boxes, bathtubs, in premises between Dudley Street and Albert Street. In the twentieth century, Sankey's grew to be one of Bilston's largest businesses.

References

1. J.A. Wylde, Bilston Enamel… A Lost Art of the Black Country, Blackcountryman, 1968, Vol.1, (2), p.9–12
2. Primrose Rostron, Black Country Beauties, Blackcountryman, 1976, Vol.9, (2), p.7–9

3. Bev Parker, www.historywebsite.co.uk (japanning)
4. William Highfield, extract from 'the Story of the japan, tin-plate working and iron brazier trade in Wolverhampton, Blackcountryman, 1972, Vol.5 (2), p.49–56
5. Henry Loveridge, Wolverhampton Trades, in Samuel Timmins (ed.), The Resources, Products and Industrial History of Birmingham and the Midland hardware District, Robert Hardwicke, 1866, p.117–24
6. Yvonne Jones, Japanned, Papier Mâché, and Tinware, 1740–1940, Antique Collectors Club, 2012

Gas Lighting

It had been known for many years that when coal is heated in the absence of air, gas is produced. But it was left to the Scotsman, William Murdoch, in the late eighteenth century, to realise the enormous commercial potential of gas. Murdoch was employed by Boulton and Watt, the famous Birmingham-based manufacturers of steam engines, and in 1777 the twenty-five-year-old engineer was dispatched to Redruth in Cornwall to take responsibility for his employer's steam engines in that county's tin mines. Murdoch had an inventive mind – he is said to have filled the head of his pipe with coal and ignited the gas as it emerged from the stem. It was not long before he astonished his neighbours by lighting his house with coal gas. That was in 1792 and in 1798, back in Birmingham, he succeeded in lighting Boulton and Watt's Soho factory. Quick to realise its commercial importance, Boulton and Watt were soon illuminating the Salford cotton mill of Phillips and Lee with gas. And money was saved! Previously, the mill owners had paid over £2,000 per year for candle illumination, now they were paying £600 for lighting by the much brighter gas burners. At this stage, however, gas lighting was seen as suitable only for illuminating factories. But all was to change when an extrovert Moravian, Friedrich Albrecht Winzler, arrived in London. His aim was to light London's streets with gas. And his ideas soon bore fruit, for in 1807, at the Crown and Anchor Tavern in the Strand, the first meeting of The New Patriotic Imperial and National Light and Heat Company was held. It was not long before this became The Gas Light and Coke Company (GLCC). Then in 1812 it was granted a Royal Charter by the Prince Regent, on behalf of George III, giving the company the right to raise capital with limited liability, to dig up streets and lay mains to supply gas to the City, Westminster, and Southwark.[1]

Gas lights came to the Black Country when the **Birmingham and Staffordshire Gas Light Company** was founded in 1825. It built works at Swan Village in West Bromwich which at the time was the largest gas works in the country. It was situated by the branch of the Wednesbury Old Canal from which coal was delivered. Later, when the Great Western Railway built a line from Birmingham to Wolverhampton in 1854, coal was delivered by rail. The Swan Village Basin Line branched off just before Swan Village Station. Changes came in 1875 when the West Bromwich commissioners built new works at Oldbury Road, Albion, near to the canal and railway. Supply came on stream five years later.[2]

Town gas (as it was known) was separated from coal by distillation, in the absence of air, in iron retorts. To begin with, horizontal retorts were used but these could only operate by a batch system and so had to be frequently recharged. Later, vertical retorts were employed which were continuously charged at the top with coal which then fell to the bottom. The coke residue was then either sold or used to further heat the retorts. Many impurities were produced which had to be removed before the gas was sold. First, the evolved gas was passed through pipes surrounded by cold water to condense out tars, then ammonia was removed by passing through water and finally hydrogen sulphide by passing through lime water. The town gas (55% hydrogen, 30% methane and 10% carbon monoxide) was then stored over water in gas holders.

On Tuesday the 7th of April 1818, a meeting of the people of Dudley was called 'for the purpose of taking into consideration the propriety of entering into a subscription for the establishment of a Gas Light Company for lighting the said town'. Land was purchased from the Dudley family at 'Cook's Tettenhall' at Pit's Hole for a gas holder and other equipment and firms were asked to tender for the 'supply of cast iron pipes, laying down, joining and completing the same and making good the pavement, and for building a gasometer'. In 1851, the **Town of Dudley Gas Light Company** works was listed in a trade directory as being in Fountain Street, Dudley. The **Brierley Hill and District Gas Light Company** was absorbed by the Dudley company in 1930. In Smethwick, the Birmingham and Staffordshire Gas Light Co provided gas for 112 streetlamps. In 1876, an Act empowered works to be built in Rabone Lane, which opened in 1881.[3]

Many gas works, built to provide street lighting, came about because of governmental improvement acts. Such was the case in **Walsall**, when, in 1826, improvement commissioners built a gas works at a cost of £4,000 on the site where Arboretum Road now stands. It was built in part to the designs of J.U. Rastrick, civil engineer and builder of the famous railway locomotive, the *Stourbridge Lion*. To meet an increasing demand for gas, the 'Walsall Improvement Act of 1848' authorised the building of new gas works in Wolverhampton Street. It was able to produce 150 million cubic feet of gas every year and up to 1887, together with its distribution mains had cost £52,000. In 1876, by the terms of 'The Walsall Gas Purchase and Borough Extension Act' powers were acquired from the Birmingham and Staffordshire Gas Lighting Co for new works at Pleck costing £58,000.[4]

In 1819, the **Wolverhampton Gas Light Company** was founded when fifty-seven prominent Wolverhampton citizens put up money as subscribers. They included John Peter Mander, the paint manufacturer. The engineer was John Grafton, who had previously taken out patents for the purification of gas. Mains were laid by the firm of Ready and Dixon. Gas began to be supplied in 1821 from the works in Horseley Fields which had two gas holders. To celebrate, a gigantic cast iron column, 40ft in height, was constructed in High Green with a gas lantern on its top. The whole thing turned out to be a folly as its height prevented it from throwing light to the ground. It survived until 1840, when it was demolished. In 1823, the town's theatre at the rear of the Swan Inn, High Green, was illuminated with gas light. Wolverhampton local authority was paying the gas company £350 per annum for street lighting in 1823, increasing to £420 three years later. To begin with, during winter months, only twenty-two nights a month were lit; the remainder had to rely on moonlight. The corporation attempted to purchase the gas company in the 1860s. They were put off by the asking price. The gas works at Horseley Fields continued in operation until 1900.[5]

A gas works was established at Stourbridge in 1835 close to the end of the Stourbridge Town branch of the Stourbridge Canal. Railway sidings were added in 1858 and the works were purchased by the town in 1895.[6]

Towards the end of the nineteenth century, gas companies began promoting the use of gas for cooking. Cannons of Deepfields, Bilston, began manufacturing in 1895 – see Hollow Ware. In 1895, a Tipton man, William Brownhill, patented the first penny-in-the-slot prepayment meter.[7]

References

1. Geoff Marshall, London's Industrial Heritage, The History Press, 2013, p.27–30
2. W.B. Stephens, Victoria County History, A History of the County of Warwick, Vol.7, p.352

3. Dudley, Brierley Hill and District Gas Company, records at Dudley Archives and Local History Service
4. F.W. Willmore, History of Walsall, 1887, p.195–7
5. Bev Parker, www.historywebsite.co.uk (A Brief History of Gas Supply)
6. Ray Shill, Birmingham and the Black Country's Canalside Industries, Tempus, 2005, p.123
7. David Eveleigh, Private Communication

Gun Trade[1,2,3]

Birmingham is usually thought of as the centre of the gun trade. However, in the 1820s, over one thousand gun makers were recorded as working in the trade in Wednesbury, Darlaston and West Bromwich. Geoff Stevens described the manufacture from old and discarded horse-shoe nails. They were welded together to form a solid lump which was drawn between rollers to form a skelp (strip) of iron one inch across and ¼ inch thick. The skelp was then twisted around a mandrel (rotating shaft) to form a helix. A tube was formed by welding together. Later in the century, a method pioneered by the Dublin gun maker, John Rigby, was used. Strips of wrought iron were welded to form a bar. One end was secured in a clamp while the other attached to a rotated spindle to produce a helical twist. Two twisted bars (one left hand the other with right hand twist) were welded to form the barrel.

The slave trade was an unpleasant aspect of the Black Country's gun-making trade. Gun locks and barrels were supplied to firms in Birmingham such as Farmer and Galton, who made and sold the finished article. Vast numbers of slave ships would then leave Liverpool, Bristol and London bound for the West Coast of Africa and laden with manufactured goods, chiefly guns, cotton and spirits. They would be exchanged for black slaves who would then be transported to the West Indies to work – provided they were lucky enough to survive the journey – on the sugar plantations. Sugar, rum, cotton, etc. would then be shipped to Bristol, Liverpool and London for the merchants in this evil trade to grow rich. Seventy-one ships left Liverpool in 1754, and it is estimated that 150,000 guns were exchanged each year in this vicious trade. The area 'Guns Village' and Guns Lane are present-day reminders in West Bromwich. The slave trade was abolished in 1807, but gun making still thrived because of demand during the French wars. The industry declined steadily in the nineteenth century, but the resilience of the Black Country man was typified when he transferred his gun barrel-making ability to that of making tubes.

References

1. Geoff Stevens, West Bromwich Gun Trade, Blackcountryman, 1974, Vol.7 (1), p.20–8
2. W.A. Richards, Black Country Guns and the Slave Trade, Blackcountryman, 1975, Vol.8 (1), p.7–13
3. F.W. Hackwood, Wednesbury Workshops, 1889, p.41

Hollow-ware

Hollow-ware is a generic term for pots, pans, kettles and the like.

Cannon Industries of Deepfields, Bilston, grew out of the firm established in 1826 by Edward and Stephen Sheldon. In 1884, the company was known as Cannon Hollow-ware Co. Ltd., and made saucepans, kettles and other kitchen utensils. By 1895, the firm was making gas stoves and cookers. The company expanded in the twentieth century, employing about one thousand workers, and made sanitary ware, including baths, basins and lavatories. In the twentieth century, it was making gas cookers. Its situation, near to the Coseley Tunnel, aided transport links with Birmingham.[1]

Izon & Co. began in Duke Street in Birmingham and in 1780 moved to West Bromwich. About seven or eight workmen moved as well but were not welcomed by the local people who refused them lodgings, forcing the company to build accommodation for them.

The old established firm of **Archibald Kenrick** were also in West Bromwich.[2]

Archibald Kenrick senior was born in Wrexham in 1760 but by 1780 he had moved to Birmingham working as a buckle maker. He set up an iron foundry in Spon Lane, West Bromwich, making cooking utensils, later joined by his son, also Archibald.

William Bullock established a foundry making hollow-ware at Spon Lane in 1805, on the Wolverhampton branch of the Birmingham Canal. (At the time it was the sole route between Wolverhampton and Birmingham.) It was taken over by **George Salter & Co.** in 1885.[3] **Thomas & Charles Clark** were at the Shakespeare Foundry at Horseley Fields, Wolverhampton. They were founded in 1795 and in 1839 patented an enamel for lining cooking vessels without the use of lead oxide or arsenic.[4]

References

1. Harold Parsons, This Cannon has Fired for almost 150 Years, Blackcountryman, 1973, Vol.6 (3), p.13–16
2. www.gracesguide.co.uk Archibald Kenrick
3. Ray Shill, Birmingham and the Black Country's Canalside Industries, Tempus, 2005, p.53-4
4. Bev Parker, www.historywebsite.co.uk/Museum/Metalware/Clark/Shakespearefoundry

Leather[1,2,3,4,5,6]

To the outside world, Walsall is best known for its leather industry, particularly the manufacture of saddles. The nickname of Walsall Football Club, the Saddlers, is evidence enough. The trade developed as a logical diversification for the town's loriners.

Although Walsall has never been particularly well known for tanning (leather tended to be imported to the town) there were tanners in Walsall from an early date. John Lyddiat – three times mayor in the late sixteenth century – was a local tanner. Apart from animal skins, the process needed a plentiful supply of wood, bark and water. Tanneries, therefore, tended to be sited close to the stream that ran through the town. There were three recorded in Hatherton Street in 1886, one known as the **Albion Tannery**, and all backing onto the Ford Brook. Nearby was **Handford Greatrex**, also using the Ford Brook and sited where Safeway supermarket is today. Others were in Park Street and Darwall Street – the stench coming from them all too familiar to Walsall people.

Here are typical details of the process. (All those of you with a squeamish nature, stop reading now.) After the poor beast was slaughtered, its flesh was sold to the butcher and the hide to the tanner. The horns were first removed and sold to comb makers. Then it was the job of the 'flesher' to scrape the hide to remove small pieces of flesh. The hide was then 'unhaired' by soaking in a quicklime solution for several days, after which the roots were sufficiently loosened for the hair to be easily pulled out. 'Graining' was the next job, where the hide was soaked in a dilute solution of sulphuric acid to open the pores. Following this, the pelt, as it was now known, was left to soak in tanning pits containing a solution of oak bark. The solution, appropriately known as 'ooze', seeped into the pores from surface to surface. After several months in the tanning pit, the leather, as it now was, was removed, hung up to dry and finally pressed between rollers.

The finest leather is still made with oak bark, but now more advanced techniques are employed, such as the addition of chromium salts or imported extracts from plants such as sumac, to quicken the process up. Now, tanning takes just a few days rather than the many months of earlier years. The allied trade of currying entails treating the raw leather with fat or grease to make it strong, flexible, water resistant and suitable for many applications.

Typically, in the mid-nineteenth century, a ten-hour day and a fifty-hour week would be worked. Men would be paid about 25s a week with women, usually employed to stitch, at only 7s. In the early days of the industry, much work would be 'put out', that is work would be done at home, usually by women, who would be paid – invariably very poorly – by the number of articles they produced.

Thomas Newton claimed to be the first manufacturer of riding saddles in Walsall. He realised there were 'black saddlers' in Walsall who made saddles for working horses, but there were no 'brown saddlers' making riding saddles. He therefore suggested to his father that they should start making riding saddles and in 1829, at the age of eighteen, inherited the family business. Ann French has researched the life of Thomas Newton and produced an excellent booklet. She describes his life with his demanding wife ('I would prefer to live in Bayswater') and tells of orders from the Indian Army and Woolwich Arsenal as well as his exhibits at the Crystal Palace. Thomas Newton eventually sold his business to **Overton Brothers**.

When the railway came to Walsall, trade expanded and a concentration of leather workshops grew up around Station Street. Michael Glasson, who has written extensively on the leather industry in Walsall, has compiled a Leather Quarter Trail and rightly observes that the area should be carefully preserved and thoughtfully developed. In this way, it could be a valuable resource for the town in a similar manner to the successful Jewellery Quarter in Birmingham. Many well-known manufacturers operated from this area to take advantage of the transport links provided by the railway. They included **Hobday and Smith**, wholesale saddlers and harness makers of Navigation Street and **D Mason and Sons** of Greatrex House in Marsh Street. Masons made the dog harness used by

Scott on his ill-fated Antarctic Expedition and provided saddles for the British Army in the First World War. Prominent at the end of Navigation Street was the **Ravenscraig Currying Works**, built in 1903 by Scottish industrialists and still carrying the name Boak on its water tower today. As well as saddles, **Boaks** made bags, belts, braces, bridles and cases and specialised in the production of pig skin for saddle seats.

Trade expanded throughout the nineteenth century and mushroomed towards the end of that century. The 1801 census records that twenty-nine people were making saddles or harnesses in Walsall; by 1861 it was 523, increasing to 3,492 in 1881 and reaching 6,830 (employed by 150 firms) in 1901. It is very easy to see why. There were literally millions of horses employed in the Victorian age for all manner of purposes, be it hauling ploughs on farmland, carting goods around from factory to shops, drawing well-to-do people in carriages or making deliveries to private houses. There were also the demands of war. Walsall saddles were used in the Crimean, Franco-Prussian and Boer Wars.

Sewing machines came into use soon after 1860 and their adoption increased leather production still further. **Charles Myring** had premises in the leather quarter in Station Street. He took out a patent for using sewing machines to increase production of leather-covered buckles. The trade was at its peak in the late nineteenth century, and rather than putting work out for people to work from home, large factories began to be built. There were many in the town such as **E.T. Holden and Son** who had premises in Park Street, where the Saddler's Shopping Centre is now. They were founded in 1819 and were both tanners and curriers. Sir E.T. Holden took over the business founded by his father, was three-time Mayor of Walsall and MP in 1891. The company relocated to Scotland in 1970. **D. Mason and Son** were another large manufacturer. Founded in Birmingham in 1853, they opened in Walsall's leather quarter in 1902. In 1928, Masons acquired the **London Saddlery Works** in Goodall Street. It was established in Walsall in 1886 by John Leckie and supplied leather goods all over the world. The South Staffordshire Advertiser described a visit to the company and commented 'saddles being constructed to meet the wishes, peculiar needs, prejudices and requirements of Kaffirs, Boers, Indians, South Americans and last but not least English Officers'. The Goodall Street works closed in the 1960s. In 1953, Masons supplied lorinery and harness for the coronation ceremony.

Not that life was easy for leather workers. In 1889, the House of Lords Select Committee on the Sweated Trades took a look at Walsall's leather industry and

Rowland Mason of D Masons and Sons was called to give evidence. Throughout the industry, women fared much worse than men. Typical pay was 10s per week, half that of men.

Craftsmen developed **Horse Brasses.** At first, designs were simple, such as a star or a heart shape but later became more complex. The bear and ragged staff is the badge of Walsall and its one-time lord of the manor, the Earl of Warwick. To show civic pride, it often featured as a horse brass. Walsall founders made the first cast-horse brasses in the mid-nineteenth century. An accurate drawing of the design was prepared first which was then converted into a hard three-dimensional pattern strong enough to leave a firm, clear impression in the casting sand. Anthony Beebee Senior of **Stanley Brothers**, Walsall, modelled in plasticine on the back of a dinner plate. He then covered in Plaster of Paris and set hard to form a negative mould into which molten lead was poured. Horse Brasses are now collectors pieces and incorporate all sorts of designs.

The motor car made its first appearance early in the twentieth century and led to the inevitable decline of Walsall's saddle trade. But manufacturers were resourceful and diversified into making fancy leather goods and light leather goods such as watch straps, handbags, purses and wallets.

By the mid-twentieth century, Walsall's leather trade was facing stiff competition from overseas producers, particularly from South East Asia, and many firms ceased production. Those that remained concentrated on the upper end of the market, making luxury goods with high-quality leather. Then, in the late twentieth century, the market for saddles revived again because of the increasing popularity of horse riding for pleasure. Walsall once again took its place as the country's undisputed centre of the saddle trade.

Given the quality of leather goods made in Walsall, it is no surprise that there are several Royal Warrant Holders in the town. **Jabez Cliff and Company** were made Royal Warrant Holders in 1990. The company was founded in 1873 by Jabez Cliff, with premises in Portland Street. By 1906, they had moved to Lower Forster Street, having absorbed the long- established saddle makers, **J.A. Barnsby**. It was Sir Cliff Tibbits, grandson of the founder, who ran the company through much of the twentieth century and saw it diversify to make many other leather articles such as sports goods and suitcases. The company produced footballs for the Cup Final in the 1930s and supplied zip-up leather holdalls for the famous female aviation pilot, Amy Johnson. **G. Ettingers** and **Launers** are other Royal Warrant Holders.

Albert Jagger Ltd is typical of companies in Walsall who began making accessories for horse-drawn vehicles but then diversified. They started in 1887, manufacturing carriage lamps and other products for the horse-drawn coach building trade, but early in the twentieth century began concentrating on parts for commercial vehicles.

They were based at the Centaur Works in Green Lane, described by Peter Arnold in his Buildings of Walsall as 'built in an elegant Free Style, with a slight Art Nouveau accent'. In 1946, the company was sold to Douglas Cooper but still trades today as Albert Jagger. The company logo is the centaur, the half man half horse beast of Greek mythology. I am reliably informed that many years ago a female employee was heard to exclaim in her broad Black Country accent, "y'ave to be arf oss to work 'ere." That said, Jaggers has always been renowned for the loyalty of its staff; one member joined in 1888 and didn't retire until 1951!

The original Centaur Works are still there today but in 2001 splendid new premises, also known as Centaur Works, were opened nearby in Green Lane. Jaggers export throughout the world and have branches in Bloxwich, Lancashire, Hampshire and New Zealand.

References

1. Geoff Marshall, Walsall, An Illustrated History, Tempus, 2008, p.74–6
2. Ann French, Walsall Werk, Walsall Local History Centre, 1997
3. Michael Glasson, Walsall Leather Quarter Trail, Walsall MBC, 2001
4. Michael Glasson, Walsall Leather Industry: The World's Saddlers, Tempus, 2001
5. Peter Arnold, A Guide to the Buildings of Walsall, Tempus, 2003
6. Peter C D Brears, Horse Brasses, Country Life Books, 1981

Limestone[1,2,3,4]

Limestone is used as a flux in the smelting of iron ore in blast furnaces, combining with impurities to form a slag which can easily be separated from the molten iron. And with the coming of the industrial revolution demand increased dramatically, especially when John 'Iron Mad' Wilkinson opened his giant iron works in Bilston. But limestone has many uses. In its raw state it is employed as a building material. Frequently, however, it is calcined by burning (more

A Multitude of Industries

accurately heating) in a kiln to produce quicklime. When quicklime is mixed with water and sand, mortar is formed. It was widely employed as a fertiliser in agriculture to reduce the acidity of soil and finds application in candle making, glass manufacture, the bleaching of cloth and in the leather industry.

The chemical name of limestone is calcium carbonate, $CaCO_3$. In the process known as calcining, or lime burning, the raw ore is heated in a kiln to a temperature of approximately 1,000°C, carbon dioxide is driven off and quicklime, CaO, is formed:

$$CaCO_3 \rightarrow CaO + CO_2$$

This reacts vigorously with water to form slaked lime:

$$CaO + H_2O \rightarrow Ca(OH)_2$$

Which, when mixed with sand, gives mortar.

In the early days of the industry, limestone would be worked from open-cast quarries, then later, as demand increased, by sinking shafts and mining.

Dr Plot, on his visit to Walsall in 1686, describes how 'the stone is dug all about Walsall, particularly at Rushall… it is broken up with iron weights knocked in at the partitions with great sledges and prized up with great levers… where some weigh at least 180 pounds'.

He goes on to describe the calcining process:

'When they have gotten the stone, they burn it in oblong pits made in the ground, about seven yards long, three wide and but six or seven foot deep at the butt of the pit. Wherein they lay first a little wood or gorse to keep the coal from the ground, which is laid under the stone, the stratum but thin, not above three inches thick, then a stratum of stone about six inches deep, the next floor of coal they make ten inches thick, and the layer of stone above that eighteen inches thick; the next of coal above that is usually about a foot thick and the next floor of stone over it double the thickness; then the fourth layer of coal is but ten inches and the fourth of stone but eighteen; then above all another stratum of coal about two or three inches, which they cover with parget or mortar made with slaked lime and water, to keep in the heat. The coal laid in this manner with the stone, burning it gradually into lime in about a week's time. Which sort of lime pit has this peculiar convenience above all others I ever yet saw that they can take away the lime that is first burnt while the rest is on fire and can make up the butt of the pit while 'tis yet burning at the mouth.'

While lime kilns in nineteenth century Walsall were brick lined and somewhat sturdier, the chemistry was still the same as in Plot's day.

Limestone mining is an ancient industry. St Matthews Church stands on an outcrop of the stone and it has been suggested that limestone quarried here and at Daw End in Rushall was used by the Romans when they built Letocetum (Wall) and to construct Watling Street. And there is good evidence for this because Roman coins have been found at both locations.

Walsall was once a major centre of limestone mining. In 1325, it was recorded that Lord of the Manor, 'Thomas le Rous grants to Robert Bonde three acres of his waste land at the Birchels, on condition that he should not make any mines of limestone in the same'. The clear implication of Le Rous's decree is that limestone was being quarried in other parts of the town, may be by the lord himself! Then in the 1460s, when St Matthew's Church was being rebuilt, calcined lime from Walsall quarries was used in its construction.

Mining was carried out in several separate, but not necessarily well-defined areas, in Walsall and Daw End in Rushall. In the town centre there were workings at Church Hill and between Ablewell Street and the Chuckery. The latter area was known as Lime Pit Bank. Both quarrying and lime burning went on and Lime Street is a present-day reminder of an industry that seems to have died out in the late eighteenth century in this part of town. Just before the last war, when air raids were feared, the idea was mooted that underground tunnels beneath Church Hill – the long-since abandoned limestone mines – should be brought back to life and reused as air raid shelters. The idea came to nothing.

At about the same time as the Church Hill and Lime Pit Bank quarries became redundant, the area of town close to the present-day Arboretum began to be exploited. The Persehouse family were the local landowners. They had already leased land for mining and in the late eighteenth century were succeeded by the Walhouse family. In 1771, John Walhouse began mining the limestone. The works he built became known as the **Butts Lime Works**. There were also workings at the adjoining Moss Close. The works operated for about fifty years and supplied limestone to the burgeoning iron industry. A tramway was built between the quarry and Walsall's newly built canal and horses would haul wagon loads of stone to the canal for distribution to furnaces throughout the Black Country. The Butts Lime Works had closed by 1845 and today the Hatherton Lake in the Arboretum is a reminder of what was once the largest openwork limestone quarry in the town. Tragically, on the 8th of July 1845, John Hyatt Harvey, Mayor of Walsall, was drowned while bathing in the lake. Later, in 1874, the whole area was converted into the Arboretum.

Rich deposits of limestone are found along the eastern borders of Walsall and were extensively quarried at **Hay Head** (the Aldridge end of Longwood Lane). There were smaller workings in the late Middle Ages at Wood End (on the present-day Sutton Road near to the Longhorn pub).

At Hay Head, limestone was extracted from an early date and was burnt for lime in open-pit kilns nearby. In 1795, they were described as 'on a very extensive plan, inexhaustible in quantity and of a very superior quality'. It was around this time that John Wilkinson enters the story. His Bradley furnaces had an insatiable thirst for limestone, and it was because of this that, together with the Earl of Bradford, he took an interest in the Hay Head mines. Both he and the Earl backed the digging of the Wyrley and Essington Canal, completed in 1794, 'to open communication with several mines of coal, limestone and other minerals and will be of great utility'. The canal's extension to Hay Head was soon opened and an arm of it (still visible today) extended to the quarry. Wilkinson was then able to transport his limestone north by the canal directly to his furnaces at Bilston. Hay Head closed by 1865 but remains of this once-thriving industry can still be seen on the nature walk that passes through the workings. The canal also provided transport for the extensive limestone mines at Rushall- Park Lime Pits (now a beauty spot) and Linley Mine.

Thomas Pearce, in his History and Directory of Walsall, tells us of limestone mines 'on the left-hand side of the road leading from Walsall to Wolverhampton near the end of the Birmingham Navigation'. They were the property of the Earl of Bradford and were 'in the occupancy of Thomas Price of Bescot Hall'. Pearce goes on to say that they 'consist of a solid bed of stone of near ten yards thick, of excellent quality'.

The largest mines near to Walsall's town centre in the early nineteenth century were situated in the Littleton Street, Hatherton Street and Portland Street area. By this time, shafts were being sunk and the limestone mined by the pillar and stall technique. James Watt's steam engines would be used to drain water from the workings. There seem to have been at least three separate enterprises. **Birchills Lime Works** was on the corner of Birchills and Green

Lane; **Hatherton Works** were between Hatherton Street and Wisemore and **Portland Street Lime Works** opened north of this in 1860. It later merged with the Hatherton works. The Hatherton mines were opened in about 1804, probably by James Adams and in 1851 passed to a local coal master called Elias Crapper, then becoming the **Crappers Lime Pits**. Crapper lived nearby at Lime House. Horses would be employed underground to haul the limestone in trucks. It was dangerous work and accidents were frequent as Pearce describes:

> 'The workings of the various mines give employment to a great number of hands, but it is to be lamented that the falling rock is frequently fatal to the miners and accidents often happen from the machinery.'

Limestone mining declined at the end of the nineteenth century and eventually came to an end in 1903.

Limestone was extracted extensively at Dudley. Tunnels were dug at both Castle Hill and Wren's Nest. At Castle Hill the main caverns are the 144 steps (Dark Cavern), Singing Cavern, Big Ben and the Flooded Mines. At Wren's Nest Hill there is Light Cavern, Cherry Hole, Fish and Chip Hole, Letter Box and Lion's Den. In 1786, an underground canal was cut to meet the expanding demand for limestone. It is 1¾ miles long and connects the Birmingham Canal Navigation at Tipton with the Dudley and Stourbridge canal. A branch off this tunnel was completed in 1792 into the heart of Castle Hill. In the mid-nineteenth century, more than one hundred boats passed through every day carrying up to thirty tons of limestone. In 1805, a second branch was cut to Wren's Nest with an extension cut in 1813.

Limestone was extracted by blasting with gun powder. A hole, about 1 to 2 inches in diameter and 2ft deep was dug by ramming an iron bar into the limestone with a sledgehammer and then filled with gun powder. Once the miner had lit the fuse, he scampered out of the way to safety to await the explosion. The scattered limestone was loaded onto carts, taken by tramway to canal boats and thence to the outside world.

References

1. Geoff Marshall, Walsall, An Illustrated History, Tempus, 2008, p.37–40
2. Thomas Pearce, The History and Directory of Walsall, 1813

3. Anon., Short History of Dudley Mines, Blackcountryman, 1970, Vol.3 (4), p.51–4
4. Robert Plot, The Natural History of Staffordshire, 1686

Lorinery[1,2]

The manufacture of bits, stirrups and spurs became Walsall's first staple industry. It was known as lorinery and those that practiced it were known as loriners (from the Latin, lorum, a thong or strap). Leland in 1540 commented that 'there were many bit makers and smiths in the town'. Not that Walsall can, at this time, be thought of solely as an industrial town, for agriculture was still important, as illustrated by complaints made against Walsall loriners in 1600, who were in the habit of giving up metal work for six months in summer so that they could help in gathering the harvest.

In the eighteenth century, the trade became highly specialised and loriners would concentrate on making one item. For instance, Sketchley and Adams' Directory of 1770 tells us there were nineteen spur and rowel (the spiked wheel of a spur) makers, eleven stirrup makers, five-bit makers and eighteen snaffle (a type of bit) makers in the town. A pattern emerged of horse furniture being forged in a series of independent small workshops, perhaps at the rear of their owners' homes or in a crowded courtyard. Only a handful of men would be employed in each workshop. For instance, in 1860, there were 250 different firms engaged in the manufacture of horse furniture and approximately one thousand people employed, an average of only four per workshop.

Many loriners would sell their bits and spurs locally but it was also very common for middlemen to be used. They were known as chapmen and they both supplied iron to the metal worker and then bought the finished product from him to sell it on. Many travelled around the country, selling the metalware of a host of manufacturers. They were often resented by the nailers and locksmiths of the Black Country, but Walsall's loriners welcomed their involvement 'for the better utterance of our said wares… readily wrought and resting upon us… especially at such times of year as in the winter season when our wares rest most upon us unuttered'. It seems that the chapmen also charged a fair price for iron, for the Walsall men continue 'that the rates for iron are not excessive and the supply of iron by the chapmen enabled the poorest sort to exercise the said craft'. The lot of the Walsall craftsman also appears favourable when compared with his farm working cousin, as Richard Baxter wrote in 1691: 'Though the labour of the smiths be hard it is in a dry house and by fits and but as nothing in comparison with mowing which constantly pulls forth a man's whole strength and little in comparison with threshing and reaping.'

Throughout the nineteenth century, Walsall was without doubt the country's leading centre for the manufacture of bits, stirrups and spurs. As noted by Robinson, 'it is questionable whether a score of bit makers could be found outside the Borough of Walsall'.

The use of malleable iron for the manufacture of bits, stirrups and other articles came to Walsall in the early nineteenth century. It is a confusing term because wrought iron is usually thought of as malleable. But in Walsall and the Black Country in general, malleable iron refers to iron cast in moulds. The technique was pioneered in Sheffield and involves melting the iron in a clay crucible and then pouring it into a mould of sand. Under normal circumstances, cast iron would be too brittle to fashion but in this process it is placed in an annealing oven for five or six days. The finished product, now known as Lucas Metal, is quite malleable and can be bent into different shapes. Workers were divided into groups according to the job they did or the article they made. There were casters, forgers, filers and finishers who made every conceivable sort of bit or stirrup. Stirrups for racing or hunting were more highly priced. Special designs were patented so that, in case of accident, the foot would be released quickly, so preventing the rider from being dragged along the ground by a horse that had bolted. **Hampson and Scott** prided themselves in making the most successful of all safety stirrups and boasted that no other safety stirrup had so great a sale. By 1889, they had sold over 30,000, including stirrups to the Empress of Russia and the Prince of Wales. The firm started in Dudley Street in 1794 and a gilt sign proudly recorded that they were 'Bit Maker to H.R.H. the Prince of Wales, afterwards George IV'. Hampson and Scott moved to the Clarence Works in Whittimere Street in 1876 but closed in the 1920s. Safeway supermarket now occupies the site. Another Walsall firm, **J.H. Hawkins and Co**. of Marsh Street and Station Street prided themselves in making 'never rust' bits, stirrups and spurs. They were prize winners at the Great Exhibition in Hyde Park in 1851 and supplied their saddler's ironmongery to the British Army in both the Crimean War and the Indian Mutiny.

In 1889, Robinson recorded that there were fifty firms making bits, but the total number of men employed was only 450, an average of only nine men per workshop. A similar pattern was found with stirrup makers, with thirty manufacturers and 250 operatives, an average of eight per workshop. In the twentieth century, manufacture began to be concentrated into somewhat larger units. In 1905, there were fifty firms employing 1,000 people. Large firms emerged such as the well-known **Matthew Harvey and Co. Ltd**. of Windmill Street and Bath Street, once holders of the Royal Warrant for supplying horse bits, who in 1914 employed six hundred people.

In the nineteenth century, it was common for children to work in the lorinery industry. A vivid account of the life of a child was given in 1864 by Samuel Dennill, a child working as a caster's assistant in a local lorinery factory. He told that 'I was ten last April. I have worked about a year and a half. I come at six and go every night at seven. On Thursday, Friday we stop at eight. On Saturday we give over work at four, but I stop to sweep up till about seven. I get 2s 6d a week. I can read a little, but I can't read the Testament yet. I go to school on Sundays. I was two years at school before I came to work'. Even after the Education Act of 1870, which stipulated compulsory education for all children, it was common – either through financial hardship or because they just wanted extra money – for parents not to send their children to school and instead, pack them off to work.

References

1. Geoff Marshall, Walsall, An Illustrated History, Tempus, 2008, p.70–1
2. W. Henry Robinson, Guide to Walsall, 1889

Nuts, Bolts and Springs[1, 2]

Nuts and bolts were made by the million in the Black Country. The **Patent Nut and Bolt Company** was at Smethwick. In 1858, Arthur Keen married Hannah, the daughter of the wealthy iron founder and cannon manufacturer, Thomas Astbury. Astbury was quick to see the potential of a nut-making machine that the American, Francis Watkins, had invented and provided money for Watkins to go into partnership with Arthur Keen at Victoria Works, Rolfe Street in Smethwick. There was a fire at the works in 1859, which prompted a move to the London Works near Birmingham. As well as nuts and bolts, the company supplied fastening for the International Exhibition of 1862 and later took over **Weston & Grace** of West Bromwich. But Arthur Keen went from strength to strength. He became the Keen in the mighty **Guest Keen and Nettlefolds.**

Darlaston was renowned as a centre of the nut and bolt and related industries. In 1870, Charles Richards joined forces with William Butler, making nuts and bolts at the Lion Works in Foster Street. The firm eventually became known as **Charles Richards & Sons Ltd** and soon expanded by acquiring Oak Works and Phoenix Works. Many of their products were purchased by the burgeoning railway companies. By 1881, they were employing 130 people. In about 1882, they moved into Imperial Works, a factory on the site of the liquidated Darlaston Steel and Iron Company. It was sited between the Walsall Canal and the LNWR railway.

The **Darlaston Nut & Bolt Company** was founded in 1859 and had premises at the Tower Works in Bright Street, near Kings Hill Park. The firm's manager was David Etchells who, in 1870, left to set up **David Etchells & Son Ltd**, at Bull Piece Works, in Station Street. The firm was described in a trade directory as manufacturers of engineers' bright, shaped nuts, black nuts, bright washers, etc. also machinery for making bolts and nuts.

There were many other similar companies in the Black Country, including the **Steel Nut & Joseph Hampton Ltd.**, of Woden Works, Franchise Street Wednesbury; **Samuel Platt Ltd.,** of Kings Hill Foundry, Wednesbury, who made machinery associated with the manufacture of nuts bolts and tubes and **Wilkes Ltd.**, which was founded in 1840. They took over **Joseph Simpson & Co.** and in the late nineteenth century, as well as nuts and bolts, were making railway fastenings at their James Bridge factory.

The Salter family came from Bridgnorth but in 1760, Richard and William Salter began making springs in a cottage in Bilston. In 1770, **Salters** moved to West Bromwich, making springs, pocket steelyards (spring balances) and bayonets. When William died, the firm was taken over by George Salter and became known as George Salters. In 1838, the first of many weighing equipment patents were taken out. By 1840, Salters were making vertical roasting jacks, muskets, domestic weighing apparatus and steam pressure gauges. Salters had a cricket team, known as W B Strollers. It later became West Bromwich Albion Football Club and went on to win the FA Cup in 1886 with Salter employees in the team. Salters adopted the Staffordshire knot, pieced by an arrow, as its trademark in 1884 and made its first typewriter in 1895

References

1. Bev Parker, www.historywebsite.co.uk and companies as above.
2. www.gracesguide.co.uk and compnies as above.

A Multitude of Industries

Tube Making[1,2,3,4,5,6,7]

Tube making was one of Wednesbury's foremost industries. In 1811, John Russell, landlord at the Turk's Head Inn and gun-barrel maker, began manufacturing wrought-iron tubes. Gas was beginning to be used for lighting and Russell identified a market in the burgeoning industry where tubes were needed for its distribution. At the time, wrought-iron tube manufacture was a very laborious task; only short lengths of about four feet could be made. The technique involved bringing flat iron strip to red heat, bending it round a cylindrical mandrel and hammer welding the two sides together. Tubes of greater length were made by tapering them and inserting one into another. In 1816, John and his brother, James Russell, founded a tube works in Wednesbury, on the corner of Wellcroft Street and Church Hill. The problem they faced, however, was that the traditional method of manufacture was laborious, and its tubes were unable to withstand high hydraulic pressures. James Russell addressed the second issue by developing a hand-forged socket to join one length of tube to the next. Meanwhile, Cornelius Whitehouse was working at the Wednesbury Forge of Edward Elwell (see above). He was born in Oldbury in 1795, the son of a gunsmith and edge-tool maker. Whitehouse realised that if he used the hollow furnace found at the edge tool manufacturers, he could heat several feet of strip to a uniform temperature. He then bent the strip to a U and passed it through a conical shaped die to produce a perfectly cylindrical tube. Cornelius Whitehouse approached his employers to see if they were interested in his invention. Elwells declined but suggested he should get in touch with James Russell. This Whitehouse did and a patent for the invention was taken out in 1825. It was assigned to Russell who agreed to pay Whitehouse an annuity of £50 per year for the duration of the patent and gave him a managerial appointment at his **Crown Tube Works** at High Bullen. In time, the two Russell brothers went their separate ways, John remaining at Wellcroft Works, trading as **John Russell & Co.**

The impact of Cornelius's invention revolutionised the tube-making industry. Workers who had previously made 100ft of tubing in 4ft lengths could now, in the same time, make 1,600ft lengths in 8ft sections. The Crown Tube Works increased its output by 2,000% and became the largest manufacturer in the world. Wednesbury was now entitled to call itself 'Tube Town'. Cornelius Whitehouse went on to make other inventions: he pioneered methods of making wrought-iron tube fittings such as bends or T-pieces. He also enabled tubes to be joined by screw threads, a screw thread on the inside of one end joined to another with its screw thread on the outside.

Many tried to copy the Crown Tube Works methods and some even resorted to spying. Rival firms bought up houses opposite the factory so that they could observe the comings and goings. Russell was forced to take the Walsall firm of Cowley and Dixon to court over infringements of his patent. He was successful and received £6,000 in damages. In 1839, he tried to extend his patent against stiff opposition. Many rival firms fought against an extension and the case went to the High Court. Many eminent scientists and engineers spoke up in favour of Russell, including Marc Brunel, father of Isambard Kingdom Brunel. With the proviso that Whitehouse's annuity be increased to £500 per year, judgment was in favour of Russell and the patent was extended. When Russell and Whitehouse rode back into Wednesbury with the news, they were greeted with scenes of wild excitement. Bands played and an ox was roasted in the marketplace. It was little wonder: full employment was now guaranteed. In 1824, the Crown Tube Works made 3,000ft of wrought-iron tubing; it was 793,000ft in 1831, and 4,228,000ft in 1858.

By 1849, Whitehouse had left the Crown Works and opened on his own behalf at the **Globe Tube Works** in Holloway Bank. Regrettably, Whitehouse lacked financial expertise and the business failed. James Russell died aged seventy-five and was succeeded by his sons. The Crown Works continued and in 1889 employed 1,100 people.

In the mid-nineteenth century, employees of the Crown Tube Works were encouraged to make tube fittings at their own homes, or in other words as outworkers. One such was **John Knowles**. He was born in Wednesbury in 1826 and, according to White's Directory was, by 1855, running his own business as an iron gas-tube fitting manufacturer and selling his products to the Crown Tube Works. He teamed up with a man called C. Russell and the pair operated from premises in Walsall Street, Wednesbury, on land belonging to Lloyds Foster & Co., which on Russell's death, Knowles purchased. Sockets were made from rolls of iron strip of width appropriate to the socket to be forged. Thickness depended on the pressure it was designed to withstand. Steam pipes needed a greater thickness than water pipes and were painted red to distinguish them. A length of strip was cut (with a slight overlap) to match the circumference of the fitting. It was forged to a U and folded over a mandrel before being forged and welded with the aid of an Oliver. John Knowles retired in 1906 and handed over the firm to his two sons. Knowles took an active part in Wednesbury life and was three times its Mayor.

In 1829, Edward and William Dixon began making apparatus in Birmingham Street, Walsall, for the newly established gas industry. Within a year they were making gas tubing and pipes. So was born the Walsall metal-tubing industry for which the town became justly renowned. The firm later became **Lambert Brothers** and made metal tubing for many applications at their **Alpha Tube Works** in Green Lane on the Wyrley and Essington Canal. Pipes and tubing of every description were made, ranging from gas pipes, water pipes and boiler tubes to chandeliers and bedsprings. In the late nineteenth century, an order was taken from Russia for an eight-mile length of piping to enable oil to be pumped from the well to the sea. Steps were taken at this time to prepare metal tubes resistant to corrosion. In Barff's process the metal tube was coated with a deposit of magnetic iron. The tubes were tested by submerging them in the canal for up to six months – after which time they were still as good as new. Other firms were soon to open and in the same way as Lamberts they tended to be sited alongside the canal. The **Alma Tube Works** backed onto the Walsall Canal in Pleck Road near Rollingmill Street and was soon joined by the **Walsall Tube Works** and Gill and Russell's **Cyclops Tube Works**. The Alma Works were eventually taken over by **Stewarts and Lloyds** who then concentrated their tube production at their Corby Works in Northamptonshire. The largest manufacturer of steel tubes in Walsall was the **Talbot-Stead Tube Company**. The firm was founded in 1906 by William Talbot and Geoffrey Stead on a forty-acre site in Green Lane. Making seamless steel tubes for railway locomotives and tubes for marine boilers, the company supplied a quarter of all the tubes used by the Royal Navy in the First World War, as well as all those used by the Italian and Japanese Navies. Many well-known ships were powered with the aid of Talbot-Stead tubes, including HMS *Renown*, HMS *Nelson* – at one time the largest battleship in the world – and the famous *Queen Mary*.

References

1. www.gracesguide.co.uk and companies as above
2. F. W. Hackwood, Wednesbury Workshops, 1889
3. B. Hawkley, Great Men of the Industrial Revolution, Cornelius Whitehouse, Iron & Steel, XL, May 1968, p.193–6
4. K.W. Knowles, John Knowles and the Wrought Iron Tube Fitting Trade, Journal West Midlands Regional Studies, Vol.11, 1968, p.77

5. S.J. Langley, The Wednesbury Tube Trade, University of Birmingham Historical Journal, Vol.11, 1950, p.163–77
6. Geoff Marshall, Walsall, an Illustrated History, Tempus, 2008, p.73–4
7. Bev Parker, www.historywebsite.co.uk (and companies as above)

Water Supply[1,2,3,4,5,6]

In 1832 and again in 1849, many in the Black Country fell victim to cholera. It is easy to see why: drinking water was taken from wherever it could be found; people drank canal water, water pumped from mine shafts, water from the River Tame and many other sources. At the time, the cause of cholera was not understood. It was widely believed that most disease, including cholera, was caused by impure air, the so-called miasma theory. It wasn't until later in the nineteenth century that it was firmly established – despite the work of John Snow in London – that cholera was a waterborne disease caused by drinking water polluted by sewage. The effect on the Black Country's expanding population was devastating. At Bilston in 1832, there were 723 deaths and in 1849, 749 in Tipton.

By the terms of the Town of Dudley Act, which received royal assent in 1791, water was to be supplied free of charge to all the town's inhabitants. A scheme was devised by William Thomas Hateley, whereby water was to be taken from a spring at Rowley and conveyed to Waddams Pool in the centre of the town. In the event, the commissioners received a report, instigated by the Earl of Dudley, that the plan was inoperative. Waddams Pool was filled in and that was the end of the matter.

In the early nineteenth century, more attempts were made to establish a waterworks company, but ratepayers frequently objected on the grounds of expense; one declaring, 'water will never be brought to this town except at great expense'. But eventually, public spirited people lobbied parliament and on the 16th of June 1834, royal assent was given allowing the formation of the **Dudley Waterworks Company**. Capital of £20,000 was authorised with shares at £50 each. The first meeting of the company was held at the Dudley Arms Hotel and William Richardson was appointed engineer. He had previously built Dudley Gas Works in 1821. Water was collected from a series of springs and conveyed to a reservoir, Parkes Hall, at Woodsetton. It was then pumped via mains in Eve Lane and Burton Road to a reservoir at Shavers End and thence by gravity to subscribers. In Dudley, 1,800 houses were supplied, with 1,200 in Bilston and Sedgley. Prices, however, were too high for the many poor in the area and supply was not dependable.

Meanwhile, the **Wolverhampton Waterworks** were formed in 1845, with premises at Regis Road in Tettenhall. Promoters included Charles Mander and the engineer was Thomas Wicksteed, who had previously worked at the East London Waterworks. About 800,000 gallons of water were pumped every day to reservoirs. Supply was intermittent: from 7am to 5pm during weekdays and all weekends. In 1846, Wicksteed left the company and was replaced by his apprentice, Henry John Marten, who soon began work to construct the Goldthorn Hill Reservoir and so ensure a constant supply. A series of difficulties arose when, for the best of reasons, Wolverhampton Corporation decided it wished to take the waterworks company into its own hands. The corporation had found a new supply from the River Worfe at Cosford, but its plans were interrupted by the emergence of another company, the **Water Supply Company,** who also wished to take water from Cosford. In the event, parliament rejected the Corporations Bill and came down in favour of the one from the Water Supply Company, which immediately amalgamated with the original Waterworks Company. The Corporation was left with hefty costs but eventually, in 1867, purchased the combined Waterworks Company. At this time, it was taking water from the River Worfe and pumping it to Summerhouse Hill from whence it fell by gravity to the Tettenhall and Goldthorn Hill reservoirs. The water, however, was of poor quality and insufficient for the town's needs and so, in 1876, Henry Marten was engaged once more. Marten sunk two artesian wells which were successful in supplying between three and four million gallons per day.

Two water supply improvement schemes came under consideration in the mid-nineteenth century. The first was from the consulting engineer at the Dudley Waterworks Company, John Robinson McClean. He had constructed the South Staffordshire Railway and proposed using water from the River Trent. Raising sufficient capital proved to be problematic. The other scheme was from Henry John Marten who, as we have seen, was successful in providing a constant supply to Wolverhampton. Three men promoted the undertaking, Edward Bagnall Dimmack, Samuel Holden Blackwell and Charles Geach. Edward Dimmack owned Parkfield Iron Works in Bilston and was Marten's father-in-law, Samuel Holden Blackwell was a coal owner, ironmaster and mining engineer in the Black Country and an expert on the geology of the area. Charles Geach was manager of the Birmingham and Midland Bank, founder of the Patent Shaft

& Axletree Company and partner in the Woodside Foundry of Bramah and Cochrane, supplier of iron for the Crystal Palace and Brunel's Great Eastern. These three men, in 1851, proposed to parliament the formation of the **South Staffordshire Mining District Water Company**. The bill was turned down by parliament but afterwards the engineers of the Dudley Waterworks and the South Staffordshire Mining District Water Company agreed to combine as the **South Staffordshire Waterworks Company**. Various water sources were investigated, including the rivers Severn and Tame and the Eastbrook and Pones Mill Stream at Lichfield, the latter finding favour. It was intended that water should be supplied to Lichfield, Walsall, Wednesbury, Darlaston, Bilston, Willenhall, Sedgley, West Bromwich, Tipton, Dudley, Oldbury and Rowley Regis via mains running alongside railway lines. A bill was placed before parliament in 1853 and despite objections from the Birmingham Canal Company, the Birmingham and Staffordshire Gas Light Company and the Earl of Lichfield, royal assent was granted on the 4th of August 1853. The company had capital of £160,000, made up of shares a £10 each. Reservoirs were planned for Ogley Hay, Walsall, Tipton and Wednesbury. A pumping shaft was sunk at Sandfield near Lichfield. On the 26th of October 1858, water reached Walsall and by 1862, all its proposed extent.

References

1. J. Van Leerzem and B. Williams, The History of the South Staffordshire Waterworks Company, Blackcountryman, 1985, Vol.18, (4), p.22–25
2. ibid, in www.southstaffswaterarchives.org.uk
3. Bev Parker, www.historywebsite.co.uk   (and companies as above)
4. www.gracesguide.co.uk (and companies as above)
5. C.J.L Elwell, The South Staffordshire Waterworks, Blackcountryman, 1980, Vol.13 (3) p.20–5
6. ibid, Blackcountryman, 1980, Vol.13 (4) p.38–43

NINE

Canals

Canals played a vital part in the Black Country becoming an important centre of the Industrial Revolution. Before they were dug, the area's coal and iron had to be transported by packhorses along rough and rutted tracks. There were obvious limits to the amount carried. Carriage along waterways changed everything.

The Birmingham Canal

On the 28th of January 1767, a group of like-minded individuals sat down at the Swan Inn, Birmingham, to plan a canal to link Birmingham with the Staffordshire and Worcestershire Canal. It would pass through the coalfields of South Staffordshire and so enable transport of coal to Birmingham and beyond. It was a project sorely needed. The preamble to the *Birmingham Canal Minute Book* summarised 'the advantages the inhabitants (of Birmingham) would receive not only in reducing the price of the carriage of coals and other commodities, but also the price of provisions by rendering useless the great number of horses that are now kept and employed for such purposes'.[1] An Act of Parliament was duly granted on the 24th of February 1768 'for making a navigable canal or cut from Birmingham to Bilston and from thence to Aldersley, there to communicate with the canal now making between the rivers Trent and Severn and for making collateral cuts up to several coal mines'.[2] By August of the following year, £55,000 had been raised in 550 shares of £100 each. The Act stipulated that no one person should possess more than ten shares. Many well-known men were associated with the enterprise, including Matthew Boulton, Samuel Galton the Birmingham gun manufacturer and Josiah Wedgwood of Wedgwood pottery fame.[2]

James Brindley (1716–1772) was engaged as surveyor. Brindley was well experienced in canal construction. He had set up in business on his own in 1742 in Leek and had been commissioned in 1761 to build a canal for the 3rd Duke of Bridgewater, England's first, to carry coal from Worsley to Manchester.

Brindley's preferred route for the Birmingham canal ran from New-Hall, over Birmingham Heath, to near Smethwick, Oldbury, Tipton Green, Bilston and thence to the Staffordshire and Worcestershire canal at Aldersley. Branches were intended to different coal works; there were to be branches to Wednesbury from Oldbury and to Ocker Hill from Toll-End. An early problem of having to dig a tunnel through sand at the hill at Smethwick was averted when it proved possible to carry the canal 'over the hill'; Brindley commenting that by such means 'there would be no more delay than (in) tunnelling'. This part of the line is known as the 'summit', where the canal is at the 491ft level.[3]

The Act specified tonnage rates. All goods were to be charged at no more than $1\frac{1}{2}$d per ton per mile with the exception of limestone, which was charged $\frac{1}{2}$d. Certain materials were given free passage, such as manure for persons whose lands had been taken to build the canal and, in certain cases, for materials for roads. There were also charges for wharfage. No charge was levied for a stay of goods up to six hours. Beyond that, it was $\frac{1}{2}$d per ton for coal, stone and brick and $1\frac{1}{2}$d for other goods, with a maximum stay of six days. It was intended that boats using the canal should be similar to those on other waterways, the proprietors specifying a length of 70ft and a width of 7ft, also stipulating, to avoid loss of water, that no boats of shorter length should pass through any lock without the consent of the proprietors. The proprietors were obviously conscious of the threat of subsidence, the Act specifying that 'no mines are to be opened within twelve yards of the canal; but mines that run under the canal may be worked, so long as the tunnel does not exceed 6ft in height and 4ft in breadth'. The issue was brought into focus when it was recorded that part of the line to Wednesbury 'had been destroyed by the falling in of the ground, from under which the coal had been taken, and is not likely to be repaired, or further useful, the mines there being all worked out'. Water was supplied to the canal from a reservoir at Smethwick and later from Titford.[4]

The Wednesbury Canal

The first priority was to build a canal from Wednesbury so that coal from the mines in and around that town could be efficiently transported to Birmingham. Coal was needed not only to fuel the household grate, but also to power the steam engines soon to be pioneered by James Watt and Matthew Boulton. Most of the work for the ten-mile route to Paradise Street in Birmingham, which opened on the 6th of November 1769, would be supervised by Brindley's assistants, Robert Whitworth (1734–1799) and Samuel Simcock. They were both experienced men. Whitworth was influenced by John Smeaton and had probably worked with Brindley on the Calder and Hebble Navigation. Simcock had assisted Brindley, who was his father-in-law, on the Oxford Canal.

The canal's route can be traced on Ordnance Survey maps; particularly useful are the original 1:2500 series reproduced by Alan Godfrey Maps. The maps, dating from the late nineteenth to the early twentieth century, also highlight how many Black Country industries chose to locate close to the canal. Industries mentioned are those identified on these maps.

The Wednesbury Canal branch ran for $4^3/_4$ miles from the main canal. It left the main Birmingham Canal at Spon Lane and headed north-west, passing the Bromford Iron Works (see chapter: Iron) and Hamblet's Blue Brick Works (see chapter: Multitude of Industries) then north towards Greets Green. It then wound its way north to Swan Village, passed beneath Great Bridge Street, West Bromwich (and the present-day Black Country New Road) to reach Golds Green and finally Balls Hill Basin. As well as collieries, many brick works were passed en route. In 1826, just north of Great Bridge Street, the Ridgacre Branch was cut. It headed north-east for 0.75 miles. From it the Dartmouth Branch ran north, via collieries and three iron works, for 0.6 miles. From the end of the Ridgacre branch the Halford Branch ran south and then east for 0.5 miles, passing the Ridgacre Oil Works, the Waterloo Iron Works, the Cyclops Ironworks, the Ridgacre Ironworks, the Hall End Ironworks and the Hall End Brick works on its journey. A very small branch, the Jesson Branch, led south from the Halford branch to coal shafts. [5, 6, 7]

Much of the Wednesbury Canal was abandoned in the mid-twentieth century. The only section remaining open to boats today is between the Birmingham Canal at Pudding Green Junction and Ryders Green where the Walsall Canal branches off. There is then a short dead end to Swan Bridge, near to the Black Country New Road.

***

To return to the main Birmingham Canal. In May 1770, the main canal was extended to meet the Staffordshire and Worcestershire Canal at Aldersley Junction. Its total length was just short of 23 miles. Customers in Birmingham would be well pleased, for the wholesale price of coal fell from between fifteen shillings and eighteen shillings per ton to about four shillings per ton. Other goods would be transported as well, including pig iron, limestone, timber and building materials. This would have given an enormous boost to trade and manufacture in Birmingham and contribute in no small way to the rapid expansion of what would eventually become Britain's second city. [8] The poet, John Freeth was inspired to write:

For true feeling joy in each breast must be wrought
When coals under five-pence per hundred are bought.

The canal left Birmingham and entered the Black Country at Smethwick, passing Boulton and Watt's Soho works on the way. There were six locks on either side of the 'summit' at Smethwick. To pump water to them, two Boulton and Watt steam engines were positioned at Bridge Street and Spon Lane. The engine at Bridge Street was the famous 'Smethwick Engine', now preserved for posterity at Birmingham's Science Museum at Millennium Point. At Spon Lane, Chance Brothers Glass Works (see chapters: Glass and Chemicals) was reached as was their associated chemical works. The canal then meanders in a south-westerly direction and passes Blakeley Hall Colliery and the Glasgow-based Tharsis Sulphur and Copper works before reaching Tat Bank.[9]

***

Titford Feeder

By 1837, a canal, just short of 2 miles in length, had been constructed to take water from the Titford Pools, via six locks, to enter the Birmingham Canal at Tat Bank. The Titford Engine House is situated at the top lock to pump water back from the Birmingham Canal. A half mile extension running southwest, the Causeway Green Branch, was made in 1858, as was the Portway Branch, running northwest.

Canals

Titford Engine House

Both branches, once serving coal mines, are now closed. Originally, the Titford Pools supplied water, via a feeder, to the Rotton Park Reservoir, and hence the Birmingham Canal at Smethwick. The Titford Canal is, at 511ft, the highest canal in the Black Country. On its banks were the Langley Maltings, which supplied malt to the Crosswells Brewery, of Stowell's Ales fame. [10] The Titford Engine House was restored in 2002 as a base for the Birmingham Canal Navigation Society.

* * *

Continuing now with the Birmingham Canal: after Tat Bank came the Oldbury Loop, a U-turn due north and another shortly afterwards to the southwest. On its journey it passed the London Iron Works, Oldbury Gas Works and the Oldbury Boiler Works. The U-turn was straightened out in 1821. The canal then continues in a north-westerly direction past the Globe Brick Works and Brades Steel Works, makers of edge tools (see chapter: Multitude of Industries). There were many brick works and collieries in this section including a tramway from the Grace Mary Collieries. This is likely to have been horse-drawn over wooden or iron rails. The canal continues in a north-westerly direction via Dudley Port and Coneygree colliery (with its tramways to the canal) towards Tipton Green. It is soon joined by Lord Dudley and Ward's Dudley Canal, constructed in 1775, to connect his lime works and colliery with the Birmingham Canal. From here, the route heads north towards Bloomfield, where it doubles back on itself past Bloomfield Iron Works (see chapter: Iron) and then north at Tipton Green Furnaces to Hope Iron Works and Colliery. Approximately three hundred yards past the Hope Works, the Ocker Hill Branch leaves eastwards for 5/8 miles to Toll End. The main canal then passes the Moat Colliery and the Gospel Oak Iron Works (see chapter: Iron), which built cast-iron columns for Liverpool's Albert Dock, then onwards via Wednesbury Oak and Bradley to Bilston. The canal then circles around Bilston's iron works – Regent, Bradley, Bankfield and Barbor's Field Furnaces – before heading south at Capponfield Iron Works to Deepfields. The section of canal between Bloomfield and Deepfields is known as the Wednesbury Oak Loop. At Deepfields the canal heads north for Wolverhampton via Ettingshall, and Horseley Fields and thence to Aldersley Junction and the Staffordshire and Worcestershire Canal.[11, 12] On its journey it passes the Staffordshire Steel and Ingot Works at Spring Dale (see chapter: Iron) the Millfield Iron Foundry, Bilston Gas Works, Mars Iron Works, Ettingshall Iron Foundry and the Chillington Iron Works (see chapter: Iron) which was linked to the canal by a tramway.

In the 1950s, the Wednesbury Oak Loop was abandoned. Its northern arm from Deepfields remains in water.

* * *

There were schemes by other companies for other canals. One was intended to run from Walsall to the Trent and Mersey Canal at Fradley, another, from Wednesbury to Fazeley and thence the Coventry Canal. Both plans came to nothing, as did the Birmingham Company's proposal for a cut from Wednesbury to Walsall. However, in 1784, the Birmingham and Fazeley Company (owners of the canal from Birmingham to Fazeley) combined with the Birmingham Company to form the Birmingham & Fazeley Canal Company. To simplify, from now I call it the Birmingham Company.[13]

The Walsall Canal

The new company immediately engaged the renowned John Smeaton (1724–1792) as engineer for the so-called Broadwaters extension from the Birmingham Canal at Ryders Green to Walsall. The contractor was John Pinkerton.[14]

(Broadwaters refers to a colliery northeast of Moxley.) Smeaton is often referred to as the 'father of civil engineering' and had previously successfully designed a series of canals and bridges. The branch, which eventually became the Walsall Canal, was built in sections. The first to the coal mines at Moxley, opened in 1785. Eight locks were needed at Ryders Green to enable the level of water to fall as the canal headed northwest towards Great Bridge. After the Ryders Green locks the Haines Branch led southwest to serve collieries. At Eagle Lane the canal passes beneath a fine brick bridge, built in 1825, probably by Thomas Telford. Further on at the Toll End Junction, the Toll End Communication Canal branches west to meet the Tipton Green Branch near to the original Horseley Iron Works (see chapter: Iron). (The Tipton Green Branch connects with the old main line of the Birmingham Canal so enabling a connection with the Walsall canal.) After the Toll End Junction, and just before the Tame Valley Canal heads in an easterly direction, the Ocker Hill Tunnel branch heads to the west.

The route continues north, past many brick works before skirting to the west of Wednesbury. Here, the Gospel Oak Branch branches west to Gospel Oak Colliery and to the east the Monway Branch to serve the Monway Iron and Steel Works (see chapter: Iron). Just beyond, at Moorcroft Junction, the Bradley Branch led southwest to collieries. It included a series of locks and terminated at

Walsall Canal, Rydres Green, Looking North

Junction of Walsall and Wednesbury Canal, Ryders Green

the Wednesbury Oak loop of the old main line of the Birmingham Canal. Jacob Twigg and Joseph Smith were engaged as contractors for the two sections from Broadwaters to Walsall.[15] It passes to the west of Darlaston to reach Moxley just after the Bull's Bridge Iron Works and the Albert Iron Works. The section to Walsall was completed by 1800. It passed many iron works north of Darlaston Green – New Priestfield Iron Works, Victoria Iron Works, Crescent Iron Works, Albert Iron Works, London & North Western Works (bolts and nuts) and Darlaston Steel & Iron Works – before reaching the Anson Canal which branched off to the northeast. Walsall was reached at Pleck. On its way into the town the canal passed the Staffordshire Galvanising Works, Alma Tube Works, Cyclops Tube and Iron Works [16,17]

* * *

All this activity put increasing pressure on the locks at Smethwick on the main Birmingham Canal. In the 1780s, the height of the 'summit' was reduced when John Smeaton built a cutting enabling three locks to be removed on both sides. The height of the hill was thereby reduced by 18ft. The endeavour impressed Aris's Birmingham Gazette which commented: 'So vast and seemingly impractical undertaking has, we believe, never before been attempted in this kingdom; mountains have been raised and levelled and a canal of a well's depth has been cut almost under the canal.' It was indeed a staggering achievement. Traffic was not interrupted because Smeaton sunk rows of coffer dams (planks of wood) into the middle of the canal. Earth was extracted from one side, but the other was left in water to allow boats to pass, albeit in turn.[18, 19]

After the connection to Walsall had been made, thought was given to straightening out the section of the Birmingham Canal between Bloomfield and Deepfields. It would have avoided the four-mile curve northeast of Coseley and enabled new coalfields to be exploited but, in the event, the project was put on hold. By the mid-1820s, the Birmingham Company saw the need to improve the canal as a whole and the great Thomas Telford (1757–1834) was brought in to advise. Telford had an enviable reputation, not only for canal building but also for building roads. He was dubbed the Colossus of Roads, a clear reference to the Colossus of Rhodes! On first setting eyes on the Birmingham Canal he called it 'little better than a crooked ditch'. There were many shortcomings: the line to Wolverhampton was frequently closed for maintenance, often for days at a time. Telford made a series of recommendations: 1. A new reservoir at Rotton Park (now Edgbaston Reservoir); 2. A shorter and improved line between Birmingham and Smethwick; 3. Getting rid of the Summit at Smethwick by cutting through the hill; 4. A new canal from Smethwick to Tipton at the 453ft level passing beneath the original canal and then via an embankment to Tipton, through three locks and 5. A deep cutting between Bloomfield and Deepfields.[20]

First to be completed was the section between Birmingham and Smethwick, and the reservoir at Rotton Park. It certainly impressed all who attended the opening ceremony of the first section. According to the company's minute book:

> 'The facilities and dispatch afforded by the double towing path, the walling of the sides of the canal, the capaciousness of the bridges and solidity of the masonry and the rapid and masterly manner in which the whole has been executed… it has been stated that these works… were second to no other works in the kingdom.' [21]

The reservoir had a capacity of three hundred million gallons and fed water via Telford's feeder canal (the engine arm) over an aqueduct across Telford's new canal to the Old Main Line. The aqueduct was designed by Telford with cast iron from the Horseley Ironworks at Tipton. Next came the great cutting at Smethwick. At its maximum, it had a depth of 71ft. Over it in West Smethwick, and carrying the Roebuck Lane, is Telford's Galton Bridge, at the time the largest canal bridge in the world, with an arch of span 151ft. After opening in December 1829, boats laden with coal could make the $7\frac{1}{4}$-mile journey to Birmingham from the Wednesbury collieries – facilitated by absence of locks – in two hours. Before the $9\frac{1}{4}$-mile journey through twelve locks had taken $5\frac{1}{2}$ hours. In 1892, the two Boulton and Watt engines previously mentioned, were replaced by the New Smethwick Pumping Station. Two steam engines lifted water from the 453ft level (Telford's line) to the 473ft level (Brindley's line as modified by Smeaton). The pumping station went out of service in 1920 but can still be seen between the two canals just past Brass house Lane and is now a small museum run by Sandwell Metropolitan Borough Council. At Spon Lane the new line passed beneath Brindley's line at the Steward Aqueduct and continued past the Bromford Ironworks. Telford's line cut across the old Wednesbury line between Hambletts Blue Brick Works and the Albion Blue Brick Works, with the Wednesbury line making a loop past Izon's Foundry, manufacturers of hollow ware (see chapter: multitude of Industries). Predictably, the loop was known as Izon's Loop. The main canal then heads north in a straight line towards Tipton, passing the Gower Branch (south) and the Dunkirk Branch (north). These changes removed all locks between Birmingham and Tipton. The Rattlechain Brick Works and the Stour Valley New Brick Works were passed before reaching the Netherton Tunnel Branch and finally Tipton. Later, in 1834, alterations were made between Bloomfield and Deepfields and a 360-yard tunnel was dug beneath Coseley. Beyond the tunnel, the new line was joined by the old line coming in from Bilston, and thence to Wolverhampton as already described. [22,23,24] Telford's modifications reduced the distance from Wolverhampton to Birmingham from $22\frac{5}{8}$ miles to $15\frac{5}{8}$ miles

Wyrley and Essington Canal

The Wyrley and Essington Canal received parliamentary consent in the thirty-second year of the reign of King George III (1792). The Act specified making a 'navigable canal from Wyrley Bank in the County of Stafford, to communicate with the Birmingham Canal at or near the town of Wolverhampton, and also certain collateral cuts from the said intended canal'. The route was surveyed by William Pitt. It ran 'from Wyrley Bank, over Essington Wood and Snead (Sneyd) Common to Bloxwich, and from thence to or near Birchil (Birchills) in the parish of Walsall and also a cut from such intended canal near Snead Common, by Wednesfield to communicate with the Birmingham Canal near Wolverhampton'. The junction at Wolverhampton was at Horseley Fields. The Birmingham Company was obviously anxious to preserve its water levels, for the Act specified that, for a boat to pass, the level of water in the Wyrley and Essington was to be at least 6 inches higher than that in the Birmingham canal. Furthermore, there was a man stationed to ensure compliance on pain of a fine of up to £5. £25,000 was raised in two hundred shares of £125, much subscribed by the Wolverhampton bankers, Molineux and Horden and the coal-owning Vernon family. Powers were given to raise further money. Two years later, a further Act was passed enabling the company to extend eastwards, a little north of Birchills to Pelsall, the coal mines at Brownhills, then Lichfield and the Coventry canal at Huddlesford. (Strictly speaking the extended canal cannot be thought of as being in the Black Country.) In its early days, the Wyrley and Essington Company was hampered by lack of water, particularly when the Sneyd Reservoir overflowed. These problems were overcome after the Cannock Reservoir (Chasewater) was built in 1800. Branches were made to the valuable limestone quarries at Daw End, Rushall, and to Lord Hay's land. Although the canal opened up a direct link with the ports of London, Bristol, Liverpool and Hull, the Curley Wyrley (as it is now often affectionately known) didn't really thrive until the Cannock coal mines were developed. It did have one thing in its favour, however, and that was plenty of surplus water from the Cannock Reservoir, which it sold to neighbouring companies.[25,26]

Tame Valley Canal

The Tame Valley Canal was opened as part of the solution to deal with the logjam at Farmer's Bridge in the centre of Birmingham which was hindering through traffic. Apart from serving Hamstead Colliery, for most of its length it is out of our area. It ran from Doe Bank Junction on the Walsall Canal at Ocker Hill, via Hamstead and Perry Barr to meet with the Fazeley line at Salford, near Nechells. The line opened in 1844, is $8^{1}/_{2}$ miles long and cost £40,000.[27]

Rushall Canal

In 1847, the Rushall Canal opened from the Wyrley and Essington at Daw End to join the Tame Valley, thereby opening up traffic from the coal mines at Cannock. It begins at the Hay Head limestone quarries and runs through open countryside in a straight line through a non-industrial part of Walsall to meet the Tame Valley Canal near to the present-day intersection of the M6 and M5[28].

* * *

Beginning in 1820, suggestions began to be made that the Wyrley and Essington should amalgamate with the Birmingham Company. There was pressure for a link from Birchills Wharf to Walsall and from there to the Birmingham canal. After lobbying from Walsall Town Council and 'landowners, mine holders, coalmasters, ironmasters, carriers and others in the town and neighbourhood of Walsall', the companies amalgamated in 1840 and three junctions were constructed. These were: first the Walsall link, then the Bentley Canal and finally the Rushall canal (see above) from Daw End to the Tame Valley line. The **Walsall Link** connected the north end of the Walsall Canal over the short distance to Birchills and the Wyrley and Essington. The **Bentley Canal** began at the Anson Canal (a branch of the Birmingham to Walsall canal) and ran through Bentley, passing Hopyard Colliery and Clarkes Lane for Willenhall. It served the Spring Heath Brick Works and the Short Bank Brick Works and then headed in a westerly direction to a branch to the Neachells Colliery. It met the Wyrley and Essington Canal at Wednesfield Junction. The **Anson Canal** was authorised as part of the original Birmingham Canal Act in 1768 but was not constructed until 1830. It was surveyed by Thomas Telford and constructed by Thomas Townsend at a cost of about £10,000. It ran from the Walsall Canal, north of Darlaston in a straight line to the Bentley quarries, blast furnaces and coal mines. When these fell into disuse it later supplied cooling water to the Birchills Power Station and later, the new Walsall Power Station. After leaving school, I worked in the laboratory at the power station; many the times have I sampled and analysed the Anson! [29]

The heyday of the Birmingham Canal Navigation was the mid-nineteenth century, when it consisted of over 160 miles of canal, including 206 locks, seventeen pumping stations, seven tunnels and six reservoirs.

The Stourbridge Canal

The Stourbridge Canal was constructed to bring Black Country coal and other materials, such as ironstone and limestone, either to Stourbridge or to the Staffordshire and Worcestershire Canal at Stourport and thence to towns to the south such as Worcester, Gloucester or Stratford upon Avon. To head off opposition from coal owners in Shropshire – who used the Staffordshire and Worcestershire Canal to transport coal from their collieries – the promoters secured petitions of support from those towns. As well as local landowners (Dudley, Foley, Hodgetts and Stamford), promoters included manufacturers such as John Foster. At first there was strong opposition from the Birmingham Company and a bill presented in 1775 was withdrawn. Nevertheless, one year later, an Act of Parliament was passed for the Stourbridge Canal and John Whitworth was taken on as surveyor. At the same session of parliament and on the same day (the 2nd of April 1776) an Act was passed for the establishment of the Dudley Canal. The two companies have always been closely associated. The proprietors raised £30,000 made up of three hundred shares of £100, with the proviso that no one person should own more than ten shares. Six years later, a further £7,500 was raised, increasing the share price to £125. Later, further capital was raised, giving a total of £43,000. The Act specified that the Staffordshire and Worcestershire Company would charge 2d per ton of coal entering its canal from the Stourbridge Canal, in contrast to 1½d for coal which entered from further north, i.e. from Shropshire. To counter this handicap, the Stourbridge Company considered ways to increase their market by bypassing the Staffs and Worcester all together and opening a new canal to run 26 miles from Stourbridge to the south of Worcester and from there to the River Severn and London. Opposition was fierce and the bill failed to get through parliament, much to the relief of the Staffs and Worcester – church bells rang out in Wolverhampton, Kidderminster and Stourton. The Stourbridge Company benefitted from the opening of iron works and collieries near its banks, allowing it to contribute to the cost of the Gad's Green reservoir and to pay mine owners to pump floodwater out of their collieries to top up the water level of the canal. Apart from some financial mismanagement in the early nineteenth century, when a toll collector had to be brought home to face the music after he had absconded to New York with £1,200, the company did well financially.[30,31]

By the end of the eighteenth century, a surge of new mining activity in the Shut End and Bromley area led to more coal being transported by road or tramway to the Fens branch of the Stourbridge Canal at Brockmoor. In 1836, the Stourbridge carried 144,606 tons of coal, 64,000 tons of which went onwards to the Staffs and Worcester, the balance for the furnaces and household grates on the line itself.

To further exploit the collieries that were opening in the Shut End district, plans were laid for a Stourbridge Extension canal. A survey was made by Samuel Hodgkinson, but the canal company was overtaken by events when, in 1829, Lord Dudley built a railway from the coal mines at and around Shut End to the Staffs and Worcester Canal at the Ashwood Basin. The Shutt End railway (also known as the Pensnett Railway) was just over 3 miles in length and was worked by the famous locomotive, the Agenoria. Put off by this, the canal company waited until 1836 before resurrecting the scheme and proposing a line to link the Stourbridge with the Birmingham Canal at Bloomfield. A new company was set up with £125,000 capital. It suggested a 5¾-mile line from Brockmoor via Corbyn's Hall, Straits Green and Cotwallend and then through a one-mile tunnel to Bloomfield and the Birmingham Canal. Coal from the new mines in the Kingswinford area could then be brought to markets either north or south. What eventually emerged, however, was a far more modest scheme, scaled down to run from Brockmoor to Old Oak Farm, just beyond Shut End and with small branches to Sandhills and Bromley. In June 1837, an Act of Parliament came onto the statute book and by 1841 the work was completed. The Stourbridge Extension was profitable in its early years but suffered when the Kingswinford branch of the Oxford Worcester and Wolverhampton Railway, running parallel with the extension, opened in 1860. It was also hampered because it offered no through route to the north and other waterways, added to which, mining activity declined along its course.[32]

The Stourbridge Canal is described in the same way as the Birmingham canal; industries identified on Ordnance Survey maps of the late nineteenth and early twentieth century are pointed out.

Stourbridge Main Line

The Stourbridge Canal leaves Stourton on its journey from the Staffordshire and Worcester Canal. There are four locks at Stourton with a fall of 43ft 3 inches. It then passes through splendid open countryside before crossing the River Stour

Stourbridge Canal, Rural Scene Between Stourton and Stourbridge

via a brick-built aqueduct just before the Wordsley junction.

To the south is the Stourbridge Branch (see later). From Wordsley Junction, the main canal then ascends 145ft northeast through a series of sixteen locks. It passed three glass works – the Wordsley Flint Glass Works (sometimes known as the London House), the Red House Glass Works and the White House Works. On its journey to the Leys, it passes a basin to serve the Nagersfield firebrick works and colliery. Then came the Bottle and Glass public house. (The pub has now gone but has been reinstalled at the Black Country Museum.) At the Leys, the main branch turns east by the Brockmoor Foundry (formerly the Eagle Foundry), passes Cricketfield Colliery where it turns south to the Brierley Iron Works and Foundry to reach Brettell Lane. There was originally a tunnel to carry the canal beneath the road but now Brettell Lane passes overhead by a bridge. Wheeley's Basin joins the canal at the point where it turns eastwards.

Wheeley's basin takes its name from the iron works which once stood here, later replaced by brick works. Although the canals' parliamentary Acts stipulated that mines should not be dug beneath or within twelve yards of the canal, the Black

Country canals were particularly susceptible to subsidence. There were old and forgotten workings or regulations were simply ignored. On the 14th of November 1803, serious subsidence occurred at Wheeley's basin. Known as a 'crowner in', the floor of the basin collapsed. The result was that 3 miles of canal water – from the Delph locks to Wide waters – poured into the chasm of old mine workings.

After Wheeley's basin, the main canal passed Clattershall brick works before it passed other brick works and the Brierley Hill District Gas Light Company to reach the Delph locks..[33,34]

The Fens Branch

The Fens Branch heads northeast from Leys junction. It was built at the same time as the main canal and also served as a feeder. It left the Leys iron foundry, the Albert iron works and a brick-and-tile works before reaching Cookley's Iron and Tin Plate Works. It was then crossed by the soon-to-be-built Kingswinford branch of the Oxford Worcester and Wolverhampton railway before it reached Haywood's Bridge and the Bromley Colliery and Bromley Iron Works. The canal terminated at the elongated Brockmoor Basin, also appropriately known as Wide Waters, with the disused Himley Colliery to its west. Water was fed from the Grove Pool, at the far end of which were sidings of the Pensnett Railway. Water was supplemented by supplies from the Middle Pool and Fens Pool, both a little to the east.[35,36]

The Stourbridge Branch

The Stourbridge Branch leaves the Wordsley Junction and then heads southeast for Stourbridge. It soon passes the Dial Glass Works on the east bank followed by Audnam's Iron and Brass Foundry and the Dial Iron Works on the west bank. It was crossed by the Kinver Light Railway with the Dennis Hall Glass Works close by to the east. The canal then turns to the east at the site of the well-known works of John Bradley & Co., famed for the construction of the Stourbridge Lion and Agenoria (see chapter: Iron). The Stourbridge Gas Works stood close to the canal's terminus where coal would have been delivered and tar exported on Thomas Clayton's tar boats. Bonded Warehouses stood at the end of the line where dutiable goods could be stored and tax paid when they left for the outside world. This lovely building, dating from 1799, has been restored and is now the home of the Stourbridge Navigation Trust.[37,38]

The Stourbridge Extension Canal

The line leaves the Fens Branch at Cookley's Iron and Tin Plate works and heads in a north-westerly direction. The first section is known as the Bromley Basin. A small basin ran off from the beginning of the Bromley Basin, running parallel with the main Stourbridge Canal, which served the Leys Iron Foundry via a tramway. After about two hundred yards, the Bromley Branch is reached which veers off to the southwest. The branch served a number of collieries: Slaters Hall, Crab Lane, Burrows, Little Meadow, Coal Leasows, many of which had been worked out by the end of the nineteenth century. The Stourbridge Extension Line continues past the disused Tiledhouse Colliery to the west before reaching the Bromley Brick Works. To the east were the New Bromley Colliery and another Tiledhouse Colliery, both of which, according to the 1901 Ordnance Map were still in operation. According to the map, the Bromley Colliery had a tramway which led to the Fens Branch near to Haywoods Bridge. The Standhills Branch leaves from the Bromley Brick Works and winds its way in a westerly direction past Standhills Colliery and Ketley Brick Works and quarry.[39,40] After the Standhills Branch, the Extension Canal continued northwards to serve collieries at Corbyn's Hall and Shut End. It fell into decline when the collieries closed.

The Dudley Canal

The Dudley Canal was an enterprise destined to be part and parcel with the Stourbridge Canal. Its Act gained Royal Assent on the same day as the Stourbridge Canal. Thomas Dadford (1730–1809), who had already worked on the Stourbridge Canal, was appointed engineer and surveyor. Dadford was yet another pupil of James Brindley, who had worked with him on the Staffordshire and Worcestershire and was senior member of what became a family of canal engineers.

Dudley Canal (Line 1)

The line began as two small branches in fields near to Parkhead, southwest of Dudley, and then ran south for about $2\frac{1}{2}$ miles to join the main branch of the Stourbridge canal ending at Black Delph. It was completed in June 1779. Once more, industries are identified on the route from the late-nineteenth and early twentieth century Ordnance Survey maps. Soon after the Parkhead Junction were the Hurst Collieries and the Hurst Fire Brick Works where the canal veers to the west and then south past the Cochrane's Woodside Iron Works (see chapter: Iron) and the Brierley Hill Iron Works of Hill and Smith. The canal then circles around the vast Round Oak Works (see chapter: Iron) passing first the New Level Furnaces and then the Old Level furnaces. (The name Level refers to the way coal was extracted by a drift (level) mine into the outcrop of thick coal.) Saltwells Colliery and Wallows Colliery were passed before Ninelocks Iron Work. The line then descends via the Delph Locks, south of Brierley Hill, to join the Stourbridge Canal.[41,42]

To increase their market, the proprietors of both the Stourbridge and Dudley companies determined to extend the $2\frac{1}{2}$-mile Dudley Canal to join with the Birmingham Canal. They were fortunate in that Lord Dudley and Ward had a private canal (a small cut on the south side of the main Birmingham Canal at Tipton) which he used to transport limestone from his Wren's Nest and Castle Hill quarries and coal from his Tipton mines. The proprietors' plan was to extend the existing line northwards, via locks, at Parkhead and from there to build a tunnel to link with Dudley's private canal and hence the main Birmingham Canal. This would give them the prospect of increased trade by transporting coal and other material directly to Stourton and by passing the Aldersley to Stourton link on the Staffs and Worcester.[43]

Predictably, strong objections came from the Staffs and Worcester, who complained 'that the line of the proposed extension does not pass through or near any mines of limestone or coal which have not at present the benefit of water carriage'. They also questioned the efficiency of the proposed tunnel, highlighting 'the difficulty and delay of passing through the intended tunnel… with no saving of time'.[44] The Dudley Company put up a stout defence, stressing that:

> '(1) coals from the Tipton Collieries will be brought to the Stourport market, which they cannot be at present because of the distance (2) limestone will be delivered at Stewpony (Stourton) at 1s 2d per ton rather than 2s 7d (3) ironstone will be sent from the mines on the Dudley Canal to Tipton at 9d per ton; whereas the conveyance by Aldersley amounts to 6s 3d and by land carriage 2s 6d per ton (4) merchandise will be conveyed from Birmingham to the Severn,

upwards of 15 miles nearer than by way of Aldersley, which will be a considerable saving in freight and time and (5) the Stourbridge clay for furnace bricks and melting pots, iron, glass and other merchandise will be sent to Birmingham by a water carriage of 16 mile only; whereas the present water carriage by Aldersley is near 40 miles.'[45]

The Act for the extension was passed, but not before compensation tonnages had been granted to the Staffs and Worcs and the Birmingham. The specification for the Dudley Tunnel was that its width was to be 9ft 3in; it had headroom of 7ft and a depth of water of 5ft 6 inches. John Pinketton was awarded the contract but regrettably was found wanting. There followed a period of uncertainty and wrangling, culminating in the tunnel not being built in a straight line. This arose because the tunnel was dug by sinking twelve vertical shafts, joined up at the bottom by miners digging horizontally. Josiah Clowes (1735–1794) (another pupil of Brindley who came with the experience of surveying the Sapperton Tunnel on the Thames and Severn Canal) was taken on to put matters right and the tunnel was duly completed in 1792. Water was supplied by feeders from a reservoir built at Gad's Green. The tunnel is 3,172 yards in length, and cost about £50,000. The Dudley Tunnel became something of a tourist attraction, but commercially it was not without its setbacks. Limestone boats were in the habit of blocking the tunnel. This arose because the tunnel had branches leading to Lord Dudley's limestone quarries. Hadfield refers to the Dudley Canal minute book which states that impediments were caused by 'loading of limestone into boats at Charley Starkey's Quarry in the tunnel, by empty limestone boats being left afloat in the tunnel and by boats loaded with limestone being left in the canal near the stop lock at Tipton'. The impediment seems to have been resolved by 1799 but there was still the problem of subsidence, requiring the tunnel to be closed until repairs were put in place. The tunnel was only designed for one-way traffic and so a period of four hours (later reduced to three) was allocated for a series of boats to travel through in one direction, after which the direction of travel was reversed. Haulage by a cable, powered by a steam engine, was suggested but expense ruled it out. [46]

Dudley Canal (Line 2)

Much to the fury of the Birmingham Company, the Dudley Company took steps to protect its interests by negotiating with the Birmingham & Worcester

Canal Company to propose 'a navigable canal from the Dudley Canal at Netherton, to a place called the Coombes in the parish of Halesowen to join with the Birmingham and Worcester at Selly Oak, with two collateral cuts to communicate with said canal'. (The Birmingham and Worcester Canal runs south from Birmingham to Worcester and the River Severn. It does not run through the Black Country.) A cost of £90,000 was estimated, £28,500 of which was contributed by the Dudley Company who agreed to carry out the work and the balance by the Birmingham & Worcester. John Snape (1737–1816) was engaged as surveyor. The line led south from Netherton at Parkhead to Windmill End, where a short collateral cut was made to Baptist End. At Gosty Hill in Old Hill the canal passed through a tunnel of 537 yards' length and from there to Halesowen and through the 3,795-yard Lapal Tunnel to join the Birmingham & Worcester at Selly Oak. There was some difficulty in getting the Act through parliament, with the expected objections coming from the Birmingham Company and the Staffs and Worcester. The ironmasters of Wolverhampton raised similar protests; fearful of the inexpensive coal they enjoyed becoming available to a wider number of customers. But 'canal mania' was at its height and despite being labelled by those opposed as 'a new system of gambling', the Act came onto the statute book in 1793. A number of engineers worked on the project: first Josiah Clowes and after he died, John Underhill, who was given charge of the Lapal Tunnel with Benjamin Timmins supervising the rest. Poor Underhill had no end of problems with the tunnel, not only with water but also with sand. Thirty shafts were sunk, and three beam engines pumped out the water. The Committee of Works drew upon Greek mythology to illustrate their troubles, likening clearing the tunnel to that of clearing an Aegean Stable. Costs far exceeded initial expectations and another Act was needed to raise further funds. Eventually, work was completed, a wharf was built at Halesowen and the line opened in 1798. Once again, however, subsidence caused complications in the tunnel, forcing it to close in both 1801 and 1805. The length of time taken to travel through was also an issue, solved up to a point by pumping water through with the aid of a steam pump and thereby creating a current of water. It was the company's hope that apart from access to the Severn, there would also be a route to London when the Stratford-upon-Avon Canal opened. By adjusting tonnage rates, the Dudley Company made every effort to encourage trade through the Lapal Tunnel rather than the alternate journey through the Dudley Tunnel and then via Tipton to Birmingham.[47]

Once more, industries on the Dudley Canal (Line 2) can be identified from the Alan Godfrey Ordnance Maps. Beginning at Parkhead, the line heads south, passing Netherton Iron Works and collieries. South of Blackbrook bridge, a branch leads westwards to link with the Dudley Line 1 Canal. At this point Line 2 goes southeast, passing a coal wharf and tramway linking with the Yew Tree Colliery. It then heads south and then east, passing the Marine works, manufacturers of chains, cable and anchors. The Saltwell Collieries are in this area and are linked to the canal by tramways and canal basins; there is also a small branch to the Lloyds Proving House (see chapter: Chains). The canal then passes the Primrosebridge chain works before turning north for the Netherton chain and anchor works and Bumble Hole where it turns southeast. (The curve was straightened out when the Netherton Tunnel was constructed.) The canal passes inclines from collieries at Warren's Hall Colliery and Springfield, then the Birmingham Pottery, before heading south past Gawn Colliery. The route then goes by the Old Hill Iron Works and Pearson's Colliery and the Powkelane Brick Works. Further collieries are passed before the canal veers eastward at the South Staffordshire Mines Drainage Works for the Gorsty Hill Tunnel, Coombeswood Tube Works and Halesowen.[48]

* * *

In the 1840s, canal mania was replaced by railway mania. Britain's first trunk line, the Grand Junction Railway between Birmingham and Liverpool, had opened in 1837 and was followed one year later by the London to Birmingham Railway. By the 1840s, facing increasing competition from furnaces in South Wales and Scotland, Black Country iron masters began to lobby for a railway line to connect with these two lines. The B.C.N and the London & Birmingham offered to build one, proposing a line from Shrewsbury to Wolverhampton and then along the line of the Birmingham canal to Birmingham with a branch from Dudley Port to Dudley. Another line was to run from Smethwick to Stourport. In addition, plans were being made for the Oxford, Worcester and Wolverhampton Railway. The latter would run through the heart of the Black Country from Stourbridge to Wolverhampton via Brierley Hill, Dudley and Tipton. This, and the proposed line running alongside the Birmingham Canal, was just too great a threat to the Dudley Canal Company. In 1846, it amalgamated with the Birmingham Canal Company.[49] A mode of working then developed – given that railways were not suited to short haul journeys – where coal and iron was taken by canal to railway interchanges and then onwards by rail to the final destination. One such interchange was the railway-canal depot at Horseley Fields in Wolverhampton, which connected the canal with the railway line to Walsall. It was constructed by the Midland Railway Company in about 1880 to enable canal-based industries access to the railway network. There was a similar one on the Dudley to Selly Oak canal at Coombes Wood, Halesowen.[50]

The final major expansion of the Birmingham Canal Navigation (BCN) was the Netherton Tunnel, agreed in 1855. Tunnelling began on New Year's Eve when Lord Dudley, in the company of three hundred onlookers, thrust his shovel into the ground to remove the first clod of earth. Work on the 3,027-yard tunnel was completed on the 20th of August 1858 and cost £302,000. It was illuminated by gas light (later electricity) and was 27ft wide. Like the Coseley Tunnel it had two towing paths. It was the last canal tunnel to be built in this country.[51]

Like the Dudley Company, the Stourbridge Canal Company objected to the Oxford, Worcester and Wolverhampton railway line and also the proposed Great Western line from Stourbridge to Kidderminster. The Stourbridge Extension Canal, in contrast, was fortunate in that thriving iron works lay close to its banks. The Oxford, Worcester and Wolverhampton railway saw an opportunity and bought the canal for £49,000 in 1847.[52]

In 1905, the BCN gave evidence to a Royal Commission. At the time it had 159 miles of canal length, 550 private basins or small branches and 216 locks. Water was provided by the South Staffordshire Mines Drainage Commissioners and reservoirs at Cannock Chase, Edgbaston, Lodge Farm and Sneyd, and thirteen of its own pumping stations transferring its own water to a higher level. Journeys were, for the most part, local: of 7,546,453 tons carried, 6,170,288 was either loaded or discharged on the BCN itself. Of the latter amount, 1,108,172 tons were loaded either from or to railway basins, of which the LNWR had thirteen, the GWR had ten and the Midland three. [53]

* * *

Many worked on the Black Country's canals. Their spiritual and physical wellbeing was looked after by the Incorporated Seamen and Boatmen's Friend Society, founded in 1846. The society set up mission halls and there were three on the Birmingham Canal network. One still remains on the Walsall Canal at Top Lock between Birchills and the town. Four religious services were held every Sunday as well as a Sunday School for children living on cabin-boats. In contrast to short haul canal boats, cabin-boats were vessels transporting cargo over long distances. They provided accommodation for the whole family, who lived permanently on the boat. During the week, mission halls were often referred to as 'Coffee Rooms'. Food, tea and washing facilities were on hand and some provided stables for canal horses to rest.[54]

As well as boats carrying cargo, passenger boats also plied the canals. They were known as flyboats, the 'stagecoaches' of the canals. They were pulled by two horses and offered first- and second-class accommodation. A service operated between Birmingham and Wolverhampton for businessmen, passengers travelling in comfort in cabins heated by hot water pipes. So-called flyboats had priority over all other boats and pleasure cruises were run for a day out in the countryside.[55]

Thomas Monk was a well-known Black Country boat builder. He was born in 1765, the son of a River Severn boat builder. He moved from Stourport, where he would have witnessed boats on the Staffs and Worcester Canal, to set up in a boat yard in Tipton at Pitchfork Bridge, near to present day Vernon Avenue. As his fame grew, his boats were named 'Monkey Boats' and were well known throughout all the country's waterways. Thomas married and had eight sons and a daughter. His sons entered the business and then expanded it by establishing boat yards throughout the Black Country. Monk introduced cabins to his boats, first as small shelters for the helmsman and later as full-scale living accommodation. As well as building boats he also started a passenger service from Factory Bridge in Tipton to the Wagon and Horses, by Friday Bridge, in Birmingham. The 'Euphrates' worked the service under its captain, John Jeven. The journey took two hours with a fare of 1s 6d first class and 1s second class. Passengers were conveyed from Dudley by horse-drawn omnibus and boarded at Dudley Port – hence its name. On the 22nd of August 1846, a pleasure cruise was arranged from Birmingham to Dudley Castle and the limestone mines tunnel. Included in the treat was an instrumental concert in one of the caverns.[56]

* * *

In the early 1960s, I was working at Walsall Power Station. Coal arrived by lorry or rail; but now and again a canal-boat load of coal arrived. The problem was – in contrast to railway wagons or a lorry – canal boats could not be tipped up and the coal had to be laboriously removed by a grab. Nevertheless it was always a treat when one turned up.

Decline accelerated in the twentieth century. The Lapal Tunnel closed in 1917 and in 1951 commercial traffic came to an end on the Dudley Canal; many basins and some branches were also abandoned. But there is still much to enjoy on the Black Country's network of canals. There is also a large literature, particularly from Ray Shill and Charles Hadfield. Andy Tidy's canal hunter series (see YouTube) is also an excellent source of information.

References

1. Birmingham Canal Minute Book, Preamble.
2. Charles Hadfield, the Canals of the West Midlands, David & Charles, 3rd Ed.1985, p.64-5.
3. Birmingham Canal Minute Book, 9 June 1768.
4. 8 Geo III c.38.
5. Charles Hadfield, p.65
6. R.H.Davies, The Birmingham Canal Navigations Through Time, Amberley, 2010, p. 19-21.
7. Alan Godfrey Maps, www.alangodfreymaps.co.uk (Oldbury & Spon Lane, 1904; Greets Green, 1902; Great Bridge & Toll End, 1902; West Bromwich North, 1885).
8. Charles Hadfield, p. 67-69.
9. Alan Godfrey Maps, (Birmingham, Winson Green & Hockley, 1888; Smethwick, 1913; The Hawthorns, 1886; Oldbury &Spon Lane, 1904).
10. R.H.Davies, p. 40-1
11. Alan Godfrey Maps, (Brades Village, 1902; Greets Green, 1902; Dudley Castle & Tipton Green, 1901; Tipton, 1884; Bradley, Coseley & Wednesbury Oak, 1901; Bilston, 1884 ; Sedgley NE & Deepfields 1901; Ettingshall) 1901; Wolverhampton SE 1885)
12. R.H.Davies, p. 31-2.
13. Charles Hadfield, p. 70-2.
14. Ray Shill, Birmingham and the Black Country's Canalside Industries, Tempus, 2005, p 33
15. ibid., p. 44
16. Charles Hadfield, , p. 72, 85.
17. Alan Godfrey Maps, (Greets Green, 1902; Great Bridge & Toll End, 1902; Wednesbury, 1913; Darlaston & king's Hill, 1901; Walsall (SW) & Pleck, 1901).

18. Aris's Birmingham Gazette, 22 June 1789
19. Andy Tidy, The Smethwick Summits, in www.bcnsociety.com/canal-hunter.
20. Charles Hadfield, p. 85-8.
21. Birmingham Canal Proprietors' Minute Book, 28 September 1827.
22. Charles Hadfied, p. 87-89.
23. Michael Pearson, Canal Companion, Stourport Ring, Central Waterways Supplies of Rugby, 6th Edition, 2003, p. 15-25.
24. R.H.Davies, p. 19-21, 31-32, 40-41.
25. Charles Hadfield, p. 94-99
26. Michael Pearson, p. 68-73
27. Charles Hadfield, p.89
28. ibid., p.99
29. ibid., p. 98-99.
30. Graham Fisher, Jewels on the Cut, Sparrow Publishing, 2010,13-25
31. Charles Hadfield, p. 73-5.
32. ibid., p.100-103
33. J. Ian Langford, A Towpath Guide to the Stourbridge Canal, Lapal Publications, 1992, p. 9-21
34. Alan Godfrey Maps, (Wordsley, 1901; Brierley Hill West, 1882)
35. J.Ian Langford, p. 29-31
36. Alan Godfrey Maps, (Brockmoor & Bromley,1901)
37. J.Ian Langford, p. 23-28
38. Alan Godfrey Maps, (Wordsley,1901; Stourbridge North, 1901)
39. J. Ian Langford, p. 33-38
40. Alan Godfrey Maps, (Brockmoor & Bromley,1901; Shut End & Tansey Green,1903)
41. J.Ian Langford and H. Jack Haden, The Dudley and Stourbridge Canals, a Bi-Centenary Commemorative Booklet, 1979, p. 15-23.
42. Alan Godfrey Maps, (Dudley West, 1881; Round Oak, 1914; Brierley Hill East, 1882)
43. Charles Hadfield, p. 76
44. Reasons offered by the Staffordshire and Worcestershire Canal Company against the proposed Extension, Document available in British Library
45. Reply to the Reasons offered by the Staffordshire and Worcestershire Canal Company against the Dudley Canal Extension, Document available in British Library.
46. Charles Hadfield, p. 77-80
47. ibid., p. 106-114

48. Alan Godfrey Maps, (Round Oak,1914; Brierley Hill,1882; Cradley Heath,1881; Netherton,1901; Cradley South,1901; Coombeswood,1914)
49. Charles Hadfield, p. 252-8
50. A.F Moseley, Narrow Boat to Freightliner, Blackcountryman, 1970, vol3(4) p.5
51. Charles Hadfield, p. 260-1
52. ibid., p 264-268
53. ibid., p. 262-3
54. Hugh Potter, Boatmen's Missions in the Black Country, Blackcountryman, 1975, Vol 8(1), p. 26
55. Primrose Rostron, Travel by Flyboat, Blackcountryman, 1975, Vol 8 (4) p. 7
56. J. Ian Langford, Thomas Monk, Boat Builder and Canal Carrier, Blackcountryman, 1978, Vol. 11(1), p. 6.

TEN
Railways

The first railway to come to the Black Country – albeit to the fringe of our area – was the **Grand Junction Railway (GJR).** It ran from Birmingham to Liverpool and was the first trunk route to open in this country. Predictably, there was opposition from canal companies, who put out scare stories of fire-breathing dragons pouring poisonous fumes into the countryside. The line was authorised by parliament on the 6th of May 1833, the same day as the **London to Birmingham Railway (L&B).** Of the two lines, the Grand Junction was less expensive, costing £18,846 per mile, mainly because, for much of its length, it ran on level ground, in contrast to the L&B which had to contend with expensive tunnels, cuttings and embankments.

Two famous railway engineers were associated with the 82½-mile route of the GJR, George Stephenson (1781–1848) and Joseph Locke (1805–1860). George Stephenson, always known as the 'Father of Railways' had, with his son, Robert Stephenson (1803–1859), pioneered the Stockton and Darlington Railway and built the engine, *Locomotion*, as well as the Liverpool and Manchester Railway and the *Rocket*. It was Stephenson who settled on a gauge of 4ft 8½ ins, which become the standard gauge, both in this country and throughout the world. Locke was the younger man and had worked for the Stephensons on the Liverpool and Manchester Railway. Joseph Locke worked under Stephenson on the GJR, but after a while a rift developed between the two men and, as a consequence, the railway company decided that both men should be joint surveyors, with Stephenson doing the north of the line and

Locke the south. Stephenson would have none of it, with the result that Joseph Locke became chief engineer for the entire line.

The GJR left Birmingham from a temporary station at Vauxhall. It ran through Perry Barr to Bescot and then to the outskirts of Wolverhampton at Wednesfield Heath. For reasons best known to the company, the line avoided sizeable towns like Walsall and Wolverhampton. It did, however, pass through Stafford on its way north, but its distance from the centre of Wolverhampton became an early cause of complaint. The residents of Wolverhampton began campaigning for an alternative route to London. The GJR opened on the 4th of July 1837 with the locomotive *Wildfire* proudly entering Birmingham after a twenty-one-gun salute at Stafford.

The promoters of both the GJR and the L&B (which opened on the 17th of September 1838) both recognised the benefit of a through route to Liverpool, Manchester and the north. This led to an Act of Parliament authorising a junction of the track of both companies at the Curzon Street terminus of the L&B. The Curzon Street terminus was connected to the original terminus of the GJR at Vauxhall by a viaduct.

In 1841, the GJR appointed Captain Mark Huish as its secretary. 'Captain' refers to his previous service with the East India Company and the formidable Huish went on to have a commanding influence on the GJR and the soon to be founded London and North West Railway. The GJR was very profitable, paying a dividend of 10%, with a capital value of £5.75m when it eventually merged with other companies. The merger was in 1846, when the L&B, the Manchester and Birmingham Railway (operating between Manchester and Crewe, where it linked with the GJR) and the GJR combining to form the **London and North West Railway (LNWR).** Meanwhile, an altogether different sort of railway was taking shape in the south of England between London and Bristol.

***

The **Great Western Railway Company GWR)**, otherwise known as God's Wonderful Railway, was founded in 1833 and authorised by Act of Parliament on the 31st of August 1835. Its first line was the London to Bristol route, surveyed by the famous engineer, Isambard Kingdom Brunel (1806–1859). It had a track gauge of 7ft ¼ inch, known as broad gauge, which gave a much smoother ride.

The GWR had ambitions to take their trains to the Midlands of England and further north, so challenging the monopoly of the L&B. In pursuit of this objective, instead of building a direct line from London to Bristol, after Reading the line headed northwest to Swindon via Didcot. From Didcot Junction, a spur line was built to Oxford. The terminus at Oxford was a little to the south of the city centre and south of the river, near to Folly Bridge. The spur line opened on the 12th of June 1844. Negotiations then began between the GWR and the GJR, the latter company wishing to extend its interests to London. Talks foundered\ after the GJR amalgamated with the L&B to form the LNWR. The directors of the GWR, however, went ahead regardless and promoted a new company, the **Birmingham and Oxford Junction Railway Company (B&O).** Money was put up by the GWR and the line ran north from Oxford, via Banbury, Fenny Compton, Warwick and Solihull to Bordesley, just outside Birmingham city centre. As part of the previous negotiations, the GWR pushed for the line to end at Curzon Street Station. As things turned out, this proved to be impossible and so a further Act was authorised by parliament, the Birmingham Extension Act. The Act approved a line from Bordesley, via a tunnel beneath Birmingham city centre, to a new station which later became known as Snow Hill. The new line was known as the **Birmingham Extension**. Both Acts received Royal Assent on the same day, the 3rd of August 1846. The Birmingham Extension then combined with the B&O with authorised capital of £1m, £700,000 for the costly subterranean extension and £300,000 for the B&O.

There were many other railway companies that secured Acts of Parliament on the 3rd of August 1846, one of which was particularly relevant to the GWR. It was for a new line running from the new station (Snow Hill) at the end of the Birmingham Extension to Wolverhampton known as the **Birmingham, Wolverhampton and Dudley Railway, (BW &D).** The line passed through the heart of the Black Country. Its route to Wolverhampton station, which became known as Wolverhampton Low Level, was via Hockley, Handsworth and Smethwick, West Bromwich, Swan Village, Wednesbury and Bilston to meet up with the proposed **Oxford, Worcester and Wolverhampton Railway (OWW)** at Priestfield before running into Wolverhampton. A branch led from Swan Village Junction, Great Bridge and Horseley Fields to Dudley. From Great Bridge it ran on the same line as the **South Staffordshire Railway (SSR)**, (see later). As promoted, the BW&D was intended as a local line to serve industries on its route, such as iron works and collieries. The line opened in 1854 and in 1862 a small station was added between Wednesbury and Bilston, called Bradley and Moxley[1]. The little station closed during the First World War, never to reopen.

But it was obvious to all, not least the LNWR, that a potential through route to the north was now open for the GWR to exploit. The LNWR put up a rear-guard action to resist the through route when their general manager, the robust Mark Huish, tried to buy up shares in the B&O and so take a controlling interest. The move failed and plans were made for the B&O to amalgamate with the BW&D early in 1847 and then to be sold to the GWR. Despite further objections from the LNWR, who saw their monopoly slipping away, royal assent for the takeover came on the 31st of August 1848.

John Robinson McClean (1813–1873) was appointed chief engineer of the BW&D. Born in Belfast, he was educated at Glasgow University, was chief engineer and later sole owner of the South Staffordshire Railway (see later). He also built the South Staffordshire Water Works. To begin with, the line was broad gauge, becoming narrow gauge from the 1st of November 1864. Construction began in 1851, but the BW&D did not get off to a good start. The line was due to open in 1854, but one week before, Captain Douglas Galton (1822–1899), captain in the Royal Engineers, friend and colleague of Florence Nightingale, and Secretary to the Railway Department of the Board of Trade, came to inspect. One day later, as a locomotive and two wagons passed over a bridge between Soho and Handsworth, the bridge collapsed into the Winson Green Road below. Brunel was duly called in and condemned five of McClean's bridges as unsafe. After the bridges were strengthened, the line eventually opened on the 14th of November 1854, the same day as the **Wolverhampton Junction Railway.** This short section of track between Cannock Road junction and Stafford Road in Wolverhampton enabled the GWR to have access to the **Shrewsbury and Birmingham Railway (S&B)** line and hence to Wales and points north.

The S&B had every intention of asserting its right of entry from Shrewsbury to Birmingham via Wolverhampton and wanted a line of its own. Their proposals were supported by the Dalhousie Company in a report submitted in 1845 to the Railway Department of the Board of Trade, and a line was surveyed by Robert Stephenson and William Baker. It served Darlaston and got the support of many in the Black Country including the Tipton ironmaster, Robert Bradley. But parliamentary authorisation, once more on the 3rd of August 1846, only gave the S&B a route of 29 miles from Shrewsbury to Wolverhampton. They were repeatedly frustrated in their attempt to reach Birmingham by both the London & North West Railway (LNWR) and the Birmingham, Wolverhampton and Stour Valley Line.

***

Birmingham, Wolverhampton & Stour Valley Line was incorporated on the 3rd of August 1846. The inclusion of the term Stour Valley in its title is somewhat incongruous. It refers to a projected line from Smethwick to Stourbridge along the valley of the River Stour. In fact, this line never materialised; nevertheless 'Stour' remained in the line's title. The route ran from Birmingham New Street (originally called Queen Street) to Smethwick, Spon Lane, Oldbury, Dudley Port, Tipton, Deepfields, Ettingshall Road and Bilston. The Shrewsbury & Birmingham were to have a 25% stake in the line as were the LNWR. A further 25% was provided by the canal companies and the remaining 25% from private sources.

Almost immediately, wrangling and conflict began between the LNWR and the S&B. The two companies each had an equal share of the half mile section which ran into Wolverhampton High Level Station. Much to the indignation of the S&B, the LNWR refused to complete this short section of the Stour Valley line and thus, by their inaction, prevented the S&B from gaining access to Birmingham. At Wolverhampton, the S&B had little choice but to transfer goods to canal barges on the Birmingham Canal, which ran alongside the High-Level Station. They made use of the Victoria Basin which had been constructed for this purpose. What followed well illustrates the bitter rivalry between the two companies, a rivalry bordering on farce. The *Wolverhampton Chronicle* of Wednesday the 17th of July 1850, relates events[2]:

'A dispute has within the last few days arisen between the London and North Western and the Shrewsbury and Birmingham companies as to certain means proposed to be adopted by the latter company for transferring the mineral traffic from the line, near the Wolverhampton temporary station to the adjoining canal… the directors of the S&B determined on laying down rails or planks by the side of their embankment at their temporary station for the purpose of communicating with the canal and thus forwarding their traffic to its destination. On Friday afternoon Mr. Moore of the firm of Hoof Hill and Moore, contractors for the construction of the Stour Valley Line, came to the spot and said that he would not allow the proposed works to proceed. A number of his men were assembled on the embankment for the purpose of supporting him.'

Moore was taken into custody and after extensive deliberations was ordered not to contemplate a breach of the peace; the magistrate adding that Moore would be personally liable for the consequences of such a breach and that it would be no excuse to say that he was authorised by William Baker, the LNWR's chief engineer.

A riot ensued on the 7th of July 1850, when S&B men, attempting to lay planks to ease the passage of goods from train to barge, were met with vigorous resistance from workmen engaged by the LNWR. Despite the Riot Act being read by Wolverhampton's Mayor, peace was not restored; further along the line there were reports of a fight on the track, wagons were overturned, men were injured, and it took a charge by cutlass-bearing police to restore order.

The root cause of the resistance of the LNWR was their wish to thwart any attempts of the GWR to compete with their lines to the north, which the latter company would be able to do by linking with the S&B. Trouble rumbled on for many months The S&B (now amalgamated with the GWR) became ever more determined for their trains to reach Birmingham, the LNWR putting all sorts of obstacles in the way. In the end, in desperation, the S&B sent a train regardless; it ended in farce, coming buffer to buffer against the LNWR's *Swift* heading in the opposite direction. S&B trains did eventually reach Birmingham New Street on the 4th of February 1854, despite a heavy rent being imposed to use that station. The unfair rent was overturned on appeal.

***

The Oxford, Worcester and Wolverhampton Railway (OWWR) ran from Wolverton Junction (near Oxford), a distance of 89 miles to Bushbury, north of Wolverhampton. It was built in stages; the section from Oxford to Worcester was via Shipton and Evesham, from Worcester to Stourbridge via Droitwich and Kidderminster. The Black Country was entered at Stourbridge, the line then proceeding via Brettell Lane, Brierley Hill, Round Oak, Netherton, Dudley, Tipton, Daisy Bank, Bilston, Priestfield and Bushbury. At Priestfield the OWWR met the BW&D coming out of Birmingham Snow Hill. A spur was built (authorised on the 14th of August 1848) to take both lines into Wolverhampton Low Level Station, which was shared with the S&B. There was a branch line to Kingswinford and Lord Dudley's Pensnett Railway.

Isambard Kingdom Brunel was commissioned to survey the line. He estimated a capital of £1,500,000, which turned out to be far short of what was needed. The provisional arrangement was that the GWR would lease the line for 999 years, paying a rent of 3.5% of the capital in addition to 50% of profits. Shares were issued at £50 each; Francis Rufford became chairman, and he proposed the line should be broad gauge. Early planning, however, coincided with a Royal Commission instigated by the Radical MP, Richard Cobden. It reported in February 1846 and came down in favour of the now standard gauge of 4ft 8½in, a decision which caused the OWWR delay and confusion.

The line was beset with difficulties. Lack of progress prompted the Railway Commissioners to intervene, resulting in the Board of Trade, in 1849, instructing the GWR to complete the line. Despite legal action, the GWR declined to do so. Then, in 1851, Lord Ward, Earl of Dudley, became chairman and more money was raised. It was at this time that Edward Ladd Betts (1815–1872) and Samuel Morton Peto (1809–1889) were engaged as contractors. Both were experienced railway engineers. Betts had worked on the Grand Junction Railway for George Stephenson; Peto was best known for building Nelson's Column in Trafalgar Square and Charles Barry's Houses of Parliament. In 1848, they went into partnership and were awarded the contract to build the line onwards from Tipton and south of Worcester. Messrs Treadwells were engaged to finish the middle section. Peto had connections with a London solicitor, John Parson, and both of them joined the board. Parson then engaged in some rather dubious business negotiations with the LNWR, in breach of the company's authorisation Act, resulting in Lord Ward resigning as chairman after only one month in post. The company was also facing financial difficulty leading to Parson urging shareholders to agree to sell to the GWR at a discount. The GWR declined the offer and to make matters worse £24,000, held in a Stourbridge Bank, was lost when the bank failed. Brunel also resigned in 1852; he did not get on with Betts or Peto and was succeeded by John Fowler. But Brunel's influence remained; he had designed the timber viaducts at Brettell Lane, Stambermill and Parkhead.

There was still no rolling stock when the line was due to open in 1852. In response, John Fowler appointed the London based carriage builder, C.C Williams, to take control of the working of the line. David Joy was then appointed as locomotive superintendent, who immediately set about acquiring rolling stock, four locomotives at first, *Jenny, Jack of Newbury, Canary* and *Mudlark*, followed by twenty more from the firm of R.W. Hawthorn in Newcastle.

The line from Evesham to Stourbridge opened on the 1st of May 1852, with a special train packed with dignitaries. Church bells rang out and the route was thronged with onlookers. Normal services began two days later, as did a regular service on the Stourbridge to Dudley section in December. One year later, connection was made from Dudley to Tipton, including the Tipton curve, which enabled the line to join the LNWR's Stour Valley line and thereby to Wolverhampton High Level. Wolverhampton (Low Level) was also reached via the BW&D from Priestfield. In 1854, the line was complete; *The Times* newspaper reporting that, on the 13th of April 1854, a broad-gauge train travelled along the entire length of the mixed track from Oxford to Wolverhampton. It proved to be the only one, for no other reason than the OWW only having standard gauge rolling stock. Four years later, the GWR gave up broad gauge rails all together. Early in 1855, David Joy and C.C. Williams left, Joy to be replaced by Frederick Hayward.

On Monday the 23rd of August 1858, a serious accident occurred in the vicinity of Round Oak, causing a greater loss of life than any accident before. Seventeen carriages of an excursion train, heading towards Wolverhampton, split from the main train and careered back down the incline to collide into a following train. Fourteen people lost their lives and many more were injured. The accident report, by Captain H.W. Tyler of the Royal Engineers, highlighted casual attitudes of working practices.

In 1858, north of Stourbridge and Brettell Lane, an extension was made to Kingswinford. The line ran alongside the Stourbridge Extension Canal and was later extended to the Earl of Dudley's, **Pensnett Railway.**

In 1860, a number of railway companies, including the OWWR, merged to become the **West Midland Railway.** The authorising Act also provided for an extension of the OWWR (the **Stourbridge Extension**) to run from Stourbridge to Cradley Heath via Lye. One year later, the line was extended to Old Hill and Rowley Regis, to meet the LNWR Stour Valley line at Galton Bridge and the GWR's BW&D line at Handsworth. The entire route was opened on the 1st of April 1867, the OWW having by this time been absorbed by the GWR. The line had extensions to local coal mines – a branch to Corngreaves and another to Hayes Lane. Another branch led off at Langley Green Station. It became known as the Oldbury Railway and was primarily a freight line, ending at sidings near a branch of the old line of the Birmingham Canal.

In 1862, an Act was passed to enable a link line to be built from the Stourbridge Extension at Old Hill to the main OWWR at Dudley. It opened on the 1st of March 1878 and had a branch from Baptist End to Primrose Hill and the Withymoor Goods Station at the Dudley canal. There was an intermediate station at Windmill End, near to the entrance to the Netherton Tunnel. The station at Dudley went through a variety of names: first Netherton, then Dudley Southside and Netherton and finally Blowers Green. Also on the 1st of March 1878, a line was opened to Halesowen from Old Hill Station[3]. The two lines (there was no through route) were known as the **Dudley and Halesowen Railway.** A short branch was made for the Halesowen branch to Halesowen Basin in 1902.

In 1879, to remove the inconvenience of Stourbridge Station being some distance from the town itself, a further short extension was made from the so called 'Stourbridge Station' to a station in the town centre. The latter station became known as **Stourbridge Town**, while the original station was renamed **Stourbridge Junction**.

* * *

By the mid-nineteenth century, railway companies began examining ways of extending their networks at local level. There was no direct service from Walsall to Wolverhampton. This was rectified by the **Wolverhampton and Walsall Railway (W&WR).** It was a joint enterprise between the LNWR and the Midland Railway. (The important Midland Railway was formed on the 10th of May 1844 by the merger of the Midland Counties Railway, the North Midland Railway, and the Birmingham and Derby Junction Railway. The Birmingham and Gloucester Railway joined two years later.) The line was authorised on the 29th of June 1865 and ran for 8 miles from Walsall to Wolverhampton (High Level), with intermediate stations at North Walsall, Bentley, Short Heath (Clark's Lane), Willenhall (Market Place), Wednesfield and Heath Town. The line opened on the 1st of November 1872. Three years later, it was purchased by the LNWR only to be sold back to the Midland one year later. The Midland also reached Walsall with a line – strictly speaking out of our area – from Castle Bromwich via Sutton Park, Streetly, and Aldridge. On this latter line, trains had to reverse in and out of Walsall but there was a direct route to Wolverhampton via a junction from Lichfield Road to North Walsall.

The LNWR opened a direct route from Walsall to Wolverhampton in 1881 with a curve from the South Staffordshire Line (see later) at Pleck to the former GJR line and another at Portobello to the Midland line at Heath Town.

* * *

The 4th Viscount Dudley and Ward mined extensive deposits of coal at Shutt End. After a succession of Enclosure Acts, he reached an agreement with James Foster of John Bradley and Co., who also had interests in the area, to build a mineral railway from Shutt End to the Staffordshire and Worcestershire Canal at Ashwood Basin. It was known as the **Shutt End Railway** or **Kingswinford Railway** and was of standard gauge[4]. The line opened on the 2nd of June 1829 and was about 3 miles in length. There were two steep inclines at both ends and a level section in between. Loaded coal wagons would be allowed to fall by gravity down each incline. Simultaneously, a rope attached to the rear wagon would haul empty wagons up each incline by a pulley system It took 3½ minutes to haul wagons up the eastern incline and 1¾ minutes at the Ashwood Basin incline, both of gradient of about 1/28. The middle section was about 2 miles in length and was worked by the famous Stourbridge locomotive, the *Agenoria*, designed by John Urpeth Rastrick of the firm of Rastrick and Foster. *Agenoria* gave loyal service for thirty-five years between 1829 and 1864.

Agenoria *(Keith Hodgkins Collection)*

By the 1840s, it was realised that further railways were needed to serve the expanding Pensnett collieries. In response, the **Pensnett Railway** was born, designed by F.P. Mackellan and built by the contractor, William Hughes[5]. It consisted of a series of lines, eventually some 40 miles in length, which served collieries, factories and other industries. There was a line from Old Park Colliery, west of Dudley, which ran south to the east of Fens Pool to reach the New Level furnaces at Round Oak. Another line headed northwest from Round Oak to serve the Himley coalfields and a further line south from Round Oak towards Nine Locks.

In 1852, the Oxford, Worcester and Wolverhampton Railway (OWWR) in its journey from Stourbridge to Dudley passed through Round Oak. It crossed the Pensnett Railway (already in place there since 1845) at right angles, much to the displeasure of Captain D Galton, the inspecting officer, who found the arrangement 'most objectionable' and 'a constant source of anxiety'. But control of the crossing was in the hands of the OWWR and its successor, the GWR and there the matter rested.

By the 1850s, mining in the Saltwells area was expanding and the Pensnett Railway was extended eastwards from Round Oak in the direction of Saltwells. A branch headed south, via Mushroom Green, to join the main Stourbridge Extension Railway at Cradley Station.

In 1865, the Kingswinford Railway connected with the Pensnett Railway. It joined about half a mile east of the main Wolverhampton to Stourbridge Road and headed north via Himley No. 3 Pit. The entire line was then known as the Pensnett Railway, the Kingswinford line becoming its Ashwood Branch. Also in that year, a branch was laid from the line to Old Park almost to the heart of Dudley at Wellington Wharf. Here, merchants could collect coal supplies. (Wharf is a confusing term. The wharf was land based and had nothing to do with water.) Various other extensions were made in the late nineteenth century and in 1912 Baggeridge Colliery opened, served by an extension built by the GWR, but remaining the property of the Pensnett Railway.

The Pensnett Railway obtained its rolling stock and locomotives from a number of suppliers, including E.B. Wilson of Leeds, who supplied *Alma* at a cost of £1,835. In 1858, E.B. Wilson went out of business and the works were taken over by Manning Wardle who supplied further engines.

* * *

The **South Staffordshire Railway (SSR)** ran from Wychnor Junction, north of Lichfield (where it connected with the Midland Railway) to Dudley, where it joined the OWWR. It was authorised on the 3rd of August 1846 and was an amalgamation of the Trent Valley, Midlands and the Grand Junction Company. It entered the Black Country at Walsall and then headed to Wednesbury, Great Bridge, Dudley Port and Dudley. South of Walsall, at Pleck, spurs ran to James Bridge (later called Darlaston) and thence to Wolverhampton and also to Bescot and thence to Birmingham. The first section of the line to open was between Bescot and Walsall in 1847, followed by the Walsall to Wychnor in 1849. In 1851, John Robinson McClean took a twenty-five-year lease on the line. He became the first person to own a railway.

Sources Consulted

Much information was taken from the following standard works to which due acknowledgement is given

John Boynton, The Oxford, Worcester and Wolverhampton Railway, Mid-England Books, Kidderminster, 2002
Rex Christiansen, A Regional History of the Railways of Great Britain, Vol.7, The West Midlands, 2nd Edition, 1983
Paul Collins, Stourbridge and its Locomotives, 1989 (Copy at Dudley Library)
E T MacDermot, History of the Great Western Railway, published by the Great Western Railway, London, 1927

References

1. Michael Hale, Bradley and Moxley Railway Station, Blackcountryman, 1972, Vol 5 (02), p. 38
2. The Shrewsbury and Birmingham and the London and North Western Railway Companies, Railway Competition and Dispute, in Wolverhampton Chronicle, Wednesday July 17, 1850.
3. Michael Hale and Ned Williams, By Rail to Halesowen, Blackcountryman, 1972, Vol 5 (04), p.9
4. www.stourbridge.com/shutt-end-railway
5. Gale, W.K.V. (1975). A History of the Pensnett Railway. Cambridge: Goose and Son.

INDEX

Albright & Wilson, 107-10
Awls, 112-3
Bessemer Furnace, 38-40,42,51
Birmingham Canal, 145-56
Birmingham, Wolverhampton & Dudley Railway, 173-4,176,178
Birmingham, Wolverhampton & Stour Valley Railway, 174-6,178
Bloomfield Iron Works, 32-3,150
Brick Making, 113-15
Bromford Iron Works, 41,147,154
Buckles, 115-6
Burritt, Elihu, v,66,112
Canal Decline, 165-6,168
Chains, Makers Life, 72-3
Chains, Manufacture, 74,78-80
Chains, Early History, 72-3
Chains, Testing, 80-2
Chains, Women Chain Makers, 72-3,77-8
Chemical Works, 103-10
Chillington Iron Company, 35-6,47,49,150
Coal, Baggeridge Colliery, 18-9,21,181
Coal, Bell Pits, 1-2
Coal, Longwall Extraction, 3,14
Coal, Pillar and Stall Extraction, 2-3,11,14,133

Corngreaves Works, 36,52-3,178
Cort, Henry, v,28,30-1,74
Cowper Stove, 35,43,51
Darby, Abraham, v,24-5
Darlaston Iron & Steel Company, 43-4
Dudley Canal, 161-5
Dudley Family, 6-9,20,48,60,149,158,162-3,166,176-7
Dudley, Dud, 2,20,24-5,55
Edge Tools, 116-7
Enamelwork & Japanning, 117-21
F.H.Lloyd, 44
Foley, Richard, 85-7
Gas Lighting, 121-4
Gibbons, John, vi,3,34,56
Glass Works, 64-5
Glass, Early History, 58-62
Glass, Excise Duty, 62-3
Glass, Chance Brothers, vi,66-71,106-8,117,148
Gospel Oak Iron Works, 53,150-1
Grand Junction Railway, 171-3,179
Grazebrook, M.W., 40-1,50
Great Exhibition, 1851, vi, 50, 65, 68-9, 75, 99, 118, 136
Great Western Railway, 18,75,107,166,172-4,176-8,181
Gun Trade, 124-5

183

Hall, Joseph, vi,30-3,39,56
Hamstead Colliery, 17-18,155
Hickman, Alfred, 39,50-1,96
Hollow-Ware, 125-6
Horseley Iron Works, vi,37,45
Iron, Blast furnaces, 23,25,27,30-1,34-40, 42-3,45,47,49,51-2,55,130,156
John Bradley & Company, vi,35,53-4,160,180
Keir, James, 64,102-4
Leather, 126-30
Limestone Industry, 130-5
Lloyds Foster & Company, 41-4,140
Locks and Keys, Chubb, John, vi,91-4,99-100
Locks and Keys, Companies 96-100
Locks and Keys, Letter Locks, 91,94
Locks and Keys, Pin Tumber Locks, 91-2,94,97,98-9,
Locks and Keys, Warded Locks, 91,93
London & Birmingham Railway, 171-2
Lorinery, 135-7
Manby, Aaron, vi,45-6,57
Mines, Accidents, 2,8,12-4
Mines, Flooding, 3,9,13,15-6,45,157
Mines, Ventilation, 9-10,13,20
Mines, Working Conditions, 11-2
Nails, Early History, 84-5
Nails, Slitting Mill, 29,53,74,85-8
Nails, Working Conditions, 88-90
Neilson, James, 35
Newcomen, Thomas, v,3-6,20,25-7,45-6,57,151,154
Nuts, Bolts & Springs, 137-8
Open Hearth Furnace, 51
Oxford, Worcester & Wolverhampton Railway, 173,176-8,181
Patent Shaft & Axletree Company, 42,44,143
Paxton, Joseph, vi,68

Pensnett Railway, 18,48,54,158,166,176,178,181
Plot, Dr Robert, 1,3,20,22,55,59,70,131-2,135
Portland Vase, 65-6
Puddling Furnace, 28,30-2,34-6,39,41-5,48-9,51,74
Rastrick, John Urpeth, vi,34-5,49,54,122,180
Round Oak Works, 18,40,47-8,162,176,178,181
Rushall Canal, 156
Savary, Thomas 3-4
Shrubbery Iron Works, 49
Social Condition, Iron, 54
Steam Engine, v,3-5,26-9,36,40,43,45,54,103,121,133,147-8,154,163
Stourbridge Canal, 157-61
Stourbridge Lion, vi,35,54,123,160
Tame Valley Canal, 155
Titanic, 75-6
Titford Feeder, 148-9
Tube Making, 139-42
Walsall Canal, 150-4
Water Supply, 142-4
Watt, James, v,5-6,26-9,40,45,103,121,133,147-8,154
Wednesbury Canal, 147-8
Wilkinson, John, v,26-30,41,130,133
Woodside Iron Works, 37,50,144,162
Wryley & Essington Canal, 154-5

This book is printed on paper from sustainable sources managed under the Forest Stewardship Council (FSC) scheme.

It has been printed in the UK to reduce transportation miles and their impact upon the environment.

For every new title that Troubador publishes, we plant a tree to offset CO_2, partnering with the More Trees scheme.

For more about how Troubador offsets its environmental impact, see www.troubador.co.uk/sustainability-and-community